YOUR CHURCH MAGAZINE EDITOR'S CHOICE

RECOGNIZING EXCELLENCE IN HELPING CHURCHES WITH THE BUSINESS OF MINISTRY

The Zo

Church and Nonprofit Organization

Tax&Financial Guide

For 1998 Tax Returns

1999 EDITION

Dan Busby, CPA

ZondervanPublishingHouse

Grand Rapids, Michigan

A Division of HarperCollinsPublishers

THE ZONDERVAN CHURCH AND NONPROFIT ORGANIZATION TAX AND FINANCIAL GUIDE: 1999 EDITION

© Copyright 1998 by Dan Busby

For information write to:
Zondervan Publishing House
Grand Rapids, Michigan 49530

Publisher's note: This guide is published in recognition of the need for clarification of tax and other laws for churches and nonprofit organizations. Every effort has been made to publish a timely, accurate, and authoritative guide. The publisher, author, and the reviewers do not assume any legal responsibility for the accuracy of the text or any other contents.

Readers are cautioned that this book is sold with the understanding that the publisher is not rendering legal, accounting, or other professional service. Organizations with specific tax problems should seek the professional advice of a tax accountant or lawyer.

References to IRS forms and tax rates are derived from preliminary proofs of 1998 forms or 1997 forms. Some adaptation for changes may be necessary. These materials should be used solely as a guide in filling out 1998 tax and information returns. To obtain the final forms, schedules, and tables for filing returns and forms, contact the IRS or a public library.

ISBN 0-310-22538-8

All rights reserved. No part of this publication may be reproduced, stored in a retrieval system, or transmitted in any form or by any means—electronic, mechanical, photocopy, recording, or any other—except for brief quotations in printed reviews, without the prior permission of the publisher.

Printed in the United States of America

98 99 00 01 / DH / 10 9 8 7 6 5 4 3 2 1

Contents . . .

SPECIAL INDEX
FOR CHURCH TREASURERS
A guide within a guide

Information return filings

(It is easy to overlook the filing of information returns)

Financial records of the church

(Design a practical recordkeeping system that fits your church)

Charitable contributions

(Help your donors obtain the maximum tax benefits from their gifts)

Insurance for the church

(An annual insurance review with a good agent or broker is a must)

Key laws that apply to churches

(Though confusing or downright intimidating, you need a basic understanding of certain laws)

Sample Board Resolutions

CAUTION: You may need to consult with a tax or legal professional before adapting these resolutions to the specific needs of your organization.

Sample Charitable Contribution Letters and Forms

INTRODUCTION

Yes, you can understand the tax rules for churches and other nonprofit organizations. It is easier than ever with this year's edition of the Guide.

Taxes and finances can be very unpleasant aspects of your organization. You do not have time or the interest to master thousands of pages of complex tax laws and regulations. But you want a basic understanding of tax and financial reporting requirements and strategies.

This book is the one for you—written in plain English—clearly explained advice you can act on, with icons in the margins to direct your attention to the most important provisions in the book.

 Tip　This marks strategy recommendations for saving tax dollars for your organization and your employees.

 Planning Idea　This alerts you to ideas for tax, compensation, or administrative planning steps.

 Key Issue　These are the most basic provisions in the tax law that impact churches and other nonprofit organizations.

 Remember　This is a friendly reminder of information to review that you will definitely want to remember.

 Action Steps　This highlights easy-to-follow steps to structure your tax and financial planning.

 Caution　This marks subjects that you should carefully study to achieve the best tax and financial treatment.

 Warning!　This alerts you to some of the most serious tax mistakes sometimes made by churches and other nonprofit organizations.

 Cross Reference　This is a reminder that more material on a topic appears in the companion guide, the 1999 edition of *The Zondervan Minister's Tax and Financial Guide*.

1998 Recent Developments

Congress passed new tax legislation in 1998. Additionally, the year produced a number of court decisions, IRS rulings, and regulations of importance to churches and other nonprofit organizations.

1998 standard mileage rates

The optional standard mileage rates for employees, self-employed individuals, and other taxpayers to use in computing the deductible costs paid in 1998 in connection with the operation of a passenger automobile for business, charitable, medical, or moving expense purposes are as follows:

Type of Expense	1998 Rate (per mile)
Business	32.5 cents
Charitable	14 cents
Moving/Medical	10 cents

1998 per diem rates

Nonprofit employers that help their employees cover business travel expenses have two basic options: (1) The employer can pay employees the precise amount of their expenses, or (2) the employer can opt for convenience and pay a set "per diem" allowance for each day of business travel.

Per diem allowances that stay within IRS-approved rates satisfy the tax law's tough accountable plan requirements almost automatically. All the employer has to do is get records of when, where, and why the employee made the trip. The employee does not have to account for actual dollars spent or keep receipts.

Employers can opt for a two-tier set of "high-low" reimbursement rates, or they can tie tax-free travel allowances to the amount the federal government provides to its employees for travel to a particular location. An employer must pick one method or the other for each employee.

Employers can provide tax-free allowances of up to $180 ($40 for meals and $140 for lodging) for each day of travel to any of 41 high-cost destinations and up to

$113 per day ($32 for meals and $81 for lodging) for travel to any other location in the contiguous 48 states.

1998 transportation and parking limits

For 1998, a church can sell transit passes and tokens to ministers and other employees at discounts of up to $65 per month tax-free. Or, a church can just give cash in 1998 of up to $65 for passes and tokens tax-free. Also, if a church gives an employee a parking space near its premises, it is tax-free to the employee up to a value of $175 per month in 1998, up from $170 in 1997. It is also tax-free up to $175 per month if the employee rents a space near the church's premises and is reimbursed. The cost of a parking space located at the employee's residence is taxable to the employee regardless of its proximity to the employer's premises.

1998 retirement plan limits

The maximum amount employees can contribute on a tax-deferred basis to a 401(k) plan is $10,000 for 1998 (Notice 97-58).

The maximum amount of employee voluntary salary reduction contributions to 403(b) plans (tax-sheltered annuities) is $10,000 per year. This limit does not apply to pension plan contributions made by a church to a denominational pension plan on behalf of a minister. Other limits apply to these payments.

1998 token limitations

Charities can give slightly more to contributors before the donors must trim their deductions. Donations are fully deductible when benefits to donor are small and part of a fund-raiser and the charity says those benefits are insubstantial. Examples of these benefits might include mugs, key chains, posters, shirts, tote bags, and so on.

The value of the benefit to the donor cannot exceed the lesser of 2% of the gift or $71.00 (1998 inflation-adjusted amount). The donor can get a token item (T-shirt, for example) bearing the name or logo of the charity and costing $7.10 or less for contributions that exceed $35.50. (Rev. Proc. 97-57)

1998 social security taxable earnings limit

The maximum amount of taxable and creditable annual earnings subject to the social security and self-employment income tax increased to $68,400 in 1998, up from $65,400 in 1997. There is no maximum wage base for Medicare.

1998 highly compensated employee definition

The "highly compensated employee" definition is important in determining whether certain fringe benefits are taxable to employees that fall within that category. Examples of fringe benefits that may trigger additional compensation based on favoring highly compensated employees include: qualified tuition and fee discounts, educational assistance benefits, dependent care plans, group-term life benefits, and self-insured medical plans.

Employees who have compensation for the previous year in excess of $80,000 (1998 limit per Notice 97-58) and, if an employer elects, were in the top 20% of employees by compensation meet the definition.

For example, Pastor Smith received gross pay of $60,000. The church established a dependent care plan to pay for the child care of two of Pastor Smith's children. The dependent care benefit is not provided to other employees of the church. Even though the plan is clearly discriminatory, Pastor Smith does not meet the highly compensated employee definition since the gross pay is less than $80,000. Therefore, the dependent care benefit is tax free.

Restructuring of the IRS

The IRS Restructuring and Reform Act of 1998 changes how the IRS is organized and how it is controlled. It represents the most extensive restructuring of the IRS and the laws under which it operates in at least 40 years.

The IRS governance is changed by creating an independent Oversight Board. The Board will consist of six private-sector experts and it will have a strong say in strategic IRS plans, modernization, training, and collection procedures.

The present problem resolution system will be replaced with local Taxpayer Advocates who will operate independently of IRS examination, collection, and appeals functions.

The IRS will eliminate or substantially modify the geographic National-Regional-District tiered structure. In its place, the IRS Commissioner will create operating units that serve particular groups of taxpayers with similar needs (individuals, small businesses, large businesses, and tax-exempts).

The new law shifts the burden of proof to the IRS, but only in certain situations. The IRS will now generally have the burden of proof in any court proceeding on income, gift, estate or generation-skipping tax liability with respect to factual issues, provided: the taxpayer introduces credible evidence on the factual issue; maintains records and substantiates items as presently required under the Code and regulations; and cooperates with reasonable IRS requests for meetings, interviews, witnesses, information, and documents.

Employer-provided transit passes

The Transportation Equity Act for the 21st Century (P.L. 105-178) makes it easier for your organization to offer commuting benefits to more employees. Employee's can pay their commuting costs with pre-tax, not after-tax, dollars.

In the past, if you offered employees a choice between a qualified fringe benefit and cash, you not only had to tax those who opted for cash, but also include the value of the fringe benefits in the gross incomes of those who opted to take the benefit. So very few employers offered the cash option.

Under the new law, you can give employees taxable cash in lieu of any of the qualified transportation fringe benefits you offer, without changing the tax-free status of those benefits. The cash you pay in lieu of a benefit is still taxable, but the transportation fringes—as long as you follow the other qualifying conditions (see page 2 for the 1998 limits)—stay tax-free.

This change will primarily impact nonprofits providing mass transit passes, parking, or vanpooling benefits to employees.

Excessive fundraising fees cause loss of exempt status

The Tax Court retroactively revoked the exemption of a tax-exempt organization because there was inurement of the organization's net earnings to a professional fundraiser who was an insider The decision is expected to be appealed. It was a case of the professional fundraiser, Watson and Hughey which has since changed its name to Direct Response Consulting Services, of McLean, Virginia, swallowing the organization that hired it. The novel aspect of this case is that third parties can now be considered as insiders for purposes of the rules prohibiting private inurement.

Watson and Hughey received uncapped total compensation of $8 million while the organization received $2.25 million—less than 10% of the total donations. In addition, the fundraiser derived substantial income from its co-ownership rights in the exempt organization's mailing list which it obtained under the contract.

Under a five-year fundraising contract, the professional fundraiser became the exclusive fundraising agent. It advanced money for the initial fundraising efforts and even granted the exempt organization a draw against future contributions. In return, it received a percentage of the contributions, co-ownership of the exempt organization's mailing list, and brokerage fees.

The court noted that contingent fee arrangements are not the norm for charitable fundraising. The IRS's working position on contingent compensation in the exempt organization context has been that it is not per se a problem as long as there is a cap or limitation on the total compensation which the professional fundraiser can receive. (United Cancer Council, Inc. v. Commissioner 107 TC No. 17, 1997)

Court allows charity to break its promise to donor

An individual makes a substantial gift to a charitable institution on the institution's written promise that it will use the contribution for a specific purpose. A few years later the institution breaks its promise and diverts the funds to its general support. What rights does the donor have? None, said the Connecticut Supreme Court.

During 1987 and 1988, the Carl J. Herzog Foundation made gifts totaling $250,000 to the University of Bridgeport under a written agreement that the school would use the grant to provide scholarships for needy students for medical-related education. At first, the university used the grant to fund scholarships to its nursing school. However, the university ran into severe financial problems in 1990, closed the school in 1991, and began using the funds for its general purposes.

The foundation filed suit, asking the courts to order the university either to use the funds for their intended purpose, or turn them over to the Bridgeport Area Foundation, which would administer the scholarship program.

The Connecticut Supreme Court ruled against the foundation, finding that it could not bring suit to enforce the gift agreement. Donors, the court said, cannot enforce gift restrictions if they have not specified in writing that the gift will revert to them, or be given over to another donee, if the beneficiary does not use the gift as intended. This limitation is not commonly included in gift agreements because retention of control over a gift defeats the donor's ability to claim a charitable deduction for it.

The effect of this decision is to tilt the balance toward the charity's long-term institutional interests, by effectively permitting it to subvert a donor's intent—as long as the institution is willing to take the risk that neither the attorney general or the intended beneficiaries will bring suit.

Lack of appraisal costs taxpayer a charitable deduction

The IRS agreed that the fair market value of donated stock in a nonpublicly traded company was equal to $121,000 that the taxpayer took as charitable deductions; it disallowed the deductions, except for $6,500, the taxpayer's very low basis. The taxpayer had used an average per share price in contemporaneous arm's-length sales and did not obtain an appraisal.

The Tax Court had previously held that the reporting requirements of the regulation could be satisfied by substantial, and not strict, compliance. Instead, the Tax Court said that simply proving the fair market value of the donated stock does not represent substantial compliance in the absence of a qualified appraisal and a summary attached to the return. (J.T. Hewitt, 109 TC No. 12)

Deputational fundraising discussions continue with IRS

Discussions and correspondence continue between the IRS and an ad hoc committee representing various religious organizations. The committee is seeking guidance regarding both the circumstances under which contributions received by a nonprofit organization are deductible to contributors and the circumstances under which deputized fundraising methods are consistent with tax-exempt status.

It appears that a nonprofit organization using the deputational fund raising method will be required to demonstrate control over contributions received. The following criteria have been proposed as a balancing test to demonstrate effective organizational control:

 The board regularly adopts the organization's annual budget in advance, including detailed line-item breakout of all relevant categories of expenses by each ministry location and project, and subsequently oversees the budget's accomplishment and application.

✓ The board consistently exercises general responsibility for establishing and reviewing the programs and policies of the organization.

✓ There is a functioning audit review committee appointed by the board.

✓ To demonstrate adequate oversight of ministry expenditures by staff members, board approved expense reimbursement procedures are adhered to that require timely filing of periodic expense reports and review of reports by a designated staff member. The review of expense reports is based on board approved guidelines of permissible reimbursable expenses.

✓ The organization uses established procedures to determine when and for what purposes funds will be sent to foreign-based operations or unaffiliated U.S. organizations, and the organization monitors expenditures of funds sent to foreign-based operations or unaffiliated U.S. organizations to assure that the funds are being used for the intended religious and charitable purposes.

✓ The organization sets qualifications for, and recruits, employees, and trains and develops qualified applicants who wish to enter the ministry as carried on by the organization.

✓ The organization provides ongoing field training for staff members and supervision through an assigned supervisor.

✓ The organization determines employee salaries based on a board-approved wage and salary structure, which assures that no salary exceeds reasonableness standards.

✓ The organization establishes its specific ministry programs and locations with board-level action and/or approval.

✓ The organization assigns staff members to specific ministry programs and locations based upon its assessment of each staff member's gifts, skills, and training, and of the specific needs of the particular ministry program.

In 1996, the IRS initially denied tax-exempt status to Great Commission Ministries (GCM), setting off alarm bells throughout the Christian parachurch community. At issue was the common practice known as deputation, by which missionaries raise support. Under the deputized concept, individuals solicit financial pledges, which are paid to a nonprofit, such as a mission agency. The nonprofit uses those funds to pay ministry costs, benefits, and a salary to the individual engaged in ministry activity.

In 1997, the IRS decided that it will not try to defend its position in court against GCM. Therefore, it fully exonerated GCM's policies and practices and issued GCM's tax exemption determination letter. GCM reportedly expended nearly $50,000 in its 3½ year battle with the IRS.

New law protects tithes and offerings

The Religious Liberty and Charitable Donations Protection Act was prompted by a case involving Crystal Evangelical Free Church in Minneapolis, Minnesota. A bankruptcy trustee tried to force the church to return donations made in good faith by a couple who were later forced to file bankruptcy. The bankruptcy court ruled that since the couple had not received anything of value for their gifts, the donations constituted a fraudulent transfer. The amount involved was $13,450, but the church spent about $300,000 fighting for the principle involved.

The new law prevents bankruptcy courts from seizing contributions made to religious organizations and other charities by persons who later file bankruptcy. The law will protect tithes and other contributions of up to 15% of the debtor's annual income, and will also allow debtors in Chapter 13 reorganization to continue to tithe while they satisfy their debts.

State regulations for gift annuities

Are you interested in the gift annuity rules that apply in a particular state? Check out the Planned Giving Resources Web site administered by James B. Potter, a planned-giving consultant. It provides an excellent resource for the state rules that apply to gift annuities. Use www.pgresources.com.

New gift annuity rates

The Board of the American Council on Gift Annuities (ACGA) has announced a slight reduction in the suggested rates for both immediate and deferred gift annuities, effective July 1, 1998. The immediate gift annuity rate reduction is .2 to .3 percent for most ages.

The gift annuity rates are reviewed annually, but the rates are adjusted only when there are significant changes in financial markets, or when changes in expense and mortality assumptions are deemed necessary.

To obtain a free copy of the new rates, send a self-addressed envelope to the American Council on Gift Annuities, 2401 Cedar Springs Road, Dallas, TX 75201.

Deposit threshold raised from $500 to $1,000

The IRS has raised the threshold at which employment tax deposits are required, from $500 per return period to $1,000 (IR Notice 98-43). The new rules apply to Form 941, Employer's Quarterly Federal Tax Return, and applies to quarterly returns for periods beginning July 1, 1998.

Before this change, employers did not have to make deposits if they had less than $500 of accumulated employment taxes—social security, Medicare, and withheld federal income taxes—for a return period. They could instead send a payment with the return they filed for that period. Now, if an employer has an employment tax liability of less than $1,000 per return period, the employer no longer needs to make monthly deposits.

IRS gives employers a break on electronic deposits

If you are required to deposit your federal taxes via electronic funds transfer (EFT), but make a deposit using the paper Form 8109 coupon instead, the IRS considers that a failure to make the deposit. The law requires that employers with more than $50,000 of federal employment tax deposits in calendar year 1995 must use electronic funds transfer to make deposits that are due on or after July 1, 1997, and related to return periods beginning on or after January 1, 1997. Taxpayers with more than $50,000 in employment tax deposits in calendar year 1996 must use electronic funds transfer to make deposits of taxes relating to return periods beginning on or after January 1, 1998.

For taxpayers first required to make federal tax deposits electronically on or after July 1, 1997, the IRS will not impose penalties solely for the failure to make those deposits by EFT. This waiver of the failure to deposit penalty applies only to deposit obligations incurred on or before December 31, 1998. (IRS Notice 98-30)

Reporting requirements extended to payments to attorneys

Information returns must be filed with the IRS for payments to an attorney or a law firm effective with payments made in 1998. It is anticipated that the reporting would be required on Form 1099-B. The only exception to this new reporting requirement is for payments that are to be reported on either Form 1099-MISC or on Form W-2. The present exemption from reporting for payments made to corporations will not apply to payments made to attorneys.

School headmistress's housing allowance isn't excludable

The IRS has ruled that a housing allowance paid by a private school to its headmistress is not excludable from income. The school provided an allowance rather than lodging in kind, the lodging was not located on the school's premises, and the proximity to the school was not necessary for the headmistress to perform her duties. The headmistress lived in a rented apartment nine blocks from the school.

The headmistress asserted that the school fired its last headmistress, in part, because she lived too far from the school. The headmistress was willing to live on the school's premises but there was no residence available, and the school was unable to purchase lodging nearby. Several days each week, the headmistress works until about 10:00 p.m., and she is required to be available for emergencies during off-hours. Twice each month she holds meetings or entertains persons from the community at her rented apartment.

The IRS explained that the headmistress's receipt of cash instead of lodging in kind caused the transaction to fail. Moreover, the IRS wrote that the lodging doesn't satisfy the regulations because the lodging isn't located on the business premises; the apartment isn't an integral part of the school's business property, regardless of the proximity of the residence to the school; and the headmistress doesn't perform a significant portion of her duties at the residence. (Letter Ruling 9801023)

Tax Court finds minister to be an employee

The Tax Court determined that Rev. Henry Radde, a United Methodist pastor and District Superintendent, was an employee for income tax purposes. Radde contended that Weber v. Commissioner (a 1994 case), in which the court held that a Methodist minister was an employee, should be applied prospectively only (the Radde case involved 1990-91). The court rejected this contention.

The court also determined that Rev. Radde had significantly under-reported the fair rental value of church-provided housing. Accordingly the court increased the self-employment income for social security purposes. (T.C. Memo. 1997-490)

Presiding elder determined to be an employee

The position of presiding elder in a particular denomination is both administrative and advisory. A presiding elder is not assigned to a specific congregation but "serves at the pleasure" of the local bishop. In this case, the elder was assigned to supervise 27 churches.

A presiding elder conducts quarterly conferences and preaches at churches within his district. A presiding elder is also expected to advise and instruct congregations in his district as needed.

The elder took the position that he is an independent contractor for income tax purposes because "he does not report to and is not supervised by the bishop who appointed him." The IRS ruled that the presiding elder is an employee for income tax purposes. (Letter Ruling 9825002)

Chaplain services qualify housing allowance

The IRS has ruled that a chaplain, in providing for spiritual needs of the residents of a retirement community, is performing services in the exercise of ministry and that part of his compensation may be designated as a parsonage allowance.

The retirement center is exempt as a religious organization but is not affiliated with any particular church or denomination. To provide for the spiritual needs of its residents, the center employs chaplains of various denominations to perform and oversee ministerial services. They are not assigned to work for the center by their particular churches. (Private Letter Ruling 9729237)

Substantiating electronic airline tickets

With an electronic airline ticket, or "e-ticket," you can often go directly to an airport gate, show identification, and the gate agent can match your name to the reservation you made earlier. This has reduced airline costs. But you do not receive a paper ticket and sometimes no paper receipt.

The IRS generally disallows a deduction for any traveling expenses unless the taxpayer substantiates the expenses by adequate records or other sufficient evidence. Adequate records usually mean the record of the expenses such as an account book, diary, log, statement of expense, trip sheets, and other similar records as well as documentary evidence in the form of receipts or paid bills.

The IRS ruled that an itinerary and receipt issued by a travel agent or airline for a ticketless trip meet the expense substantiation rules. The documents must contain the amount, date, place, and essential character of the expense. The business nature of the trip must also be recorded to fully satisfy the accountable business expense rules. (Letter Ruling 9805007)

IRS releases regulations on intermediate sanctions

The IRS has released so-called "intermediate sanctions" regulations that affect many nonprofit organizations.

Intermediate sanctions are penalty taxes that may be imposed on individuals employed by, or associated with, a nonprofit organization who receive unreasonable compensation or are a party to an insider deal. These situations are referred to as "excess benefits transactions." Penalty taxes may also be imposed on organization managers who participate in an excess benefit transaction. Prior to the new intermediate sanctions rules, the only penalty available to the IRS when it found cases of excessive compensation was to revoke the tax-exempt status of the organization.

While very few nonprofits will ever be involved in an excess benefit transaction, the proposed regulations provide certain safe harbor rules for the presumption that a particular compensation arrangement is not an excess benefit transaction.

New green cards

The Immigration and Naturalization Service (INS) has issued 50,000 new versions of the "green card." You will see these new cards as individuals start using them as proof of work eligibility. New features to look for include:

✓   a hologram with images of the Statue of Liberty, a U.S. map, and the INS seal;

✓   a laser-etched photograph and fingerprint of the holder; and

✓   new color and new name.

The new pinkish-red cards are called "Permanent resident cards." They have the same form number (I-551) as the green "Alien registration receipt cards."

Employers should not stop accepting old green cards. Permanent residents can continue using them for proof of work-eligibility until their old card expires.

Affinity cards

The IRS is still in pursuit of tax dollars from tax-exempt organizations that sponsor affinity credit card arrangements. However, their recent decision not to appeal the Tax Court's decision in a key case (*Mississippi State Alumni v. Commissioner*, T.C. Memo 1997-37) may signal that their interest in these cases is waning. Affinity card cases still being litigated by the IRS include *Oregon State University Alumni Association, Inc. v. Commissioner* and *Alumni Association of the University of Oregon v. Commissioner*.

Joint ventures with for-profit organizations

Although a recent revenue ruling on this topic focused on hospitals, an IRS official notes the principles of the ruling may apply to other nonprofits. The ruling related to a charity that formed a Limited Liability Corporation with a for-profit corporation. The charity contributed assets to the LLC. The ruling gives an example of a charity which holds majority control of the LLC and retained their exempt status. Conversely, a charity that does not hold majority control over the LLC, the charity would lose its exempt status. (Revenue Ruling 98-15)

Management services income

The IRS has ruled that income received by a nonprofit for management services is subject to unrelated business income tax. One nonprofit organization handled the correspondence, answered telephones, maintained books and records, and provided other services for another nonprofit organization. The fees received under the management services agreement was termed unrelated business income. (Letter Ruling 9811001)

Travel tours and unrelated business income

After years of complaints by the commercial travel industry, proposed regulations on travel and tour activities have been issued. When tours aren't related to a charity's exempt purpose, the tour income will be subject to unrelated business income tax (UBIT).

To be exempt, the travel tour must have a curriculum or some other form of substantial scheduled instruction. It is important for a charity to document, at the time a tour is planned and conducted, how and why the destination is selected, how the destination ties in with the organization's exempt purpose, and what happens on the tour.

Unless a tour program can contribute very significantly to your mission, it may not be worth the hassle to set one up and claim that it is not subject to unrelated business income tax.

Moving expense reporting changes

Effective with 1998, employers will not have to report any qualified moving services they pay directly to a vendor for an employee on the employee's 1998 Form W-2. However, employers who reimburse an employee directly for qualified moving expenses must report the reimbursements in Box 13 of the Form W-2, using Code P as the identifier. Employers who pay an employee's nonqualified moving expenses, on the other hand, must include the reimbursements in Box 1 of Form W-2, regardless of whether the reimbursement was paid directly to the employee or to a third party.

If an organization directly pays moving expenses for an independent contractor or reimburses an independent contractor, the full amounts of the payment(s) must be included on Form 1099-MISC.

Effective with returns for tax year 1998, employees will report on Form 3903, "Moving Expenses," only those qualified moving expenses they pay directly, reduced by any employer reimbursements.

Qualified moving expenses are limited to the cost of transportation of household goods and personal effects and travel (including lodging but not meals) to the new residence. The new principal place of work must be at least 50 miles farther from the taxpayer's old residence than the old residence was from the taxpayer's old place of work. During the 12-month period immediately following the move, the taxpayer must be employed full-time for at least 39 weeks. If any of these tests are not met, moving expenses paid directly or reimbursed must be included in Box 1 of Form W-2 under 1998 rules.

Minimum wage increases

The federal minimum wage was increased from $4.75 to $5.15 on September 1, 1997. See pages 180–81 for a discussion of if and when the minimum wage rules apply to churches.

CHAPTER ONE

Financial Accountability

We need to practice what we preach about accountability.

In This Chapter

- Organizations promoting accountability
- Accountability to an independent board
- Accountability to donors
- Accountability to government

The public has high expectations of religious organizations. Day after day, thousands in the nonprofit community work tirelessly and selflessly to address physical and spiritual needs worldwide, only to find the public casting a wary eye on them due to the highly publicized misdeeds of a few. Donors recognize that enormous needs exist and they want to respond generously to those needs. But they also want to be sure that optimum use of their sacrificial gifts is employed by the charities they support. There is no acceptable alternative to accountability.

For large nonprofit organizations, accountability issues often relate to complex issues of private inurement or conflicts of interest. In churches and small-to-medium-nonprofits, the issues may be as basic as whether to accept a gift that appears to be a pass-through contribution for the personal benefit of a designated individual.

Financial accountability is based on the principle of stewardship. A steward-manager exercises responsible care over entrusted funds. Good stewardship rarely occurs outside a system of accountability.

Financial accountability is the natural outgrowth of proper organizational leadership. Providing clear, basic explanations of financial activity starts with the daily record of transactions and evolves to the adequate reporting to donors and boards.

U.S. laws provide special tax treatment of religious and charitable institutions. The nonprofit organization that refuses to disclose its finances is shortchanging the public from which it derives its support. It also causes suspicions about how it is using the financial resources at its disposal.

Organizations Promoting Accountability

Being a member of organizations that promote stewardship principles often enhances accountability. Several organizations provide leadership in the area of financial accountability. These organizations include the Evangelical Council for Financial Accountability (ECFA), the National Charities Information Bureau (NCIB), and the Council of Better Business Bureaus, Inc. (CBBB).

The National Committee on Planned Giving and the Committee on Gift Annuities (NCPG/CGA) have adopted model standards for those involved in planned giving. The National Society of Fund Raising Executives (NSFRE) has also prepared fund-raising guidelines.

For missionary organizations, the Interdenominational Foreign Mission Association (IFMA) and the Evangelical Fellowship of Mission Agencies (EFMA) are groups which provide accountability for members.

The strong tenets of these organizations are proper accounting, an independent and responsible volunteer board of directors, full disclosure of finances, and fair treatment for donors.

Accountability to an Independent Board

Board governance

Strong leadership often shuns accountability. Some boards do not live up to their responsibility to hold themselves accountable and to demand accountability of the organizational leadership.

Can your organization's leadership be challenged and voted down? Are the board members permissive and passive or involved and active? Are your values and policies clearly articulated? Are they operative in the organization daily? Are annual evaluations, based on predetermined goals, made of the pastor(s) or the nonprofit chief executive officer (CEO)?

A board should generally meet at least semi-annually. Some boards meet monthly. Meetings should be more than listening to the CEO's report and rubber-stamping a series of resolutions prepared by the CEO.

ECFA and NCIB members must have a board of not less than five individuals. A majority of the board must be other than employees or staff, or those related by blood or marriage, to meet ECFA standards. No more than one paid staff member may be on the board to comply with NCIB standards.

Even when employee membership on the board is slightly less than a majority, the independence of the board may be jeopardized. Employees often lack independence and objectivity in dealing with many board-level matters. The CEO is often a member of an organization's board of directors. Department heads are generally not members of the board.

Recording board actions

The actions of an organization's board and its committees should be recorded by written minutes, including the signature of the group's secretary, prepared within a few days after the meeting concludes. The minute books of some charities are almost nonexistent. Minutes of the most recent board meeting often appear to be placed in proper written form on the eve of the succeeding board meeting. Such lack of organization can be indicative of weak board governance and may leave a poor paper trail to document the board's actions.

The actions of an organization's board typically include the approval and revision of policies that should be organized and printed as the body of board policies. These policies, extracted from the board minutes, should be revised after each board meeting if new policies are adopted or previously existing policies are revised.

Financial reporting

ECFA members must have an independent annual audit according to generally accepted auditing standards (GAAS). Financial statements must be prepared following generally accepted accounting principles (GAAP). NCIB also requires a GAAP audit.

A subcommittee of the board, often called an audit review committee, should recommend the independent accountants to perform the audit (this appointment to be made by the board) and review the audit report (and management letter, if one is prepared) prior to its submission to the board. This committee should not be controlled by employees or staff members.

The board should also receive staff-prepared monthly or quarterly financial statements.

Compensation review

An annual review of the local church minister's or nonprofit organization executive's compensation package is vital. The review should focus on all elements of pay, taxable and nontaxable.

Pay and fringe benefit packages should be determined by an objective evaluation of responsibilities, goals reached, and available resources. A comparison with positions in other organizations may be helpful. National salary surveys may provide meaningful data such as National Association of Church Business Administrators Church Staff Compensation Survey, and Christian Management Association Salary Survey.

The approved compensation package should be documented in board and/or subcommittee minutes. This action should include guidelines for disbursement of compensation-related funds by the organization's treasurer.

With increased scrutiny on nonprofit salaries (see chapter 3), it is important that compensation amounts be accurately stated. Gross pay may include the following elements (some taxable and some tax-free or tax-deferred):

✓ Cash salary

✓ Fair rental value of a house, including utilities, provided by the organization

✓ Cash housing or furnishings allowance

✓ Tax-deferred payments

✓ Expense advances that exceed documented business expenses

✓ Value of the personal use of organization-owned aircraft or vehicle

✓ Value of noncash goods and services

✓ Cash bonuses

Budget process

The organization should prepare a detailed annual budget consistent with the major classifications in the financial statements and approved by the board. The budget should allow meaningful comparison with the previous year's financial statements; recast if necessary.

Responsibility for budgetary performance should be clearly assigned to management as appropriate (for example, department heads, field directors, and so on). The controller or treasurer of an organization is normally responsible for budgetary enforcement and reporting. For more information on the budgeting process, see pages 99–100.

Conflicts of interest and related party transactions

Conducting activities

Fairness in decision-making is more likely to occur in an impartial environment. Conflicts of interest and related-party transactions are often confused. However, the distinction between the two concepts is useful.

The potential for a conflict of interest arises in situations in which a person has a responsibility to promote one interest, but has a competing interest at the same time. If the competing interest is exercised over a fiduciary interest, the conflict is realized. Conflicts of interest should be avoided.

Related-party transactions are transactions that occur between two or more parties that have interlinking relationships. These transactions should be disclosed to the governing board. Transactions should be evaluated to ensure they are made on a sound economic basis. Some related-party transactions are clearly to the advantage of the organization and should be pursued. Other related-party transactions are conflicts of interest and should be avoided.

Under ECFA guidelines, transactions with related parties may be undertaken only in the following situations:

✓ The audited financial statements of the organization fully disclose material related-party transactions.

✓ Related parties are excluded from the discussion and approval of related-party transactions.

✓ Competitive bids or comparable valuations exist.

✓ The organization's board approves the transaction as being in the best interest of the organization.

Example 1: An organization purchases insurance coverage through a firm owned by a board member. This would constitute a conflict of interest unless the cost of the insurance is disclosed, the purchase is subject to proper approvals, the price is below the competition, and the purchase is in the best interests of the organization. If the purchase passes these tests, it is still a related-party transaction.

Example 2: The CEO and several employees are members of the board. When the resolution on salary and fringe-benefit adjustments comes to the board, should those affected by the resolution discuss and vote on the matter? No. To avoid the appearance of a conflict of interest, the employees should absent themselves from the meeting.

Example 3: A nonprofit board considers a significant loan to a company in which a board member has a material ownership interest. Should this loan even be considered? Only if it is in the best interest of the non-profit and allowable under state laws and the organization's by-laws.

Example 4: A church receives a significant endowment gift. The church board establishes investment policy guidelines and appoints a subcommittee of the board to carry out the routine investing of the funds.

The Investment Committee is chaired by an investment broker who sells mutual funds for which his firm receives commissions. He receives commissions on the sales from his firm. The broker recommends that the purchases of certain mutual funds be made from his firm.

This is a blatant conflict of interest even if the broker fully discloses the fees that would be paid to his firm and commissions that, in turn, would be paid to him and even if the fees are comparable to what other brokers would charge. This biased environment makes it nearly impossible to achieve fairness in decision-making.

Sample Conflict or Duality of Interest Policy Statement

All trustees, officers, agents, and employees of this organization shall disclose all real or apparent conflict or dualities of interest which they discover or which have been brought to their attention in connection with this organization's activities. "Disclosure" shall mean providing properly, to the appropriate person, a written description of the facts comprising the real or apparent conflict or duality of interest. An annual disclosure statement shall be circulated to trustees, officers, and certain identified agents and employees to assist them in considering such disclosures, but disclosure is appropriate and required whenever conflicts or dualities of interest may occur. The written notices of disclosures shall be filed with the Chief Executive Officer or such other person designated by the Chief Executive Officer to receive such notifications. All disclosures of real or apparent conflict or duality of interests shall be noted for the record in the minutes of the meeting of the top governing body.

An individual trustee, officer, agent, or employee who believes that he or she or an immediate member of his or her immediate family might have a real or apparent conflict of interest, in addition to filing a notice of disclosure, must abstain from (1) participating in discussions or deliberations with respect to the subject of the conflict (other than to present factual information or answer questions), (2) using their personal influence to affect deliberations, (3) making motions, (4) voting, (5) executing agreements, or (6) taking similar actions on behalf of the organizations where the conflict or duality of interest might pertain by law, agreement or otherwise. At the discretion of the top governing body or a committee thereof, a person with a real or apparent conflict or duality of interest may be excused from all or any portion of discussion or deliberations with respect to the subject of the conflict.

A member of the top governing body or a committee thereof, who, having disclosed a conflict or duality of interest, nevertheless shall be counted in determining the existence of a quorum at any meeting where the subject of the conflict is discussed. The minutes of the meeting shall reflect the disclosure made, the vote thereon, the abstention from participation and voting by the individual making disclosure.

There shall be no business transactions, whether the nature of employment, contract, purchase, or sale, between the organization and a trustee during his or her term in office, except in the case of employment, for a period of one year thereafter. For purposes of this section, the payment of any benefit to which the trustee might otherwise be entitled, shall not be deemed a business transaction.

The Chief Executive Officer shall ensure that all trustees, officers, agents, employees, and independent contractors of the organization are made aware of the organization's policy with respect to conflicts or duality of interest.

Sample Conflict or Duality of Interest Disclosure Annual Reporting Statement

Certification

I have read and understand Conflict or Duality of Interest Policy. I hereby declare and certify the following real or apparent conflict or dualities of interest:

Disclosure Statement

_____

_____

_____

_____

_____

_____

_____

_____

_____

_____

_____

(If necessary, attach additional documentation.)

Date _____   _____

Signature

_____

Title

Selecting board members

Information concerning prospective and current board members may reveal potential conflicts that will disqualify the individual. If a conflict is sufficiently limited, the director may simply need to abstain from voting on certain issues. If the conflict of interest is material, the election or re-election of the individual may be inappropriate.

Board compensation

Most nonprofit board members serve without compensation. This practice reinforces an important distinction of nonprofits: the assets of a nonprofit should not be used for the private enrichment of directors, members, or employees.

Board members often have travel-related expenses reimbursed. Mileage may be reimbursed up to the standard IRS business rate (32.5 cents per mile for 1998) without reporting any taxable income to the board member. Travel expenses reimbursed for the spouse of a board member represent taxable income to the board member unless the spouse qualifies for employee treatment and provides services to the nonprofit in conjunction with the trip.

Accountability to Donors

Donors are showing greater concern about the solicitation and use of their contributions. The primary areas of concern are:

Donor communication

ECFA requires that all statements made by an organization in its fund-raising appeals about the use of a gift must be honored by the organization. The donor's intent may be shaped by both the organization's communication of the appeal and by any donor instructions with the gift.

If a donor responds to a specific appeal, the assumption may be made that the donor's intent is that the funds be used as outlined in the appeal. There is a need for clear communication in the appeal to insure that the donor understands precisely how the funds will be used. Any note or correspondence accompanying the gift or conversations between the donor and donee representatives indicate donor intent.

All aspects of a proposed charitable gift should be explained fully, fairly, and accurately to the donor. Any limitations on the use of the gift should be clear and complete both in the response device and the appeal letter. These items should be included in the explanation:

 The charity's proposed use of the gift. Realistic expectations should be communicated regarding what the donor's gift will do within the programs of the donee organization.

✓ **Representations of fact.** Any description of the financial condition of the organization, or narrative about events must be current, complete, and accurate. References to past activities or events should be appropriately dated. There should be no material omissions or exaggerations of fact or use of misleading photographs or any other communication tending to create a false impression or misunderstanding.

✓ **Valuation issues and procedures.** If an appraisal is required, the donor should fully understand the procedures and who is responsible to pay for the appraisal.

✓ **Tax consequences and reporting requirements.** While tax considerations should not be the primary focus of a gift, the donor should clearly understand the current and future income, estate and gift tax consequences, and reporting requirements of the proposed gift. A charitable gift should never be represented as a tax shelter.

✓ **Alternative arrangements for making the gift.** The donor should understand the current and deferred gift options that are available.

✓ **Financial and family implications.** In addition to the tax consequences, the overall financial implications of the proposed gift and the potential impact on family members should be carefully explained.

✓ **Possible conflicts of interest.** Disclose to the donor all relationships which might constitute, or appear to constitute, conflicts of interest. The disclosure should include how and by whom each party is compensated and any cost of managing the gift.

Fund raising appeals must not create unrealistic donor expectations of what a donor's gift will actually accomplish within the limits of the organization's ministry. The following are examples of the application of donor communication principles:

Example 1: **Bible distribution:** An organization distributes Bibles and related literature as its primary purpose. Fund-raising letters appeal for funds to distribute Bibles in a particular country. The organization includes the funds raised in general income. The accounting records do not account for the costs associated with distributing Bibles in that location to determine whether or not the funds donated for that location have been used for the stipulated purpose or whether the project has been overfunded or underfunded.

The organization's handling of the gift funds is inappropriate. It should account for gifts by country with appropriate allocation of costs associated with the distribution. Any overfunding or underfunding should be identified for the particular country.

Example 2: **Child sponsorship:** A child sponsorship organization appeals to donors to support specific children and creates the impression that specific sponsorships directly benefit specific children. Instead, sponsorship funds are pooled and spent on a project basis under the philosophy of child-focused community development programs. Although there is shared benefit to the entire community by worthwhile development, only a small amount of the project budget is exclusively for the sponsored children in the community.

The fund-raising practices of this organization are inappropriate unless:

✓ It discloses to donors that child sponsorship gifts are pooled to support child-focused community development projects and that many of the benefits are shared by all the children in the community.

✓ The organization insures that sponsored children are receiving direct benefit from the development activities in the community. Community development activities must create specific improvements in the lives of the sponsored children within the community. Periodic reports should be provided to the donor which clearly explain the project activities, how they benefit the sponsored child, as well as the specific progress of the sponsored child.

✓ Donor receipts and related accounting records indicate that financial support has been provided in fulfillment of a pledge of support for the pooled sponsorship funds with a preference for an individual child.

Example 3: **Feeding the hungry:** An organization appeals for gifts to feed the hungry and indicates that a certain number of dollars will provide a certain number of meals. The organization does not separately account for the donations and costs of the meal program. The meal costs quoted are based on national rather than local factors. Much of the food and labor is donated and the gifts are primarily used for the general support of the organization rather than being limited to use in the feeding program.

The organization's fund raising practices are inappropriate. It should account for such gifts as donor-restricted and limited to use only in the feeding program. To avoid a separate accounting for the program, the organization would need to modify appeals to not give the impression that a specific amount will provide a certain number of meals. The following wording might be used for an unrestricted appeal: "This gift is to help feed, cloth, shelter, and minister to the needy at the Christmas season and throughout the year."

Accounting for restricted gifts

Donors often place temporary or permanent restrictions on gifts that limit their use to certain purposes. These stipulations may specify a use for a contributed asset that is more specific than broad limits relating to the nature of the organization, the environment in which it operates, and the purposes specified in its articles of incorporation or bylaws or comparable documents for unincorporated entities. A restricted gift generally results whenever a donor selects a giving option on a response device other than "unrestricted" or "where needed most."

Some organizations lack the proper accounting structure to account for restricted gift income and to track the funds through to the point of expenditure. This may lead to the following problems:

✓ **Inadequate accounting.** All funds given for specific purposes, projects, or programs should be accounted for separately. Charges against the gifts should be allocated based only on disclosed policies (e.g., administrative assessments or indirect costs) or for costs that are directly attributable to the purpose, project, or program.

✓ **Donations received for one project but spent on another.** Separate revenue and expense accounts must be maintained for each project to ensure the integrity of the funds.

✓ **Overfunding or underfunding of projects.** This may require communicating additional information to donors about the use of the funds. In some cases, donor approval may be needed to re-direct the use of funds. If the purpose of a designated gift cannot be fulfilled and the donor is unwilling to remove or change the designation, it may be necessary to make a refund to the donor (see page 166).

A possible disclosure for response devices and receipts is: "Contributions to (name of charity) are administered and disbursed under the supervision of the Board of Trustees/Directors. In the unlikely event that a ministry is overfunded, gifts may be used in another ministry activity as closely in keeping with your interests as possible." The use of a statement of this type

● is only appropriate when events of overfunding are unusual and infrequent,

● does not make a restricted gift unrestricted until a future event occurs, and

● does not diminish the organization's moral, social, and perhaps legal obligation to use the funds for the specified purpose, except when such an unanticipated event occurs.

✓ **Inadequate reporting to donors on projects.** ECFA requires members, on request, to provide a report, including financial information, on the project

23

for which it is soliciting gifts. Without a proper accounting system, an accurate and timely report on specific projects may be impossible to prepare.

Use of funds

Most contributors believe that their contributions are being applied to the current program needs identified by the organization, unless there is other specific representation. It is prudent management for organizations to accumulate adequate unrestricted operating funds. The needs of the constituency served should be the most important factor in determining the adequacy of reserve funds.

> **Example:** An organization has $250,000 in savings at the time a direct mail appeal asks for donations to cover operating expenses. A donor questions the ethics of the appeal. Was the appeal improper?
>
> The size of the organization would have a significant bearing on the appropriateness of the appeal. The appeal may be inappropriate if the annual budget of the organization is $50,000 (in other words, the savings account would be five times the annual budget). Yet, an organization with an annual budget of $2M may justify a savings account of $250,000 for contingencies.

NCIB standards call for net assets available for the following fiscal year to be not more than twice the current year's expenses or the next year's budget, whichever is higher.

Projects unrelated to an organization's primary purpose

Nonprofits sometimes receive funds for programs that are not part of its present or prospective ministry, but are proper according to its exempt purpose (i.e., one of the exempt purposes under the Internal Revenue Code). In these instances the organization must treat them either as restricted funds and channel them through an organization that can carry out the donor's intent, or return the funds to the donor.

Reporting for incentives and premiums

Fund-raising appeals may offer premiums or incentives in exchange for a contribution. If the value of the premiums or incentives is not insubstantial, but significant in relation to the amount of the donation, the donee organization must advise the donor of the fair market value of the premium or incentive and that the value is not deductible for tax purposes (see pages 150–51). ECFA members must comply with the IRS rules on incentives and premiums. NPGA/CGA has a general standard relating to compliance with all federal and state laws.

Reporting to donors

ECFA, NCIB, and the CBBB require an organization to provide a copy of its current financial statements upon written request. NCIB also requires that a statement of functional allocation of expenses be provided. This type of statement reflects expenses by type—salaries, fringe benefits, and travel—as well as by function.

Compensation of gift planners

Payment of finders' fees, commissions, or other fees by a donee organization to an outside gift planner as a condition for delivery of a gift is never appropriate under ECFA, NSFRE, and NCPG/CGA standards. Commission or contingency-based compensation to an organization's own employees is considered inappropriate by these organizations.

Tax-deductible gifts for a named recipient's personal benefit

According to the Internal Revenue Code and other laws and regulations governing tax-exempt organizations, tax-deductible gifts may not be used to pass money or benefits to any named individual for personal use. Individuals often want to use charitable organizations as a conduit for funds to change the character of personal, nondeductible gifts to deductible charitable contributions. Gifts for the support of specific staff individuals may be deductible as charitable contributions if the donee organization controls the funds and follows proper procedures. Chapter 7 covers this topic in more detail.

Conflict of interest on royalties

ECFA requires that an officer, director, or other principal of the organization must not receive royalties for any product used for fund-raising or promotional purposes by his or her organization. The payment of reasonable royalties for items offered for sale is permissible.

Acknowledgment of gifts-in-kind

Property or gifts-in-kind received by an organization should be acknowledged, describing the property or gift accurately *without* an estimate of the gift's market value. It is the responsibility of the donor to determine the fair market value of the property for tax purposes.

Acting in the interest of the donor

Every effort should be made to avoid accepting a gift from or entering into a contract with a prospective donor that would knowingly place a hardship on the donor, or place the donor's future well-being in jeopardy.

Financial advice

Fund-raisers should recognize that it is almost impossible to properly represent the full interests of the donor and the charitable organization simultaneously.

When dealing with persons regarding commitments on major estate assets, gift planners should seek to guide and advise donors so that they may adequately consider the broad interests of the family and the various organizations they are currently supporting before they make a final decision. Donors should be encouraged to discuss the proposed gift with competent and independent attorneys, accountants, or other professional advisors.

Accountability to Government

Almost every church and nonprofit has some reporting requirements to one or more governmental agencies. Many organizations do not fully comply with reporting guidelines.

Churches and nonprofits abhor the thought of increased governmental regulation. Yet failure to self-regulate areas such as executive compensation, unrelated business activities, fund-raising practices, and political lobbying continues to draw the attention of the IRS and Congress.

A few organizations knowingly operate in or at the edge of fraudulent areas. But most organizations have good intentions and any violations are primarily based on ignorance of laws and regulations.

Key Concepts

■ Good stewardship rarely occurs outside a system of accountability.

■ Adequate board governance is the first step to proper accountability.

■ Accountability in donor solicitation and the use of contributions is vital.

■ Fulfillment of required reporting to governmental agencies is a must.

Tax Exemption

Your tax-exempt status is extremely valuable — guard it carefully!

In This Chapter

- Tax exemption for churches
- Advantages and limitations of tax exemption
- Starting a nonprofit
- Unrelated business income
- Private benefit and private inurement
- Filing federal returns
- Filing state returns
- Political activity

Qualifying tax-exempt organizations may have many advantages. One of the most important benefits is the eligibility to attract deductible charitable contributions from individual and corporate donors. Exemption from tax liability, primarily income, sales, and property tax, is also important.

The term "nonprofit organization" covers a broad range of entities such as churches, colleges, universities, health-care providers, business leagues, veterans groups, political parties, country clubs, and united-giving campaigns. Sources of revenue, ownership structure, and activities distinguish nonprofit from for-profit organizations. The most common type of nonprofits is the charitable organization.

The nonprofit organization concept is basically a state law creation. But tax-exempt organizations are based primarily on federal law. The Internal Revenue Code does not use the word "nonprofit." The Code refers to nonprofits as exempt organizations. Certain state statutes use the term "not-for-profit." A not-for-profit organization under state law may or may not be tax-exempt under federal law.

In this book, the term "nonprofit" refers to nonprofit organizations that are exempt from federal income tax. This is key because not all nonprofit organizations are necessarily tax-exempt.

Tax Exemption for Churches

Tax law and IRS regulations do not define "religious." But the courts have defined "religious" broadly. In part, because of these constitutional concerns, some religious organizations are subject to more lenient reporting and auditing requirements under federal tax law.

The "religious" category includes churches, conventions of churches, associations of churches, church-run organizations (such as schools, hospitals, orphanages, nursing homes, publishing entities, broadcasting entities, and cemeteries), religious orders, apostolic groups, integrated auxiliaries of churches, missionary organizations, and Bible and tract societies. IRS regulations define religious worship as: "What constitutes conduct of religious worship or the ministration of sacerdotal functions depends on the interests and practices of a particular religious body constituting a church."

Although not stated in the regulations, the IRS applies the following 14 criteria to decide whether a religious organization can qualify as a "church":

✔ Distinct legal existence

✔ Recognized creed and form of worship

✔ Definite and distinct ecclesiastical government

✔ Formal code of doctrine and discipline

✔ Distinct religious history

✔ Membership not associated with any other church or denomination

✔ Organization of ordained ministers

✔ Ordained ministers selected after completing prescribed courses of studies

✔ Literature of its own

✔ Established places of worship

✔ Regular congregations

✔ Regular religious services

✔ Sunday schools for religious instruction of the young

✔ Schools for preparation of its ministers

Churches receive favored status in that they are not required to file either an application for exemption (Form 1023) or annual report (Form 990) with the IRS. A church is still subject to filing an annual report on unrelated business income (Form 990-T) and Form 5578 for private schools as well as payroll tax, sales tax, and other forms, if applicable.

Advantages and Limitations of Tax Exemption

Upon approval by the IRS, tax exemption is available to organizations that meet the requirements of the tax code. This exemption provides relief from federal income tax. This income tax exemption may or may not extend to local and state income taxes. Even if an organization receives tax-exempt status, certain federal taxes may still be imposed. Possible taxes are the unrelated business income tax, tax on certain "political" activities, and tax on excessive legislative activities.

Tax exemption advantages

Besides the basic exemption from federal income and excise tax, an organization that is recognized as a charitable organization under the Internal Revenue Code enjoys several advantages:

✓ Its donors can be offered the benefit of a deduction for contributions.

✓ It can benefit from lower postal rates on third-class bulk mailings.

✓ It is in a favored position to seek funding from foundations and other philanthropic entities, many of which will not support organizations other than those recognized under 501(c)(3).

✓ It is eligible for government grants available only to entities exempt under 501(c)(3).

✓ It often qualifies for exemption not only from state and local income tax but from property taxes (for property used directly for its exempt function) and certain sales and use taxes as well.

✓ It may qualify for exemption from the Federal Unemployment Tax Act in certain situations.

✓ Its employees may participate in 403(b) tax-sheltered annuities and 401(k) plans.

✔ It is an exclusive beneficiary of free radio and television public service announcements (PSAs) provided by local media outlets.

✔ If it is a church or a qualified church-controlled organization, it may exclude compensation to employees from the FICA social security base. The organization must be opposed on religious grounds to the payment of FICA social security taxes. The social security liability shifts to the employees of the electing organizations in the form of SECA social security tax.

Tax exemption limitations

Offsetting the advantages of tax-exempt status are some strict requirements:

✔ An organization must be engaged "primarily" in qualified charitable or educational endeavors.

✔ There are limitations to the extent to which it can engage in substantial legislative activities or other political activities.

✔ An organization may not engage in unrelated business activities or commercial activities to an impermissible extent.

✔ There is a prohibition against private inurement or private benefit.

✔ Upon dissolution, the organization's assets must be distributed for one or more exempt purposes.

Starting a Nonprofit

The choice of a nonprofit organizational form is a basic decision. Most churches are unincorporated. However, an increasing number of churches are incorporating for the purpose of limiting legal liability. Most other nonprofit organizations are corporations. While incorporation may usually be desirable, it is generally not mandatory.

Organizations using the corporate form will need articles of incorporation and bylaws. An unincorporated organization will typically have the same instruments although the articles may be in the form of a constitution.

Several planning questions should be asked. If the organization is formed for charitable purposes, is public status desired or is a private foundation acceptable? Are any business activities contemplated and to what degree will the organization be incorporated? Is an attorney competent in nonprofit matters available to help with the preparation of the legal documents? What provisions will the bylaws contain? Who will serve on the board of directors? What name will be used for the organization?

The following materials may be needed or useful when starting a church or other nonprofit organization:

Package 1023   Application for Recognition of Exemption with Instructions

Publication 557   Tax-Exempt Status for Your Organization

Obtaining an employer identification number

All entities, whether exempt from tax or not, must obtain an Employer Identification Number (EIN) by filing IRS Form SS-4. An EIN is required for each church even though churches are not required to file with the IRS for tax-exempt status. This number is not a "tax-exempt number," but is simply the organization's unique identifier in the IRS's records, similar to an individual's social security number.

When the IRS approves an organization for exemption from federal income tax (not required for churches), it will receive a "determination letter." This letter does not assign the organization a "tax-exempt number."

If an organization is a "central organization" that holds a "group exemption letter," the IRS will assign that group a four-digit number, known as its Group Exemption Number (GEN). This number must be supplied with the central organization's annual report to the IRS (updating its list of included subordinate organizations). The number also is inserted on Form 990 (if required) of the central organization and the subordinate organizations included in the group exemption.

When an organization applies for exemption from state or local income, sales, or property taxes, the state or local jurisdiction may provide a certificate or letter of exemption, which, in some jurisdictions, includes a serial number. This number is often called a "tax-exempt number." This number should not be confused with an EIN.

Application for recognition of tax-exempt status

Although churches are not required to apply to the IRS for tax-exempt status under Section 501(c)(3) of the Internal Revenue Code and are exempt from filing Form 990, it may be appropriate to apply for recognition in some situations:

✓ Independent local churches that are not a part of a national denominational body often file for tax-exempt status to provide evidence of their status. The local congregation may wish to file for group exemption if it is a parent church of other local congregations or separately organized ministries.

    National denominations typically file for group exemption to cover all local congregations. A copy of the national body's IRS determination letter may be used by the local group to provide evidence of tax-exempt status.

✓ Some donors, or their professional advisors, may ask if a local church is

31

Form **SS-4**

(Rev. February 1998)

Department of the Treasury
Internal Revenue Service

Application for Employer Identification Number

(For use by employers, corporations, partnerships, trusts, estates, churches, government agencies, certain individuals, and others. See instructions.)

▶ Keep a copy for your records.

EIN

OMB No. 1545-0003

Please type or print clearly.

1 Name of applicant (legal name) (see instructions)
Lynn Haven Church

2 Trade name of business (if different from name on line 1)

3 Executor, trustee, "care of" name

4a Mailing address (street address) (room, apt., or suite no.)
P.O. Box 4382

5a Business address (if different from address on lines 4a and 4b)
3801 North Florida Avenue

4b City, state, and ZIP code
Miami, FL 33168

5b City, state, and ZIP code
Miami, FL 33168

6 County and state where principal business is located
Dade County, Florida

7 Name of principal officer, general partner, grantor, owner, or trustor—SSN or ITIN may be required (see instructions) ▶

8a Type of entity (Check only one box.) (see instructions)

Caution: *If applicant is a limited liability company, see the instructions for line 8a.*

☐ Sole proprietor (SSN) _____
☐ Partnership
☐ REMIC
☐ State/local government
☑ Church or church-controlled organization
☐ Other nonprofit organization (specify) ▶ _____
☐ Other (specify) ▶

☐ Personal service corp.
☐ National Guard
☐ Farmers' cooperative

☐ Estate (SSN of decedent) _____
☐ Plan administrator (SSN) _____
☐ Other corporation (specify) ▶ _____
☐ Trust
☐ Federal government/military
(enter GEN if applicable) _____

8b If a corporation, name the state or foreign country (if applicable) where incorporated

State	Foreign country
Florida	

9 Reason for applying (Check only one box.) (see instructions)
☑ Started new business (specify type) ▶ _____
Church
☐ Hired employees (Check the box and see line 12.)
☐ Created a pension plan (specify type) ▶

☐ Banking purpose (specify purpose) ▶ _____
☐ Changed type of organization (specify new type) ▶ _____
☐ Purchased going business
☐ Created a trust (specify type) ▶ _____
☐ Other (specify) ▶ _____

10 Date business started or acquired (month, day, year) (see instructions)
2/1/99

11 Closing month of accounting year (see instructions)
June

12 First date wages or annuities were paid or will be paid (month, day, year). **Note:** *If applicant is a withholding agent, enter date income will first be paid to nonresident alien. (month, day, year)* . . . . ▶ **2/1/99**

13 Highest number of employees expected in the next 12 months. **Note:** *If the applicant does not expect to have any employees during the period, enter -0-. (see instructions)* . . . . ▶

Nonagricultural	Agricultural	Household
3		

14 Principal activity (see instructions) ▶

15 Is the principal business activity manufacturing? . . . . ☐ Yes ☑ No
If "Yes," principal product and raw material used ▶

16 To whom are most of the products or services sold? Please check one box.
☐ Public (retail)   ☐ Other (specify) ▶   ☐ Business (wholesale)   ☐ N/A

17a Has the applicant ever applied for an employer identification number for this or any other business? . . . . ☐ Yes ☑ No
Note: *If "Yes," please complete lines 17b and 17c.*

17b If you checked "Yes" on line 17a, give applicant's legal name and trade name shown on prior application, if different from line 1 or 2 above.
Legal name ▶   Trade name ▶

17c Approximate date when and city and state where the application was filed. Enter previous employer identification number if known.

Approximate date when filed (mo., day, year)	City and state where filed	Previous EIN

Under penalties of perjury, I declare that I have examined this application, and to the best of my knowledge and belief, it is true, correct, and complete.

Business telephone number (include area code)
305-688-7432

Fax telephone number (include area code)

Name and title (Please type or print clearly.) ▶ **Mike R. Thomas, Treasurer**

Signature ▶ *Mike R. Thomas*   Date ▶ *1/31/99*

Note: *Do not write below this line. For official use only.*

Please leave blank ▶

Geo.	Ind.	Class	Size	Reason for applying

For Paperwork Reduction Act Notice, see page 4.   Cat. No. 16055N   Form **SS-4** (Rev. 2-98)

Note: Nearly every church or other nonprofit organization needs an Employer Identification Number (EIN) obtained by filing this form.

listed in IRS Publication 78, the Cumulative List of Organizations identifying entities to which tax deductible contributions may be made. Only churches that have applied and been approved for tax-exempt status are listed in Publication 78.

There is no requirement for churches to be listed in Publication 78. However, a listing in the publication generally eliminates any question about the deductibility of contributions to the church as charitable contributions.

✓ If a local congregation ordains ministers, it may be helpful to apply for tax-exempt status. Ministers that are ordained by a local church may be required to provide evidence that the church is tax-exempt. This could be particularly true if the minister files Form 4361 applying for exemption for self-employment tax.

Churches or other charitable organizations desiring recognition of tax-exempt status should submit Form 1023. If approved, the IRS will issue a determination letter describing the category of exemption granted.

The IRS must be notified that the organization is applying for recognition of exemption within 15 months from the end of the month in which it was organized. Applications made after this deadline will not be effective before the date on which the application for recognition of exemption is filed.

Large and small organizations often find that obtaining an exemption letter from the IRS is an intimidating process. Organizations faced with the process are typically new, with a general mission in mind. The mission is often not fully developed and therefore it may not be clearly articulated. It may be helpful to have your application reviewed by a CPA or attorney before it is filed.

Determination letter request

A user fee of $465 (with Form 8718) must accompany applications for recognition of tax-exempt status where the applicant has gross receipts that annually exceed $10,000. For an organization that has had annual gross receipts of $10,000 or less during the past four years, the fee is $150. Start-ups may qualify for the reduced fee. Group exemption letter fees are $500.

Granting tax exemption

Upon approval of the application for exemption, the IRS will provide a determination letter. This letter may be an advance determination or a definitive (or final) determination. The exempt status is usually effective as of the date of formation of the organization, if filing deadlines are met.

An advance determination letter provides tentative guidance regarding status but is a final determination relating to operations and structure of the organization. An advance determination is effective for five years. Before the end of the advance determination period, the organization must show that it qualifies for nonprivate foundation status. During the advance determination period, contributors may make tax-deductible donations to the organization.

A newly created organization seeking status as a publicly supported organization is entitled to receive, if it so elects, a definitive ruling if it has completed a tax year consisting of eight full months as of the time of filing the application.

A definitive (or final) determination letter represents a determination by the IRS position that the organizational and operational plans of the nonprofit entitle it to be classified as exempt.

Group exemption

An affiliated group of organizations under the common control of a central organization can obtain a group exemption letter. Churches that are part of a denomination are not required to file a separate application for exemption if they are covered by the group letter.

The central organization is required to report annually its exempt subordinate organizations to the IRS (the IRS does not provide a particular form for this reporting). The central organization is responsible to evaluate the tax status of its subordinate groups.

Unrelated Business Income

All income of tax-exempt organizations is presumed to be tax-exempt from federal income tax unless the income is generated by an activity that is

✓ not substantially related to the organization's exempt purpose or function,

✓ a trade or business, and

✓ regularly carried on.

Unrelated business income (UBI) is permitted for tax-exempt organizations. However, churches and other nonprofits may have to pay tax on income derived from activities unrelated to their exempt purpose. UBI must not comprise a substantial part of the organization's operation. There is no specific percentage limitation on how much UBI is "substantial." However, organizations with 50% to 80% of their activities classified as unrelated have faced revocation of their tax-exempt status.

Form 990-T must be completed to report the source(s) of UBI and related expenses and to compute any tax. UBI amounts are also reportable on Form 990 (if the filing of Form 990 is required).

Although exempt from filing Form 990, churches must file Form 990-T if they have $1,000 or more of gross UBI in a year. There is a specific deduction of $1,000 in computing unrelated business taxable income. This specific deduction applies to a diocese, province of a religious order, or a convention or association of churches with respect to each parish, individual church, district, or other local unit.

Unrelated business income consequences

Some church and nonprofit executives are paranoid about UBI to the point that they feel it must be avoided altogether. Some people equate UBI with the automatic loss of exempt status. A more balanced view is to understand the purpose of the UBI and minimize the UBI tax through proper planning.

The most common adverse result of having UBI is that all or part of it may be taxed. A less frequent, but still possible, result is that the organization will lose its tax exemption. It is possible that the IRS will deny or revoke the tax-exempt status of an organization when it regularly derives over one-half of its annual revenue from unrelated activities.

Congress recognized that some nonprofits may need to engage in unrelated business activities to survive. For example, a nonprofit with unused office space might rent the space to another organization. Also, nonprofits are expected to invest surplus funds to supplement the primary sources of the organization's income.

A trade or business regularly carried on

A trade or business means any activity regularly carried on which produces income from the sale of goods and services and where there is a reasonable expectation of a profit. To decide whether a trade or business is regularly carried on, the IRS considers whether taxable organizations would carry on a business with the same frequency and continuity. Intermittent activities may escape the "regularly carried on" definition.

> **Example 1:** If a church sells sandwiches at an area bazaar for only two weeks, the IRS would not treat this as the regular conduct of a trade or business.

> **Example 2:** A one-time sale of property is not an activity that is regularly carried on and therefore does not generate unrelated business income unless the property was used in an unrelated business activity.

> **Example 3:** A church is located in the downtown section of a city. Each Saturday, the church parking lot is operated commercially to accommodate shoppers. Even though the business activity is carried on for only one day each week on a year-round basis, this constitutes the conduct of a trade or business. It is subject to the unrelated business income tax.

Substantially related

According to the IRS regulations, a trade or business must "contribute importantly to the accomplishment of the exempt purposes of an organization" if it is to

Form **990**	**Return of Organization Exempt From Income Tax**	OMB No. 1545-0047
Department of the Treasury Internal Revenue Service	Under section 501(c) of the Internal Revenue Code (except black lung benefit trust or private foundation) or section 4947(a)(1) nonexempt charitable trust	**1998** This Form is Open to Public Inspection

Note: *The organization may have to use a copy of this return to satisfy state reporting requirements.*

A For the 1997 calendar year, OR tax year period beginning _____ , 1997, and ending _____ , 19____

B Check if:	Please use IRS label or print or type. See Specific Instructions.	**C** Name of organization Athen's Children's Home	**D** Employer identification number 35-7438041
☐ Change of address ☐ Initial return ☐ Final return ☐ Amended return (required also for State reporting)		Number and street (or P.O. box if mail is not delivered to street address) — Room/suite 1212 South Palo Verde	**E** State registration number
		City, town, or post office, state, and ZIP + 4 Phoenix, AZ 85035	**F** Check ▶ ☐ if exemption application is pending

G Type of organization ▶ ☐ Exempt under section 501(c) (3) ◀ (insert number) OR ▶ ☐ section 4947(a)(1) nonexempt charitable trust

Note: *Section 501(c)(3) exempt organizations and 4947(a)(1) nonexempt charitable trusts MUST attach a completed Schedule A (Form 990).*

H (a) Is this a group return filed for affiliates? . . . . ☐ Yes ☒ No

I If either box in H is checked "Yes," enter four-digit group exemption number (GEN) ▶

(b) If "Yes," enter the number of affiliates for which this return is filed: ▶

J Accounting method: ☐ Cash ☒ Accrual ☐ Other (specify) ▶

(c) Is this a separate return filed by an organization covered by a group ruling? ☐ Yes ☒ No

K Check here ▶ ☐ if the organization's gross receipts are normally not more than $25,000. The organization need not file a return with the IRS; but if it received a Form 990 Package in the mail, it should file a return without financial data. **Some states require a complete return.**

Note: *Form 990-EZ may be used by organizations with gross receipts less than $100,000 and total assets less than $250,000 at end of year.*

Part I Revenue, Expenses, and Changes in Net Assets or Fund Balances (See Specific Instructions on page 11.)

1	Contributions, gifts, grants, and similar amounts received:		
a	Direct public support	1a	314,812
b	Indirect public support	1b	41,042
c	Government contributions (grants)	1c	
d	**Total** (add lines 1a through 1c) (attach schedule of contributors) (cash $ _____ noncash $ _____)	1d	355,854
2	Program service revenue including government fees and contracts (from Part VII, line 93)	2	
3	Membership dues and assessments	3	
4	Interest on savings and temporary cash investments	4	10,483
5	Dividends and interest from securities	5	
6a	Gross rents 6a		
b	Less: rental expenses 6b		
c	Net rental income or (loss) (subtract line 6b from line 6a)	6c	
7	Other investment income (describe ▶)	7	
8a	Gross amount from sale of assets other than inventory — (A) Securities 8a / (B) Other		
b	Less: cost or other basis and sales expenses — 8b		
c	Gain or (loss) (attach schedule) — 8c		
d	Net gain or (loss) (combine line 8c, columns (A) and (B))	8d	
9	Special events and activities (attach schedule)		
a	Gross revenue (not including $ 51,842 of contributions reported on line 1a) 9a	74,712	
b	Less: direct expenses other than fundraising expenses — 9b	29,003	
c	Net income or (loss) from special events (subtract line 9b from line 9a)	9c	45,709
10a	Gross sales of inventory, less returns and allowances 10a		
b	Less: cost of goods sold 10b		
c	Gross profit or (loss) from sales of inventory (attach schedule) (subtract line 10b from line 10a)	10c	
11	Other revenue (from Part VII, line 103)	11	
12	**Total revenue** (add lines 1d, 2, 3, 4, 5, 6c, 7, 8d, 9c, 10c, and 11)	12	412,046
13	Program services (from line 44, column (B))	13	259,028
14	Management and general (from line 44, column (C))	14	84,933
15	Fundraising (from line 44, column (D))	15	59,012
16	Payments to affiliates (attach schedule)	16	
17	**Total expenses** (add lines 16 and 44, column (A))	17	402,973
18	Excess or (deficit) for the year (subtract line 17 from line 12)	18	9,073
19	Net assets or fund balances at beginning of year (from line 73, column (A))	19	144,098
20	Other changes in net assets or fund balances (attach explanation)	20	
21	Net assets or fund balances at end of year (combine lines 18, 19, and 20)	21	153,171

For Paperwork Reduction Act Notice, see page 1 of the separate instructions.   Form **990** (1997)

Note: Form 990 has a total of five pages. Schedule A of Form 990 has five pages and is used to furnish additional information.

be considered "substantially related." Even if all the profits from a business go to support the work of the nonprofit, the profits may still be taxed.

> **Example:** If a church operates a restaurant and devotes all the proceeds to mission work, the church will not escape taxation on the restaurant's income.

Types of income that may be "related" are

✓ the sale of products made by handicapped individuals as a part of their rehabilitation;

✓ the sale of homes constructed by students enrolled in a vocational training course; and

✓ a retail grocery store operated to provide emotional therapy for disturbed adolescents.

Tours conducted by nonprofits usually create UBI. Tours may be exempt from UBI only if they are strongly educationally oriented, with reports, daily lectures, and so on. Tours with substantial recreational or social purposes are not exempt.

The definition of "unrelated trade or business" *does not* include

✓ activities in which unpaid volunteers do most of the work for an organization;

✓ activities provided primarily for the convenience of the organization's members; or

✓ activities involving the sale of merchandise mostly donated to the organization.

Rental income

Nonprofits often rent facilities, equipment, and other assets for a fee. Rental income usually represents UBI with the following exceptions:

✓ Renting to another nonprofit may be termed "related" if the rental expressly serves the landlord's exempt purposes.

✓ Mailing lists produce UBI, with specific exceptions.

✓ Rental of real estate is excluded from UBI unless the excludable property is acquired or improved with indebtedness. Rental income from the property becomes UBI to the extent of the ratio of the "average acquisition indebtedness" during the year to the total purchase price. The nonprofit may deduct the same portion of the expenses directly connected with the production of the rental income. Depreciation is allowable using only the straight-line method.

Form **990-T**

Department of the Treasury
Internal Revenue Service

Exempt Organization Business Income Tax Return
(and proxy tax under section 6033(e))

For calendar year 1997 or other tax year beginning _____, 1997, and ending _____, 19____

▶ See separate instructions.

OMB No. 1545-0687

1998

A ☐ Check box if address changed	Name of organization	**D** Employer identification number (Employees' trust, see instructions for Block D on page 6.)
Please Print or Type	Family Bible Crusades	35-4427081
B Exempt under section ☒ 501(**c**)(**3**) or ☐ 408(e) ☐ 220(e)	Number, street, and room or suite no. (If a P.O. box, see page 5 of instructions.) 400 North Sunset Avnue	**E** Unrelated business activity codes (see instructions for Block E on page 6.)
C Book value of all assets at end of year $4,384,975	City or town, state, and ZIP code Lemon Grove, CA 92045	6512

F Group exemption number (see instructions for Block F on page 6) ▶

G Check type of organization ▶ ☒ 501(c) corporation ☐ 501(c) trust ☐ Section 401(a) trust ☐ Section 408(a) trust ☐ 220(d) trust

H Describe the organization's primary unrelated business activity. ▶ *Apartment Rental*

I During the tax year, was the corporation a subsidiary in an affiliated group or a parent-subsidiary controlled group? . . . . . ▶ ☐ Yes ☒ No
If "Yes," enter the name and identifying number of the parent corporation. ▶

J The books are in care of ▶ *Family Bible Crusades*   Telephone number ▶ (   )

Part I   Unrelated Trade or Business Income

			(A) Income	(B) Expenses	(C) Net
1a	Gross receipts or sales				
b	Less returns and allowances _____ c Balance ▶	1c			
2	Cost of goods sold (Schedule A, line 7)	2			
3	Gross profit (subtract line 2 from line 1c)	3			
4a	Capital gain net income (attach Schedule D)	4a			
b	Net gain (loss) (Form 4797, Part II, line 18) (attach Form 4797)	4b			
c	Capital loss deduction for trusts	4c			
5	Income (loss) from partnerships (attach statement)	5			
6	Rent income (Schedule C)	6			
7	Unrelated debt-financed income (Schedule E)	7	79,410	52,301	27,109
8	Interest, annuities, royalties, and rents from controlled organizations (Schedule F)	8			
9	Investment income of a section 501(c)(7), (9), or (17) organization (Schedule G)	9			
10	Exploited exempt activity income (Schedule I)	10			
11	Advertising income (Schedule J)	11			
12	Other income (see page 7 of the instructions - attach schedule) . .	12			
13	TOTAL (combine lines 3 through 12)	13	79,410	52,301	27,109

Part II   Deductions Not Taken Elsewhere (See page 8 of the instructions for limitations on deductions.)
(Except for contributions, deductions must be directly connected with the unrelated business income.)

14	Compensation of officers, directors, and trustees (Schedule K)	14	
15	Salaries and wages	15	
16	Repairs and maintenance	16	
17	Bad debts	17	
18	Interest (attach schedule)	18	
19	Taxes and licenses	19	
20	Charitable contributions (see page 9 of the instructions for limitation rules)	20	
21	Depreciation (attach Form 4562) 21		
22	Less depreciation claimed on Schedule A and elsewhere on return 22a	22b	
23	Depletion	23	
24	Contributions to deferred compensation plans	24	
25	Employee benefit programs	25	
26	Excess exempt expenses (Schedule I)	26	
27	Excess readership costs (Schedule J)	27	
28	Other deductions (attach schedule)	28	
29	TOTAL DEDUCTIONS (add lines 14 through 28)	29	
30	Unrelated business taxable income before net operating loss deduction (subtract line 29 from line 13)	30	27,109
31	Net operating loss deduction	31	
32	Unrelated business taxable income before specific deduction (subtract line 31 from line 30)	32	27,109
33	Specific deduction	33	1,000
34	Unrelated business taxable income (subtract line 33 from line 32). If line 33 is greater than line 32, enter the smaller of zero or line 32	34	26,109

For Paperwork Reduction Act Notice, see instructions.   Form **990-T** (1997)

Note: Form 990-T has a total of four pages. Only page one is shown here.
Caution: Professional assistance may be needed to complete this form.

Debt-financed income

To discourage exempt organizations from borrowing money to purchase passive income items, Congress imposed a tax on debt-financed income. An organization may have debt-financed income if

✔ it incurs debt to purchase or improve an income-producing asset; and

✔ some of that debt remains within the 12 months prior to when income is received from the asset.

An organization also may have debt-financed income if it accepts gifts or bequests of mortgaged property in some circumstances.

There are exceptions to the debt-financed income rules, including

✔ substantially all (85% or more) of any property is used for an organization's exempt purposes;

✔ use of property by a related exempt organization to further its exempt purposes;

✔ life income contracts, if the remainder interest is payable to an exempt charitable organization;

✔ neighborhood land rule, if an organization acquires real property in its "neighborhood" (the neighborhood restriction does not apply to churches) mainly to use it for exempt purposes within ten years (15 years for churches).

Activities that are not taxed

Income from the following sources is generally not considered as UBI:

✔ **Passive income.** Income earned from most passive investment activities is not UBI unless the underlying property is subject to debt. Types of passive income include

• dividends, interest, and annuities

• capital gains or losses from the sale, exchange, or other disposition of property

• rents from real property (some rent is UBI if the rental property was purchased or improved subject to a mortgage)

• royalties (oil and gas working interest income generally constitute UBI)

✓ **Volunteers.** Any business where volunteers perform most of the work without compensation does not qualify as UBI. To the IRS, "substantially" means at least 85% of total work performed.

> **Example:** A used-clothing store operated by a nonprofit orphanage where volunteers do all the work in the store would likely be exempt.

✓ **Convenience.** A cafeteria, bookstore, or residence operated for the convenience of patients, visitors, employees, or students is not a business. Stores, parking lots, and other facilities may be dually used (part related and part unrelated).

✓ **Donated goods.** The sale of merchandise, mostly received as gifts or contributions, does not qualify as UBI. A justification for this exemption is that contributions of property are merely being converted into cash.

✓ **Low-cost items.** Items (costing no more than $7.10—1998 adjusted amount) distributed incidental to the solicitation of charitable contributions are not subject to UBI. The amounts received are not considered as an exchange for the low-cost articles and therefore they do not create UBI.

✓ **Mailing lists.** Mailing lists exchanged with or rented to another exempt organization are excluded from UBI, although the commercial sale of the lists will generally create UBI. The structuring of the agreement as a royalty arrangement may make the income exempt from UBI treatment.

Calculating the unrelated business income tax

Income tax rules applicable to businesses, such as depreciation method limitations and rates, apply to the UBI computation. Direct and indirect costs may be used to offset income. The first $1,000 of annual net unrelated income is exempt from taxation.

For 1998, the corporate tax rates are

Taxable Income			Tax Rate
$ 0	to	$50,000	15% plus
$ 50,001	to	$75,000	25% plus
$ 75,001	to	$100,000	34% plus
$100,001	to	$335,000	39% plus
$335,001	to	$10,000,000	34%

Unrelated business income summary

Be aware of the type of activities that may create UBI in your organization.

✓ Maintain careful records of income and related expenses (both direct and indirect, including depreciation) for any activities that might be considered unrelated to the exempt purpose of your organization. These records should include allocations of salaries and fringe benefits based on time records or, at a minimum, time estimates.

   It may be wise to keep a separate set of records on potential unrelated activities. This separate set of records would need to be submitted to the IRS only upon audit.

✓ Be sure that board minutes, contracts, and other documents reflect the organization's view of relatedness of various activities to the exempt purpose of the entity.

✓ If the organization has over $1,000 of gross UBI in a given fiscal (tax) year, file Form 990-T.

Private Benefit and Private Inurement

Tax laws and regulations impose prohibitions on nonprofit organizations concerning private benefit and private inurement.

Private benefit

Nonprofit organizations must serve public, and not private, interests. The private benefit prohibition applies to anyone outside the intended charitable class. The law does allow some private benefit if it is incidental to the public benefits involved. It is acceptable if the benefit to the public cannot be achieved without necessarily benefiting private individuals.

> **Example:** The IRS revoked exemption of a charity where it served the commercial purposes and private interests of a professional fund-raiser where the fund-raiser distributed only 3% of the amount collected to the nonprofit organization.

Private inurement

Private inurement is a subset of private benefit. This is an absolute prohibition that generally applies to a distinct class of private interests. These "insiders" may be founders, trustees or directors, officers, managers, or significant donors. Transactions involving these individuals are not necessarily prohibited, but they must be subject to reasonableness, documentation, and applicable reporting to the IRS.

Inurement arises whenever a financial benefit represents a transfer of resources to an individual solely by virtue of the individual's relationship with the organization, without regard to accomplishing its exempt purposes. When an individual receives something for nothing or less than it is worth, private inurement may have occurred. Excessive, and therefore unreasonable, compensation can also result in prohibited inurement. The IRS may ask the following questions to determine if private inurement exists:

✓ Did the expenditure further an exempt purpose, and, if so, how?

✓ Was the payment at fair market value or did it represent reasonable compensation for goods and services?

✓ Does a low- or no-interest loan to an employee or director fall within a reasonable compensation package?

✓ On an overseas trip for the nonprofit, did the employee (and perhaps a spouse) stay an additional week for a personal vacation and charge the expenses to the organization?

Example 1: An organization lost its exemption when it engaged in numerous transactions with an insider, including the purchase of a 42-foot boat for the personal use of the insider. The insider also benefitted from several real estate transactions, including donations and sales of real property to the organization which were never reflected on its books.

Example 2: A church lost its tax-exemption after it operated commercial businesses and paid substantial private expenses of its founders, including expenses for jewelry and clothing in excess of $30,000 per year. The church also purchased five luxury cars for the founders' personal use. None of these benefits were reported as personal income to the founders.

Example 3: A tax-exempt organization transfers an auto to an employee for $100. The transfer was not approved by the board and does not constitute a portion of a reasonable pay package. The fair market value of the auto is $2,000. The net difference of $1,900 is not reported to the IRS as compensation. Private inurement has occurred.

Example 4: Same facts as Example 3, except the transfer was approved by the board and properly constituted a portion of the reasonable pay package, and the $1,900 was added to the employee's Form W-2 as compensation. There is no private inurement.

A two-tiered scheme of penalty taxes is imposed on insiders who improperly benefit from excess benefit transactions and on organization managers who are involved in illegal transactions. Sanctions cannot be imposed on the organizations themselves.

A first-tier penalty tax equal to 25% of the amount of the excess benefit is followed by a tax of 200% if there is no correction of the excess benefit within a certain time period.

Filing Federal Returns

Nearly all nonprofit organizations must file an annual return with the IRS (churches are exempt from filing Form 990 or 990-EZ). The basic filing requirements are

FORM TO BE FILED	CONDITIONS
No form filed	Gross annual receipts normally under $25,000
Form 990-EZ	Gross annual receipts between $25,000 and $100,000 with total assets of less than $250,000
Form 990	Gross annual receipts over $100,000 or assets over $250,000 with gross annual receipts between $25,000 and $100,000
Form 990-T	Any organization exempt under Sec. 501(a) with $1,000 or more gross income from an unrelated trade or business
Form 1120	Any nonprofit corporation that is not tax-exempt
Form 5500	Pension, profit-sharing, medical benefit, cafeteria, and certain other plans must annually file one of several series 5500 Forms

Public inspection of information returns

The IRS has issued proposed regulations on the exempt organization disclosure rules. These regulations become effective on the date the final regulations are issued. Here are the key provisions of the regulations:

 ✓ **Materials made available for public inspection.** Nonprofits, other than private foundations, must provide access to application for tax exemption (Form 1023) and any supporting documents filed by the organization in support of its application. It also includes any letter or other documents issued by the IRS in connection with the application.

Nonprofits must also provide access to their three most recent information returns. This generally includes Forms 990, 990-EZ, and schedules and attachments filed with the IRS. There is not a requirement to disclose parts of the information returns that identify names and address of contributors to the organization. Neither does the organization have to disclose Form 990-T.

✓ **Places and times for public inspection.** Specified documents must be made available at the nonprofit's principal, regional, and district offices during normal business hours. Under the new regulations, an office will be considered a regional or district office only if (1) it has three or more paid, full-time employees or (2) the aggregate hours per week worked by its paid employees (either full-time or part-time) is 120 or more.

✓ **Responding to requests.** If a person requests copies in person, the request generally must be fulfilled on the day of the request. In unusual circumstances, an organization will be permitted to furnish the copies on the next business day. When the request is made in writing, the organization must provide the requested copies within 30 days. If the organization requires advance payment for reasonable copying and mailing fees, it can provide copies within 30 days of the date it is paid, instead of the date of the request.

✓ **Fees for providing copies.** Reasonable fees may be charged by nonprofits for copying and mailing documents. The fees cannot exceed the amounts charged by the IRS—currently, $1 for the first page and 15 cents for each subsequent page—plus actual mailing costs. An organization can require payment in advance. To protect requesters from unexpected fees, when an organization receives a request in writing without advance payment, it must obtain consent before providing copies that will result in fees of more than $20.

✓ **Documents widely available.** A nonprofit organization does not have to comply with requests for copies if it has made the appropriate materials widely available. This requirement is satisfied if the document is posted on the organization's World Wide Web page on the Internet or in another database of similar materials.

Reporting substantial organizational changes

An organization's tax-exempt status remains in effect if there are no material changes in the organization's character, purposes, or methods of operation. Significant changes should be reported by letter to the IRS soon after the changes occur.

Example: An organization received tax-exempt status for the operation of a religious radio ministry. Several years later, the organization decided to add a facility for homeless children. This change would likely be considered to be material and should be reported to the IRS.

Change in accounting methods

A nonprofit organization may adopt any reasonable method of accounting to keep its financial records that clearly reflects income. These methods include the cash receipts and disbursements method; the accrual method; or any other method (including a combination of methods) that clearly reflects income.

An organization that wishes to change from one method of accounting to another generally must secure the consent of the IRS to make that change. Consent must be obtained both for a general change of method, and for any change of method with respect to one or more particular items. Thus, a nonprofit organization that generally uses the cash method, but uses the accrual method with respect to publications for which it maintains inventories, may change its method of accounting by adopting the accrual method for all purposes. But the organization must secure the IRS's consent to do so.

To obtain the consent of the IRS to change an accounting method, the organization should file IRS Form 3115, Application for Change in Accounting Method. The form must be filed within 180 days after the beginning of the tax year in which the change is made. There is a more expeditious consent for a change from the cash to accrual method filed under Revenue Procedure 85-37.

Change of fiscal years

Generally, an exempt organization may change its fiscal year simply by timely filing Form 990 with the appropriate Internal Revenue Service Center for the "short year." The return for the short year should indicate at the top of page 1 that a change of accounting period is being made. It should be filed not later than the 15th day of the fifth month following the close of the short year.

If neither Form 990 nor Form 990-T must be filed, the ministry is not required to notify the IRS of a change in the fiscal year, with one exception. The exception applies to exempt organizations that have changed their fiscal years within the previous ten calendar years. For this exception, Form 1128 must be filed with the IRS.

Other

✓ **Form 5578.** Form 5578 may be completed and furnished to the IRS to provide information regarding nondiscrimination policies of private schools instead of completing the information at item 31 of Form 990, Schedule A. If Form 990 is not required to be filed, Form 5578 should be submitted, if applicable. Form 5578 must be filed for schools operated by a church, including preschools.

✓ **Form 8717 and 8718.** Nonprofits wishing IRS private letter rulings on exempt organization information or on employee plans must include new forms 8717 or 8718, respectively, with the appropriate fees.

✓ **Form 8282.** If a nonprofit donee sells or otherwise disposes of gift property for which an appraisal summary is required on Form 8283 within two years after receipt of the property, it generally must file Form 8282 with the IRS. See Chapter 7 for more information on these reporting rules.

✓ **Employee and nonemployee payments.** As an employer, a nonprofit organization must file federal and state forms concerning payment of compensation and the withholding of payroll taxes. Payments to nonemployees may require the filing of information returns. See Chapters 4 and 5 for more coverage on these requirements.

Filing State Returns

Separate filings are often necessary to obtain exemption from state income tax. The requirements vary from state to state. In some states it is also possible to obtain exemption from sales, use, and property taxes.

A nonprofit organization may be required to report to one or more states in relation to its exemption from or compliance with state income, sales, use, or property taxation.

Many states accept a copy of Form 990 as adequate annual reporting for tax-exempt status purposes. Annual reporting to the state in which the organization is incorporated is normally required even if there is no requirement to file Form 990 with the IRS. Check with the offices of the secretary of state and attorney general to determine required filings.

Do not send a list of major contributors to the state unless it is specifically required. While this list is not open to public inspection with respect to the federal filing, it may not be confidential for state purposes.

Political Activity

Churches and other organizations exempt from federal income tax under section 501(c)(3) of the Internal Revenue Code are prohibited from participating or intervening, directly or indirectly, in any political campaign on behalf of or in opposition to any candidate for public office.

To avoid violating the political campaign provisions of the law:

✓ Do not use a rating program to evaluate candidates.

✓ Do not endorse a candidate directly or indirectly through a sermon, speech, newsletter, or sample ballot.

✓ Do not publish a candidate's statement.

✓ Do not publish the names of candidates who agree to adhere to certain practices.

✓ Do not publish candidate responses to a questionnaire that evidences a bias on certain issues.

✓ Do not publish responses to an unbiased questionnaire focused on a narrow range of issues.

✓ Do not raise funds for a candidate.

✓ Do not provide volunteers, mailing lists, publicity, or free use of facilities unless all parties and candidates in the community receive the same services.

✓ Do not pay campaign expenses for a candidate.

✓ Do not distribute statements about candidates or display campaign literature on organization's premises.

If the IRS finds that an organization has engaged in these activities, it could result in a loss of exempt status. Also, the IRS may assess an excise tax on the amount of the funds spent on the activity.

Are there any political campaign activities that may legally be engaged in by a church or nonprofit? Forums or debates may be conducted to educate voters at which all candidates are treated equally, or a mailing list may be rented to candidates on the same basis as it is made available to others. Organizations may engage in voter registration or get-out-the-vote activities. However, it is wise to avoid defining a target group by political or ideological criteria (e.g., encouraging individuals to vote who are "registered Republicans").

Key Concepts

▦ Tax exemption is a privilege—not to be taken lightly.

▦ Churches are generally tax-exempt from federal income taxes without applying for this status.

▦ Most nonchurch organizations must apply for federal tax-exempt status.

▦ Churches and other nonprofits may be subject to the unrelated business income tax.

▦ Tax-exempt funds must not be diverted for personal use. This is called private inurement or benefit.

▦ Exemption from federal income tax does not automatically provide exemption from state taxes such as property, sales, and use tax.

| Form **5578**
(Rev. June 1998)
Department of the Treasury
Internal Revenue Service | **Annual Certification of Racial Nondiscrimination
for a Private School Exempt From Federal Income Tax**
(For use by organizations that do not file Form 990 or Form 990-EZ) | OMB No. 1545-0213

**For IRS
use ONLY** ▶ |

| For the period beginning | **July 1** | , **1998** | and ending | **June 30** | , **1999** |

1a Name of organization that operates, supervises, and/or controls school(s).

Liberty Grove Church

1b Employer identification number

Address (number and street or P.O. box no., if mail is not delivered to street address) | Room/suite

1533 North Andrews Avenue

35 : 1047863

City or town, state, and ZIP + 4 (If foreign address, list city or town, state or province, and country. Include postal code.)

Ft. Lauderdale, FL 33308

2a Name of central organization holding group exemption letter covering the school(s). (If same as 1a above, write "Same" and complete 2c.) If the organization in 1a above holds an individual exemption letter, write "Not Applicable."

Not applicable

2b Employer identification number

Address (number and street or P.O. box no., if mail is not delivered to street address) | Room/suite

2c Group exemption number (see instructions under **Definitions**)

City or town, state, and ZIP + 4 (If foreign address list city or town, state or province, and country. Include postal code.)

3a Name of school. (If more than one school, write "See Attached," and attach a list of the names, complete addresses, including postal codes, and employer identification numbers of the schools.) If same as 1a above, write "Same."

Liberty Grove Christian School

3b Employer identification number, if any

Address (number and street or P.O. box no., if mail is not delivered to street address) | Room/suite

2100 Cook Lane

City or town, state, and ZIP + 4 (If foreign address, list city or town, state or province, and country. Include postal code.)

Ft. Lauderdale, FL 33308

Under penalties of perjury, I hereby certify that I am authorized to take official action on behalf of the above school(s) and that to the best of my knowledge and belief the school(s) has (have) satisfied the applicable requirements of sections 4.01 through 4.05 of Rev. Proc. 75-50, 1975-2 C.B. 587, for the period covered by this certification.

Roy L. Crawford
(Signature)

Roy L. Crawford, Superintendent
(Type or print name and title.)

7/31/99
(Date)

General Instructions

This form is open to public inspection.

Section references are to the Internal Revenue Code.

Purpose of Form

Form 5578 may be used by organizations that operate tax-exempt private schools to provide the Internal Revenue Service with the annual certification of racial nondiscrimination required by Rev. Proc. 75-50 (the relevant part of which is reproduced in these instructions).

Who Must File

Every organization that claims exemption from Federal income tax under section 501(c)(3) of the Internal Revenue Code and that operates, supervises, or controls a private school or schools must file a certification of racial nondiscrimination. If an organization is required to file **Form 990**, Return of Organization Exempt From Income Tax, or **Form 990-EZ**, Short Form Return of Organization Exempt From Income Tax, either as a separate return or as part of a group return, the certification must be made on **Schedule A (Form 990)**, Organization Exempt Under Section 501(c)(3), rather than on this form.

An authorized official of a central organization may file one form to certify for the school activities of subordinate organizations that would otherwise be required to file on an individual basis, but only if the central organization has enough control over the schools listed on the form to ensure that the schools maintain a racially nondiscriminatory policy as to students.

Definitions

A **racially nondiscriminatory policy as to students** means that the school admits the students of any race to all the rights, privileges, programs, and activities generally accorded or made available to students at that school and that the school does not discriminate on the basis of race in the administration of its educational policies, admissions policies, scholarship and loan programs, and other school-administered programs.

The IRS considers discrimination on the basis of race to include discrimination on the basis of color or national or ethnic origin.

A **school** is an educational organization that normally maintains a regular faculty and curriculum and normally has a regularly enrolled body of pupils or students in attendance at the place where its educational activities are regularly carried on. The term includes primary, secondary, preparatory, or high schools and colleges and universities, whether operated as a separate legal entity or as an activity of a church or other organization described in Code section 501(c)(3). The term also includes preschools and any other organization that is a school as defined in Code section 170(b)(1)(A)(ii).

A **central organization** is an organization that has one or more subordinates under its general supervision or control. A subordinate is a chapter, local, post, or other unit of a central organization. A central organization may also be a subordinate, as in the case of a state organization that has subordinate units and is itself affiliated with a national organization.

The **group exemption number (GEN)** is a four-digit number issued to a central organization by the IRS. It identifies a central organization that has received a ruling from the IRS recognizing on a group basis the exemption from Federal income tax of the central organization and its covered subordinates.

When To File

Under Rev. Proc. 75-50, a certification of racial nondiscrimination must be filed annually by the 15th day of the 5th month following the end of the organization's calendar year or fiscal period.

Where To File

Mail Form 5578 to the Internal Revenue Service Center, Ogden, UT 84201-0027.

Certification Requirement

Section 4.06 of Rev. Proc. 75-50 requires an individual authorized to take official action on behalf of a school that claims to be racially nondiscriminatory as to students to certify annually, under penalties of perjury, that to the best of his or her knowledge and belief the school has satisfied the applicable requirements of sections 4.01 through 4.05 of the revenue procedure, reproduced below:

Rev. Proc. 75-50

4.01 Organizational Requirements. A school must include a statement in its charter, bylaws, or other governing instrument, or in a resolution of its governing body, that it has a racially nondiscriminatory policy as to students and therefore does not discriminate against applicants and students on the basis of race, color, and national or ethnic origin.

For Paperwork Reduction Act Notice, see back of form.   Cat. No. 42658A   Form **5578** (Rev. 6-98)

Note: Private schools must complete this form annually. This form need not be filed if Form 990 is required and item 31 of Schedule A is completed.

CHAPTER THREE

Compensation Planning

In This Chapter

- Reasonable compensation
- Organization-provided housing
- Maximizing fringe benefits
- Nondiscrimination rules
- Paying employee expenses

Compensation plans should provide tax-effective benefits. A dollar of benefit costs to the organization may be multiplied when received by the employee as tax-free or tax-deferred.

Reasonable Compensation

Employees of churches and nonprofit organizations may receive reasonable compensation for their efforts. Excessive compensation can result in private inurement and may jeopardize the tax-exempt status of the organization. Reasonable compensation is based on what would ordinarily be paid for like services by a like organization under similar circumstances.

Compensation packages over the $150,000-$200,000 level for even larger non-profit organizations could be challenged by the IRS. Lower compensation packages could be termed excessive for smaller churches or ministries.

A review of the changes in the Consumers Price Index from one year to the next may be helpful when projecting salary increases:

1984	3.9%	1989	4.6%	1994	2.7%
1985	3.8%	1990	6.1%	1995	2.5%
1986	1.1%	1991	3.1%	1996	3.3%
1987	4.4%	1992	2.9%	1997	1.7%
1988	4.4%	1993	2.7%	1998	2.0% (est.)

Organization-Provided Housing

Nonminister employees

Housing provided to nonminister employees by a church or nonprofit organization for its convenience, as a condition of employment, and on its business premises is

✓ exempt from income tax and FICA tax withholding by the church; and

✓ excluded from wages reporting by the church and employee.

If these criteria are not met, the fair rental value should be reported as compensation on Form W-2 and is subject to withholding and FICA taxation.

Minister's housing allowance

Qualified ministers receive preferred treatment for their housing. If a minister has a home provided as part of compensation, the minister pays no income tax on the rental value of the home. If a home is not provided but the minister receives a rental or housing allowance, the minister pays no tax on the allowance if it is used for housing expenses subject to certain limitations.

Every minister should have a portion of salary designated as a housing allowance. For a minister living in organization-owned housing, the housing allowance may be only a modest amount to cover incidental expenses such as maintenance, furnishings, and utilities. But a properly designated housing allowance may be worth thousands of dollars in tax savings for ministers living in their own homes or rented quarters.

Ministers may exclude the housing allowance under the following rules:

✓ The allowance must be officially designated before payment by the organization. The designation should be evidenced in writing, preferably by resolution of the top governing body, in an employment contract, or, at a minimum, in the church budget and payroll records.

   If the only reference to the housing allowance is in the organization's budget, the budget should be formally approved by the top governing body.

✓ Only actual expenses can be excluded from income. The expenses must be paid from ministerial income earned in the current year.

For extensive coverage of the minister's housing allowance, see the 1999 edition of *The Zondervan Minister's Tax and Financial Guide*.

Sample Housing Allowance Resolutions

PARSONAGE OWNED BY OR RENTED BY A CHURCH

Whereas, The Internal Revenue Code permits a minister of the gospel to exclude from gross income "the rental value of a home furnished as part of compensation" or a church-designated allowance paid as a part of compensation to the extent that actual expenses are paid from the allowance to maintain a parsonage owned or rented by the church;

Whereas, Nelson Street Church compensates the senior minister for services in the exercise of ministry; and

Whereas, Nelson Street Church provides the senior minister with the rent-free use of a parsonage owned by (rented by) the church as a portion of the compensation for services rendered to the church in the exercise of ministry;

Resolved, That the compensation of the senior minister is $2,500 per month of which $200 per month is a designated housing allowance; and

Resolved, That the designation of $200 per month as a housing allowance shall apply until otherwise provided.

HOME OWNED OR RENTED BY MINISTER

Whereas, The Internal Revenue Code permits a minister of the gospel to exclude from gross income a church-designated allowance paid as part of compensation to the extent used for actual expenses in owning or renting a home; and

Whereas, Nelson Street Church compensates the senior minister for services in the exercise of ministry;

Resolved, That the compensation of the senior minister is $3,500 per month of which $1,250 per month is a designated housing allowance; and

Resolved, That the designation of $1,250 per month as a housing allowance shall apply until otherwise provided.

EVANGELISTS

Whereas, The Internal Revenue Code permits a minister of the gospel to exclude from gross income a church-designated allowance paid as part of compensation to the extent used in owning or renting a permanent home; and

Whereas, Nelson Street Church compensates Rev. John Doe for services in the exercise of ministry as an evangelist;

Resolved, That the honorarium paid to Rev. Doe shall be $1,512 consisting of $312 travel expenses (with documentation provided to the church), $500 housing allowance, and a $700 honorarium.

Maximizing Fringe Benefits

Personal use of employer-provided vehicles

Vehicles provided by organizations to employees for business use are often used for personal purposes. The IRS (see IRS Publication 535) treats most types of personal use of an employer-provided vehicle as a noncash fringe benefit, and generally requires the fair market value of such use to be included in the employee's gross income (to the extent that the value is not reimbursed to the employer).

If the employee reimburses the employer in a chargeback system for the full dollar value of the personal use, it will cost the employee more than if the employer includes the personal use value in the income of the employee.

> **Example:** The personal use value of an automobile provided to a lay employee is determined to be $100; a chargeback system would require the employee to pay $100 to the employer. If, on the other hand, the employer includes the $100 in the employee's income, the employee will be subject to payroll taxes on $100 of income. Assuming a federal income tax rate of 31% and an FICA rate of 7.65% (based on annual gross pay of $68,400 or less for 1998) for a total of $38.65, compared with the $100 cash out-of-pocket chargeback.

Valuation of personal vehicle use

There are three special valuation rules, in addition to a set of general valuation principles, which may be used under specific circumstances for valuing the personal use of an employer-provided vehicle. This value must be included in the employee's compensation if it is not reimbursed by the employee.

Under the general valuation rule, the value is based on what the cost would be to a person leasing from a third party the same or comparable vehicle on the same or comparable terms in the same geographic area.

The special valuation rules, which are used by most employers, are:

 Cents-per-mile valuation rule. Generally, this rule may be used if the employer reasonably expects that the vehicle will be regularly used in the employer's trade or business, and if the vehicle is driven at least 10,000 miles a year and the vehicle is primarily used by employees. This valuation rule is available only if the fair market value of the vehicle, as of the date the vehicle was first made available for personal use by employees, does not exceed a specified value set by the IRS. For 1998, this value is $15,600.

The value of the personal use of the vehicle is computed by multiplying the number of miles driven for personal purposes by the current IRS standard mileage rate (32.5 cents per mile for 1998). For this valuation rule, personal use is "any use of the vehicle other than use in the employee's trade or business of being an employee of the employer."

✓ **Commuting valuation rule.** This rule may be used to determine the value of personal use only where the following conditions are met:

- The vehicle is owned or leased by the employer and is provided to one or more employees for use in connection with the employer's trade or business and is used as such.

- The employer requires the employee to commute to and/or from work in the vehicle for bona fide noncompensatory business reasons. One example of a bona fide noncompensatory business reason is the availability of the vehicle to an employee who is on-call and must have access to the vehicle when at home.

- The employer has a written policy that prohibits employees from using the vehicle for personal purposes other than for commuting or de minimis personal use such as a stop for a personal errand on the way home from work.

- The employee required to use the vehicle for commuting is not a "control" employee of the employer. A control employee is generally defined as any employee who is an officer of the employer whose compensation equals or exceeds $50,000 or is a director of the employer whose compensation equals or exceeds $100,000.

  The personal use of an employer-provided vehicle that meets the above conditions is valued at $1.50 per one-way commute.

✓ **Annual lease valuation rule.** Under this rule, the fair market value of a vehicle is determined and that value is used to determine the annual lease value amount by referring to an annual lease value table published by the IRS (see page 54). The annual lease value corresponding to this fair market value, multiplied by the personal use percentage, is the amount to be added to the employee's gross income. If the organization provides the fuel, 5.5 cents per mile must be added to the annual lease value. Amounts reimbursed by the employee are offset.

The fair market value of a vehicle owned by an employer is generally the employer's cost of purchasing the vehicle (including taxes and fees). The fair market value of a vehicle leased by an employer generally is either the manufacturer's suggested retail price less 8%, or the retail value as reported in a nationally recognized publication that regularly reports automobile retail values.

If the three special valuation rules described above do not apply, the value of the personal use must be determined by using a set of general valuation principles. Under these principles, the value must be generally equal to the amount that the employee would have to pay in a normal business transaction to obtain the same or comparable vehicle in the geographic area in which that vehicle is available for use.

ANNUAL LEASE VALUE TABLE

Annual Fair Market Value of Car			Lease Value	Fair Market Value of Car			Annual Lease Value
$0	-	$999	$600	$19,000	-	$19,999	$5,350
1,000	-	1,999	850	20,000	-	20,999	5,600
2,000	-	2,999	1,100	21,000	-	21,999	5,850
3,000	-	3,999	1,350	22,000	-	22,999	6,100
4,000	-	4,999	1,600	23,000	-	23,999	6,350
5,000	-	5,999	1,850	24,000	-	24,999	6,600
6,000	-	6,999	2,100	25,000	-	25,999	6,850
7,000	-	7,999	2,350	26,000	-	27,999	7,250
8,000	-	8,999	2,600	28,000	-	29,999	7,750
9,000	-	9,999	2,850	30,000	-	31,999	8,250
10,000	-	10,999	3,100	32,000	-	33,999	8,750
11,000	-	11,999	3,350	34,000	-	35,999	9,250
12,000	-	12,999	3,600	36,000	-	37,999	9,750
13,000	-	13,999	3,850	38,000	-	39,999	10,250
14,000	-	14,999	4,100	40,000	-	41,999	10,750
15,000	-	15,999	4,350	42,000	-	43,999	11,250
16,000	-	16,999	4,600	44,000	-	45,999	11,750
17,000	-	17,999	4,850	46,000	-	47,999	12,250
18,000	-	18,999	5,100	48,000	-	49,999	12,750

Federal income tax withholding on auto benefits

Withholding of federal income tax is required on auto benefits for lay employees unless the employee is notified that the employer elects not to withhold by January 31 of the calendar year to which the election applies or, if later, within 30 days after the employee is given the automobile. The notification must be provided in writing and the employer must still withhold social security taxes if required to normally do so. If withholding is provided, the employer can treat the compensation as regular wages subject to the regular withholding rates or as supplemental wages subject to a flat 20% rate.

Tax-sheltered annuities and 401(k) plans

Tax-sheltered annuities

Employees of churches and other nonprofit organizations may have a Section 403(b) salary reduction arrangement based on a written plan. These plans are also called tax-sheltered annuities (TSAs).

Both nonelective and elective employer contributions for a minister to a TSA are excludable for income and social security tax (SECA) purposes. Elective contributions for nonministers are subject to FICA. While permissible, after-tax employee contributions are the exception in TSAs.

There are three separate, yet interrelated, limitations on the amount of contributions to a TSA that are excludable from gross income. See the 1999 edition of *The Zondervan Minister's Tax & Financial Guide* for additional information on TSA contribution limitations.

Tax-Sheltered Annuity Agreement

In order to provide benefits for retirement, the Employee desires to have contributions made on his or her behalf to purchase a non-forfeited annuity contract from _____ .

The Employer and Employee hereby agree that, with respect to the Employee's compensation for services rendered to the Employer commencing on the annual period ending _____, 199__ such compensation shall be reduced by $_____ or _____% per _____(period).

Each Employee shall ensure that the reduction in compensation shall in no event exceed the Employee's "exclusion allowance" as defined in Section 403(b)(2), or the limitation set forth in Section 415 and 402(g) of the Internal Revenue Code.

The Employee may, from time to time, by written instruction to the Employer, change from one division to another under the annuity contract.

This agreement must be amended by an instrument in writing signed by the Employer and the Employee and may be terminated by either the Employer or the Employee upon not less than 30 days' notice to the other. No designation or redesignation of investments or withdrawal shall be construed as an amendment or termination of this Agreement.

This Agreement is not a contract of employment between the parties hereto, and no provision hereof shall restrict the right of the Employer to discharge the Employee or the right of the Employee to terminate his or her employment.

Note: The above plan includes wording related to the stringent nondiscrimination rules. However, if your organization is a church or elementary or secondary school that is controlled, operated, or principally supported by a church or convention of association of churches, the nondiscrimination rules do not apply.

401(k) plans

A church or nonprofit organization may offer a 401(k) plan to its employees. Under a 401(k) plan, an employee can elect to have the church make tax-deferred contributions (up to $10,000 for 1998) to the plan.

401(k) and 403(b) Plans Compared

Provision	401(k)	403(b)
Federal taxation of employee salary reductions	Exempt from income tax Subject to FICA Exempt from SECA	Exempt from income tax Subject to FICA Exempt from SECA
State taxation of employee salary reductions	All states exempt employee salary reductions.	A few states tax employee salary reductions.
Roll-over available to 403(b) plan	No	Yes
Roll-over available to a pension plan or 401(k) plan, including plans of businesses	Yes	No
Roll-over available to IRA	Yes	Yes
Loans	Allowable, within certain limits	Allowable, within same limits as 401(k)
Calendar year maximum on elective deferral contributions	Lesser of percentage specified in plan document or statutory limit ($10,000 in 1998).	Generally, 20% of includable compensation, not to exceed statutory limit ($10,000 in 1998). NOTE: Catch-up elections allowing up to $12,500 annually are available to employees with over 15 years of service.
Per participant maximum on annual additions, including elective deferrals and employer matching contributions	Lesser of 25% of includable compensation or $30,000	Lesser of 25% of includable compensation or $30,000. Certain modifications can be made to this limitation.
Subject to exclusion allowance limit	No	Yes
Anti-discrimination testing	Two tests are required: One is for the employee's 401(k) portion of the plan and the other is for the employer's matching 401(m) portion of the plan. These tests can limit 401(k) contributions and matching contributions made on behalf of highly compensated employees. Churches are not exempt.	Only the employer's matching 401(m) portion of the plan is subject to an anti-discrimination test. Therefore, if no employer contributions are made, anti-discrimination testing is not required. Churches are exempt.
Subject to ERISA with its Form 5500 filing and other requirements	Yes, for most employers. Churches are exempt.	Any employer can avoid coverage by stringent non-involvement in plan. Churches are exempt.

Employer-provided dependent care assistance plan

A church or nonprofit organization can provide employees with child care or disabled dependent care services to allow employees to work. The amount excludable from tax is limited to the smaller of the employee's earned income, the spouse's earned income, or $5,000 ($2,500 if married filing separately).

The dependent care assistance must be provided under a separate written plan that does not favor highly compensated employees and that meets other qualifications (see sample plan below).

Dependent care assistance payments are excluded from income if the payments cover expenses that would be deductible by the employee as child and dependent care expenses on Form 2441 if the expenses were not reimbursed. If the employee is married, both spouses must be employed. There are special rules if one spouse is a student or incapable of self-care.

Sample Dependent Care Assistance Plan

Whereas, Willowbrook Church desires to establish a dependent care assistance plan under Section 129 of the Internal Revenue Code,

Resolved, That a dependent care assistance plan shall be established as follows:

1. The plan will not discriminate in favor of highly compensated employees.
2. Notification of the availability of the plan will be provided to all eligible employees.
3. Each year, on or before January 31, the plan will furnish to each employee a written statement showing the amounts paid or expenses incurred by the employer in providing dependent care assistance to such employee during the previous calendar year.
4. Dependent care assistance will be reported in Box 10 of Form W-2.
5. If dependent care assistance is provided to highly compensated employees, only those employees must include benefits provided under the plan in gross income.
6. Payments from the plan must be for expenses that would be deductible by the employee as child and dependent care expenses incurred to enable the employee to work.
7. The plan will only cover dependents of common-law employees of the church.
8. The exclusion for dependent care assistance payments is limited to $5,000 a year ($2,500 in the case of a married individual filing separately).
9. If child care services are provided on the premises of the church, the value of the services made available to the employee is excludable from income.

Resolved, That this dependent care assistance plan shall become effective on _____, 199___.

Medical expense reimbursement plan

Organizations often provide benefit plans covering an employee's major medical expenses. Some plans even cover some dental and optometry expenses.

With even the best employee benefit plans, there are usually after-tax expenses that the employee must pay out-of-pocket. These expenses may relate to the plan deductible, co-insurance, or simply noncovered items.

A medical expense reimbursement plan (MERP) is an excellent way to pay expenses not covered under another employee benefit plan—tax-free! With a MERP, the employee merely submits the otherwise out-of-pocket medical bills to the organization and receives a reimbursement. Since the nondiscrimination rules apply to these plans, it is often wise to make the benefit available to all full-time employees. MERP payments to individuals that are self-employed for income tax purposes represent taxable income.

Here's how a medical reimbursement plan could work for your organization:

✓ **Determine the relation of the MERP to the compensation package and set any limits.** Determine if the medical reimbursement benefit will be handled as:

- strictly a salary reduction (for example, an employee chooses to have $50 withheld each month under the medical reimbursement plan and may submit documentation for medical expenses up to $600 per year for reimbursement), or

- funded by the employer in addition to present gross pay and fringe benefits (for example, the organization elects to pay up to $500 per year without any salary reduction), or

- salary reduction plus employer funding (for example, the employer agrees to pay $500 plus the employee has a salary reduction of $600 per year).

✓ **Formally adopt the plan.** The plan should be approved by the organization's top governing body annually based on the structure and amounts determined. This action would generally occur in December for the following year.

✓ **Reimburse expenses under the plan.** Employees submit documentation after the primary carrier has considered the claims. If a particular expense is noncovered under the primary plan, it could be submitted under the medical reimbursement plan without being denied by the carrier.

A MERP established with employee-provided funds is a "use it or lose it" concept. If the employee does not submit sufficient expenses in the course of a year to use up the amount set aside under the plan, the amount remaining in the plan cannot be paid over to the employee without causing all benefits paid under the plan to become taxable. Therefore, it is important that the employee estimate expenses conservatively.

Form 5500 (or 5500-C or 5500-R) must be filed for employee-funded MERPs. There is no filing requirement for employer-funded MERPs.

A medical reimbursement plan does require administrative effort to establish it, annually review it, and process claim payments. However, the benefit can easily save several hundreds of dollars per year for each employee.

Sample Medical Expense Reimbursement Plan

Whereas, Valley View Church desires to provide medical care benefits relating to expenses not covered under the medical policy of the Church;

Resolved, That Valley View Church establishes a Medical Expense Reimbursement Plan effective _____, 199__ for the benefit of all full-time employees (working at least 30 hours or more per week) and their dependents (employee's spouse and minor children) under Section 105 of the Internal Revenue Code;

Resolved, That medical reimbursement accounts shall be maintained for each full-time employee from which covered expenses (as defined in Section 213 of the Internal Revenue Code) for the employee or their dependents shall be reimbursed. Reimbursements to an employee shall not exceed $_____ during one calendar year, plus any additional amount contributed by the employee under a written salary reduction agreement to the Plan for that year;

Resolved, That there shall be only one salary reduction election by each employee each year. This election may be changed during the year only in the following situations: (1) change in family status, e.g., marriage or divorce; birth, adoption, or death of a family member; (2) change of spousal employment status and/or health plan coverage; or (3) change in coverage under the employer's own health insurance policy;

Resolved, That the submission of medical expenses must be in a form and in sufficient detail to meet the requirements of the Church. Expenses may be submitted until March 31 for the previous calendar year. At that time, any balance remaining in an employee's account as of the end of the calendar year, shall be forfeited by the employee; and

Resolved, That the plan shall be administered in a nondiscriminatory manner and shall remain in effect until modified or terminated by a later resolution.

Note: The above plan is a combined employer-funded and employee salary reduction plan.

Compensation-related loans

Some churches and nonprofit organizations make loans to employees. The loans are often restricted to the purchase of land or a residence or the construction of a residence.

Before a loan is made, the organization should determine if the transaction is legal under state law. Such loans are prohibited in many states.

If an organization receives interest of $600 or more in a year relating to a loan secured by real estate, a Form 1098 (see page 91) must be provided to the payor. For the interest to be deductible as an itemized deduction, an employee loan must be secured by the residence and properly recorded.

If an organization makes loans to employees at below-market rates, the organization may be required to report additional compensation to the employee. If the loan is below $10,000, there is no additional compensation to the borrower. For loans over $10,000, additional compensation is calculated equal to the foregone interest that would have been charged if the loan had been made at a market rate of interest. The market rate of interest is the "applicable federal rate" for loans of similar duration. The IRS publishes these rates monthly. The additional compensation must be reported on Form W-2, Box 1.

There are certain exceptions to the general rules on below-market loans. These exceptions relate to loans secured by a mortgage and employee relocation loans.

Social security tax reimbursement

Churches and nonprofit organizations often reimburse ministers for a portion or all their self-employment tax (SECA) liability. Reimbursement also may be made to lay employees for all or a portion of the FICA tax that has been withheld from their pay. Any social security reimbursement must be reported as taxable income for both income and social security tax purposes. The FICA reimbursement to a lay employee is subject to income tax and FICA withholding.

Because of the deductibility of the self-employment tax in both the income tax and self-employment tax computations, a full reimbursement is effectively less than the gross 15.3% rate:

Marginal Tax Rate	Effective SECA Rate
0%	14.13%
15	13.07
28	12.15
31	11.94

For missionaries who are not eligible for the income tax deduction of one-half of the self-employment tax due to the foreign earned-income exclusion, the full reimbursement rate is effectively 14.13%.

It is usually best to reimburse an employee for self-employment tax on a monthly or quarterly basis. An annual reimbursement may leave room for misunderstanding between the organization and the employee if the employee is no longer employed at the time the reimbursement is due.

Property transfers

✓ **Unrestricted.** If an employer transfers property (for example, a car, residence, equipment, or other property) to an employee at no charge, this constitutes taxable income to the employee. The amount of income is generally the fair market value of the property transferred.

✓ **Restricted.** To recognize and reward good work, some churches or nonprofits transfer property to an employee subject to certain restrictions. The ultimate transfer will occur only if the employee lives up to the terms of the agreement. Once the terms are met, the property is transferred free and clear. Property that is subject to substantial risk of forfeiture and is nontransferable is substantially not vested. No tax liability will occur until title to the property is vested with the employee.

The exclusion is not an exemption from tax but is a deferral of tax. When restricted property becomes substantially vested, the employee must report the transfer as taxable income. The amount reported must be equal to the excess of the fair market value of the property at the time it becomes substantially vested, over the amount the employee pays for the property.

Example: A church transfers a house to the pastor subject to the completion of 20 years of service for the church. The pastor does not report any taxable income from the transfer until the 20th year.

✓ **Property purchased from employer.** If the employer allows an employee to buy property at a price below its fair market value, the employer must include in income as extra wages the difference between the property's fair market value and the amount paid and liabilities assumed by the employee.

Moving expenses

Moving expenses reimbursed by an employer, based on substantiation, are excludable from an employee's gross income. To qualify for this exclusion, the expenses must be deductible as moving expenses if they are not reimbursed.

The definition of deductible moving expenses is quite restrictive. Amounts are excludable only to the extent they would be deductible as moving expenses, i.e., only the cost of moving household goods and travel, other than meals, from the old residence to the new residence. Distance and timing tests must also be met.

Reimbursements to nonminister employees that do not exceed deductible moving expenses are not subject to withholding. However, excess payments are subject to FICA and federal income tax withholding. Excess reimbursements to minister-employees are only subject to income tax withholding if a voluntary withholding agreement is in force.

Excess payments to minister or nonminister employees must be included as taxable compensation, for income tax purposes, on Form W-2.

Reimbursements to a self-employed individual (for income tax purposes) are reportable on Form 1099-MISC and are not deductible for purposes of the social security calculation on Schedule SE.

> **Example:** A church paid a moving company $2,200 in 1998 for an employee's move. The employer also reimbursed the employee $350. All of the expenses qualify as deductible moving expenses. The employer should report $350 on Form W-2, only in Box 13, using Code P. The $2,200 of expenses paid directly to the moving company are not reportable.

Allowances and other nonaccountable expense reimbursements

Many organizations pay periodic allowances to employees for car expenses, library, entertainment, and so on. Other organizations reimburse employees for professional expenses with no requirement to account adequately for the expenses. This is a nonaccountable plan. Allowances or reimbursements under a nonaccountable plan must be included in the taxable income of the employee and are subject to income tax and FICA withholding for nonminister employees.

Gifts

All cash gifts to employees must be included in taxable compensation. Noncash gifts of nominal value to employees are tax-free. Gifts to certain non-employees up to $25 may be tax-free.

Nondiscrimination Rules

To qualify for exclusion from income, many fringe benefits must be nondiscriminatory. This is particularly true for many types of benefits for certain key employees. Failure to comply with the nondiscrimination rules does not disqualify a fringe benefit plan entirely. The benefit simply is fully taxable for the highly compensated or key employees.

The nondiscrimination rules apply to the following types of fringe benefit plans:

✓ qualified tuition and fee discounts,

✓ eating facilities on or near the employer's premises,

✓ educational assistance benefits,

✓ dependent care plans,

✓ tax-sheltered annuities (TSAs), 401(k) plans, and other deferred compensation plans,

✓ group-term life insurance benefits,

✓ self-insured medical plans, and

✓ cafeteria plans (including medical reimbursement plans).

Fringe benefit plans that limit benefits only to officers or highly compensated employees are clearly discriminatory. An officer is an employee who is appointed, confirmed, or elected by the board of the employer. A highly compensated employee for 1998 is

✓ paid more than $80,000, or

✓ if the employer elects, was in the top 20% of paid employees for compensation for the previous year.

Paying Employee Expenses

An accountable plan is a reimbursement or expense allowance arrangement that requires (1) a business purpose for the expenses, (2) employees to substantiate the expenses, and (3) the return of any excess reimbursements.

The substantiation of expenses and return of excess reimbursements must be handled within a reasonable time. The following methods meet the "reasonable time" definition:

✓ The fixed date method applies if

• an advance is made within 30 days of when an expense is paid or incurred;

• an expense is substantiated to the employer within 60 days after the expense is paid or incurred; and

• any excess amount is returned to the employer within 120 days after the expense is paid or incurred.

✓ The periodic statement method applies if

Sample Accountable Expense Reimbursement Plan

Whereas, Income tax regulations provide that an arrangement between an employee and employer must meet the requirements of business connection, substantiation, and return of excess payments in order to be considered a reimbursement;

Whereas, Plans that meet the three requirements listed above are considered to be accountable plans, and the reimbursed expenses are generally excludable from an employee's gross compensation;

Whereas, Plans that do not meet all the requirements listed above are considered nonaccountable plans, and payments made under such plans are includable in gross employee compensation; and

Whereas, Poplar Grove Church desires to establish an accountable expense reimbursement policy in compliance with the income tax regulations;

<u>Resolved</u>, That Poplar Grove Church establish an expense reimbursement policy effective _____, 199__ whereby employees serving the church may receive advances for or reimbursement of expenses if

    A. There is a stated business purpose of the expense related to the ministry of the church and the expenses would qualify for deductions for federal income tax purposes if the expenses were not reimbursed,

    B. The employee provides adequate substantiation to the church for all expenses, and

    C. The employee returns all excess reimbursements within a reasonable time.

and,

<u>Resolved</u>, That the following methods will meet the "reasonable time" definition:

    A. An advance is made within 30 days of when an expense is paid or incurred;

    B. An expense is substantiated to the church within 60 days after the expense is paid or incurred; or

    C. An excess amount is returned to the church within 120 days after the expense is paid or incurred.

and,

<u>Resolved</u>, That substantiation of business expenses will include business purpose, business relationship (including names of persons present), cost (itemized accounting), time, and place of any individual nonlodging expense of $75 or more and for all lodging expenses. Auto mileage reimbursed must be substantiated by a daily mileage log separating business and personal miles. The church will retain the original copies related to the expenses substantiated.

Note: The above resolution includes the basic guidelines for an accountable expense reimbursement plan. If the employer desires to place a dollar limit on reimbursements to be made under the plan employee-by-employee, a separate resolution may be adopted for this purpose.

- the employer provides employees with a periodic statement that sets forth the amount paid under the arrangement in excess of substantiated expenses;

- statements are provided at least quarterly; and

- the employer requests that the employee provide substantiation for any additional expenses that have not yet been substantiated and/or return any amounts remaining unsubstantiated within 120 days of the statement.

If employees substantiate expenses and return any unused excess payments to the church or nonprofit organization, payments to the employee for business expenses have no impact on tax reporting. They are not included on Form W-2 for the employee or Form 1099-MISC for the self-employed. Although Section 179 expense deductions can be claimed by an employee on their Form 1040, Section 179 amounts are not eligible for reimbursement under an accountable expense reimbursement plan.

Nonaccountable expense reimbursement plans

If business expenses are not substantiated by the employee to the church or nonprofit organization, or if the amount of the reimbursement to the employee exceeds the actual expenses and the excess is not returned within a reasonable period of time, reporting is required.

Nonaccountable reimbursements and excess reimbursements over IRS limits must be reported as wages on Form W-2. They are generally subject to federal income tax and FICA withholding for employees other than ministers.

Accountable plans and the self-employed

Nonaccountable reimbursements and excess reimbursements over IRS limits paid to self-employed workers must be reported as compensation on Form 1099-MISC. No reporting to the IRS is required for accountable expense reimbursements to self-employed workers.

Reimbursement of an organization's operating expenses

The reimbursement of operating expenses of an organization should be distinguished from reimbursements of employee business expenses. Accountable expense reimbursement plans generally relate to payments for employee business expenses.

Many organizations set a limit on overall accountable expense plan reimbursements. If organization operating expenses are mixed with employee business expenses, the employee may be penalized.

Example: A minister uses personal funds to pay for the printing of the weekly church bulletin. This printing is a church operating expense not an employee business expense. If the church has imposed an overall expense reimbursement limit on the minister, the inclusion of the bulletin printing in the employee reimbursement plan would improperly count these dollars against the plan limit.

Per diem allowance

The federal per diem rate, which is the sum of the federal lodging rate and meals and incidental expenses rate, is $180 for 1998 for the 41 high-cost areas and $113 per day for all other areas. The federal meals and incidental expense rate is $40 for the high-cost areas and $32 for any other locality. The federal lodging rate is $140 for the high-cost areas and $81 for other localities. Allowances that do not exceed these rates need not be reported to the IRS. Although no receipts are required, employees must document the date, place, and business purpose. The high-cost areas are identified in IRS Publications 463 and 1542.

Key Concepts

- Your organization will benefit from compensation planning as you try to stretch ministry dollars to cover personnel costs.

- Maximizing tax-free fringe benefits by adequate planning is vital for your employees.

- Proper use of the housing allowance for ministers who work for your organization is crucial.

- Do not ignore the nondiscrimination rules that apply to certain fringe benefits.

- The use of an accountable expense reimbursement plan for all employees of your organization is vital.

Employer Reporting

The withholding and reporting requirements with which employers must comply are complicated. The special tax treatment of qualified ministers simply adds another level of complexity.

Churches and nonprofit organizations are generally required to withhold federal (and state and local, as applicable) income taxes and social security taxes, and pay employer social security tax on all wages paid to all full-time or part-time employees (except qualified ministers) who earn at least $100 during the year.

The Classification of Workers

Whether an individual is classified as an employee or independent contractor has far-reaching consequences. This decision determines an organization's responsibility under the Federal Insurance Contributions Act (FICA), income tax withholding responsibilities, potential coverage under the Fair Labor Standards Act (see pages 180–81), and coverage under an employer's benefit plans. Misclassification can lead to significant penalties.

Questions frequently arise about the classification of certain nonprofit workers. Seasonal workers and those working less than full-time such as secretaries, custodians,

KEY ISSUE

and musicians require special attention for classification purposes. If a worker receives pay at an hourly rate, it will be difficult to justify independent contractor status. This conclusion would be true even if the workers are part-time.

Since 1935, the IRS has relied on 20 common law factors (see bottom of this page) to determine whether workers are employees or independent contractors. Pressure continues to build on Congress and the IRS to provide clearer guidance on who can be an independent contractor and when.

Employees

If a worker is a nonministerial employee, the employer must withhold federal income tax (and state income tax, if applicable) and Federal Insurance Contributions Act (FICA) taxes; match the employee's share of FICA taxes; and, unless exempted, pay unemployment taxes on employee's wages. In addition, the employer may incur obligations for employee benefit plans such as vacation, sick pay, health insurance, and pension plan contributions.

Among other criteria, employees comply with instructions, have a continuous relationship, perform work personally, work full- or part-time, are subject to dismissal, can quit without incurring liability, are often reimbursed for expenses, and must submit reports.

Independent contractors

If the worker is classified as an independent contractor, quarterly estimated income taxes and social security taxes under the Self-Employment Contributions Act (SECA) are paid by the worker. There is no unemployment tax liability or income or social security tax withholding requirement for independent contractors.

Independent contractors normally set the order and sequence of work, set their hours of work, work for others at the same time, are paid by the job, offer their services to the public, have an opportunity for profit or loss, furnish their tools, and may do work on another's premises, and there is often substantial investment by the worker.

Common law rules

The IRS generally applies the common law rules to decide if an individual is an employee or self-employed (independent contractor) for income tax purposes. Generally the individual is an employee if the employer has the legal right to control both what and how it is done, even if the individual has considerable discretion and freedom of action.

Workers are generally considered employees if they

✓ Must follow the organization's work instructions;

✓ Receive on-the-job training;

Independent Contractor Status Myths

- *Myth*: A written contract will characterize a person as an independent contractor.

  Fact: It is the substance of the relationship that governs.

- *Myth*: Casual labor or seasonal workers are independent contractors or their classification is a matter of choice.

  Fact: There is never a choice. The classification is determined by the facts and circumstances.

- *Myth*: If a person qualifies as an independent contractor for federal payroll tax purposes, he or she is automatically exempt for Workers' Compensation and state unemployment tax purposes.

  Fact: State Workers' Compensation and unemployment tax laws are often broader and an individual may actually be covered under these laws even though qualifying as an independent contractor for federal payroll tax purposes.

✓ Provide services that must be rendered personally;

✓ Provide services that are integral to the organization;

✓ Hire, supervise, and pay assistants for the organization;

✓ Have an ongoing work relationship with the organization;

✓ Must follow set hours of work;

✓ Work full-time for the organization;

✓ Work on the organization's premises;

✓ Must do their work in an organization-determined sequence;

✓ Receive business expense reimbursements;

✓ Receive routing payments of regular amounts;

✓ Need the organization to furnish tools and materials;

✓ Do not have a major investment in job facilities;

✓ Cannot suffer a loss from their services;

✓ Work for one organization at a time;

✓ Do not offer their services to the general public;

✓ Can be fired by the organization;

✓ May quit work at any time without penalty.

Key issue: The amount of control and direction the church has over a worker's services is the most important overall issue. So some of the above factors may be given greater weight than others.

The classification of ministers

It is important that the organization decide if the services of ministers employed by the organization qualify for special tax treatment as ministerial services.

Special Tax Provisions for Ministers

● Exclusion for income tax purposes of the housing allowance and the fair rental value of a church-owned parsonage provided rent-free to clergy.

● Exemption of clergy from self-employment tax under very limited circumstances.

● Treatment of clergy (who do not elect social security exemption) as self-employed for social security tax purposes for income from ministerial services.

● Exemption of clergy compensation from mandatory income tax withholding.

● Eligibility for a voluntary income tax withholding arrangement between the minister-employee and the church.

● Potential double deduction of mortgage interest and real estate taxes as itemized deductions and as housing expenses for housing allowance purposes.

Most ordained, commissioned, or licensed ministers serving local churches will qualify for the above six special tax provisions with respect to services performed in the exercise of ministry. The IRS and courts apply certain tests to ministers serving local churches including whether the minister administers the sacraments, conducts worship services, is considered a spiritual leader by the church, and if the minister performs management services in the "control, conduct, or maintenance of a religious organization." It may not be necessary for a minister to meet all of these tests to qualify for the special tax treatment. For a complete discussion of this topic, see the 1999 edition of *The Zondervan Minister's Tax & Financial Guide.*

Ordained, commissioned, or licensed ministers not serving local churches may qualify as ministers for federal tax purposes without meeting additional tests if their duties include the following:

✔ Administration of church denominations and their integral agencies, including teaching or administration in parochial schools, colleges, or universities that are under the authority of a church or denomination.

✔ Performing services for an institution that is not an integral agency of a church pursuant to an assignment or designation by ecclesiastical superiors, but only if the services relate to church purposes.

If a church does not assign or designate the minister's services, they will be qualified services only if they involve performing sacerdotal functions or conducting religious worship.

Sample Board Resolution for Ministerial Assignment

Whereas, _____Name of assigning church_____ recognizes the calling of _____Name of minister assigned_____ as a minister and is (ordained, licensed, or commissioned) and

Whereas, We believe that the assignment of ____Name of minister assigned____ will further the efforts and mission of our church and we desire to provide support and encouragement;

Resolved, That _____Name of minister assigned_____ is hereby assigned to ____Name of ministry to which assigned____ effective_____, 199__ to serve as _____Position Title_____ and

Resolved, That this assignment is made for a period of one year upon which time it will be reviewed and may be renewed, and

Resolved, That this assignment is contingent upon the quarterly submission of activity and financial reports by ____Name of minister assigned____ to our church.

Reporting Compensation

Minister-employees

Form W-2s are annually provided to minister-employees. There is no requirement to withhold income taxes, but they may be withheld under a voluntary agreement. Social security taxes are not withheld.

Nonminister-employees

If an employee does not qualify for tax treatment as a minister, the organization is liable to withhold and pay FICA and income taxes. Certain FICA tax exceptions are discussed later.

Nonemployees

A self-employed minister and other self-employed recipients of compensation should receive Form 1099-MISC instead of Form W-2 (if the person has received compensation of at least $600 for the year).

Payroll Tax Withholding

FICA social security

Most churches and nonprofit organizations must withhold FICA taxes from their employees' wages and pay it to the IRS along with the employer's share of the tax. Minister-employees are an exception to this rule. In 1998 both the employer and the employee pay a 6.2% tax rate on the social security wage base of up to $68,400. Similarly, both the employer and the employee pay a 1.45% medicare tax rate on all pay above $68,400. The rates remain the same for 1999. The 1999 social security wage base is estimated to be $71,400.

There are a few exceptions to the imposition of FICA. Generally wages paid to an employee of less than $100 in a calendar year are not subject to FICA. Services excluded from FICA include

✓ services performed by a minister of a church in the exercise of ministry or by a member of a religious order in the exercise of duties required by such order;

✓ services performed in the employ of a church or church-controlled organization that is opposed for religious reasons to the payment of social security taxes (see later discussion of filing Form 8274);

✓ services performed by a student in the employ of a school, college, or university.

Churches and church-controlled organizations opposed to social security taxes

In 1984 the law was changed to allow qualifying churches and church-controlled organizations to claim exemption from payment of FICA taxes. An organization must certify opposition "for religious reasons to the payment of employer social security taxes." Very few organizations qualify to file Form 8274.

Organizations in existence on September 30, 1984, were required to file Form 8274 by October 30, 1984. Any organization created after September 30, 1984, must file before the first date on which a quarterly employment tax return is due from the organization.

Organizations desiring to revoke their exemption made earlier by filing Form 8274 should file Form 941 with full payment of social security taxes for that quarter.

Federal income tax

Most nonprofit organizations are exempt from the payment of federal income tax on the organization's income (see page 34 for the tax on unrelated business income). But they must withhold and pay federal, state, and local income taxes on the wages paid to each employee. Minister-employees are an exception to this rule.

An employee-minister may have a voluntary withholding agreement with a church or nonprofit employer relating to the minister's income taxes. An agreement to withhold income taxes from wages must be in writing. There is no required form for the agreement. A minister may request voluntary withholding by submitting Form W-4 (Employee Withholding Allowance Certificate) to the employer indicating the additional amount to be withheld in excess of the tax table or the written request may be in another form.

The self-employed minister for income tax purposes reports and pays income taxes through the estimated tax (Form 1040-ES) procedure. There is no provision for federal income tax withholding from payments made to independent contractors, even on a voluntary basis.

Federal income taxes for all employees (except ministers) are calculated based on the chart and tables shown in IRS Publication 15. State and local income taxes are usually required to be withheld according to state withholding tables.

✓ **Form W-4.** All employees, part- or full-time, must complete a W-4 form. (Ministers are an exception to this requirement unless a voluntary withholding arrangement is used.) The withholding allowance information completed on this form gives the basis to determine the amount of income tax to be withheld.

All Form W-4s on which employees claim exempt status (and the

Form **W-4**
Department of the Treasury
Internal Revenue Service

Employee's Withholding Allowance Certificate
▶ **For Privacy Act and Paperwork Reduction Act Notice, see page 2.**

OMB No. 1545-0010

1998

1 Type or print your first name and middle initial	Last name	2 Your social security number
Walter R.	Knight	511 : 20 : 7943

Home address (number and street or rural route)	3 ☐ Single ☑ Married ☐ Married, but withhold at higher Single rate.
601 Oakridge Boulevard	Note: *If married, but legally separated, or spouse is a nonresident alien, check the Single box.*

City or town, state, and ZIP code	4 If your last name differs from that on your social security card, check
Vinton, VA 24179	here and call 1-800-772-1213 for a new card . . . . . . ▶ ☐

5	Total number of allowances you are claiming (from line H above or from the worksheets on page 2 if they apply) .	5	4
6	Additional amount, if any, you want withheld from each paycheck	6 $	

7 I claim exemption from withholding for 1998, and I certify that I meet **BOTH** of the following conditions for exemption:
- Last year I had a right to a refund of **ALL** Federal income tax withheld because I had **NO** tax liability **AND**
- This year I expect a refund of **ALL** Federal income tax withheld because I expect to have **NO** tax liability.

If you meet both conditions, enter "EXEMPT" here . . . . ▶ | 7 |

Under penalties of perjury, I certify that I am entitled to the number of withholding allowances claimed on this certificate or entitled to claim exempt status.

Employee's signature ▶ *Walter R. Knight*   Date ▶ *1/1* , 19 **99**

8 Employer's name and address (Employer: Complete 8 and 10 only if sending to the IRS)	9 Office code (optional)	10 Employer identification number

Note: This form must be completed by all lay employees, full- or part-time by February 18 of each year. If a minister completes this form, it can be the basis to determine income tax withholding under a voluntary agreement.

Form **W-5**
Department of the Treasury
Internal Revenue Service

Earned Income Credit Advance Payment Certificate
▶**Use the current year's certificate only.**
▶ **Give this certificate to your employer.**
▶ **This certificate expires on December 31, 1998.**

OMB No. 1545-1342

1998

Type or print your full name	Your social security number
Daniel L. Wheeler	304-78-6481

Note: *If you get advance payments of the earned income credit for 1998, you **must** file a 1998 Federal income tax return. To get advance payments, you **must** have a qualifying child and your filing status must be any status **except** married filing a separate return.*

		Yes	No
1	I expect to be able to claim the earned income credit for 1998, I do not have another Form W-5 in effect with any other current employer, and I choose to get advance EIC payments	X	
2	Do you have a qualifying child?	X	
3	Are you married?	X	
4	If you are married, does your spouse have a Form W-5 in effect for 1998 with any employer?		X

Under penalties of perjury, I declare that the information I have furnished above is, to the best of my knowledge, true, correct, and complete.

Signature ▶ *Daniel L. Wheeler*   Date ▶ 1/1/99

Note: This form should be completed if an employee elects to receive advance payments of the earned income credit.

employees' wages would normally exceed $200 weekly) or claim more than 10 withholding allowances must be filed with the IRS.

✓ **Form W-5.** An eligible employee uses Form W-5 to elect to receive advance payments of the earned income credit (EIC). Employees may be eligible for the EIC when they are expecting 1998 taxable and nontaxable earned income less than $9,770 if there is no qualifying child, less than $25,760 if there is one qualifying child, or less than $29,290 if there are two or more qualifying children.

The portion of your housing allowance excluded from the Form W-2 and the fair rental value of church-provided housing must be included when calculating the EIC. Also includable are 403(b) and 401(k) voluntary tax-sheltered annuity deferrals.

If eligible for the earned income credit, an employee may choose to receive an advance instead of waiting until they file their annual Form 1040.

✓ **Form W-7.** Certain individuals who are not eligible for a social security number (SSN) may obtain an Individual Taxpayer Identification Number. The following individuals may file Form W-7: (1) nonresident aliens who are required to file a U.S. tax return, (2) nonresident aliens who are filing a U.S. tax return only to claim a refund, (3) individuals being claimed as dependents on U.S. tax returns and who are not eligible to obtain a social security number, (4) individuals being claimed as husbands or wives for exemptions on U.S. tax returns and who are not eligible to obtain a SSN, and (5) U.S. residents who must file a U.S. tax return but are not eligible for a SSN.

Self-employment tax

Self-employment taxes (SECA) should never be withheld from the salary of an employee. But under the voluntary withholding agreement for ministers' federal income taxes, additional federal income tax may be withheld sufficient to cover the minister's self-employment tax liability. When these withheld amounts are paid to the IRS, they must be identified as "federal income tax withheld" (and not social security taxes withheld).

Personal liability for payroll taxes

Church and nonprofit officers and employees may be personally liable if payroll taxes are not withheld and paid to the IRS. If the organization has willfully failed to withhold and pay the taxes, the IRS has the authority to assess a 100% penalty of withheld income and social security taxes.

This penalty may be assessed against the individual responsible for withholding and paying the taxes, even if the person is an unpaid volunteer such as a church treasurer.

Depositing Withheld Payroll Taxes

The basic rules for depositing payroll taxes are

✓ If your total accumulated and unpaid employment tax is less than $1,000 in a calendar quarter, taxes can be paid directly to the IRS when the organization files Form 941. These forms are due one month after the end of each calendar quarter.

✓ If payroll taxes are over $1,000 for a quarter, deposits must be made monthly or before the 15th day of each month for the payroll paid during the preceding month. Large organizations with total employment taxes of over $50,000 per year are subject to more frequent deposits. (See page 8 in the Recent Developments section for certain penalty relief provided by the IRS for organizations subject to electronic funds transfer requirements.)

To determine if an organization is a monthly depositor under the new rules, you must determine if the accumulated liabilities in the "look-back period" reached a threshold of $50,000. Those with an accumulated liability of less than $50,000 in the look-back period are generally monthly depositors (except those qualifying for quarterly deposits with liabilities of $1,000 or less).

A new organization (or one filing payroll tax returns for the first time) will be required to file monthly until a "look-back" period is established. A look-back period begins on July 1 and ends on June 30 of the preceding calendar year.

The cost of missing deposit deadlines can be very high. Besides interest, the organization can be hit with penalties at progressively stiffer rates. These range from 2% if you deposit the money within five days of the due date, to 15% if it is not deposited within 10 days of the first delinquency notice or on the day that the IRS demands immediate payment, whichever is earlier.

Deposit coupons

✓ **Form 8109.** Use Form 8109 deposit coupons to make deposits of the taxes covered by the following forms: Form 941, Form 990-T, and Schedule A.

The preprinted name and address of the organization and the Employer's Identification Number (EIN) appear on the coupons. Deliver or mail the completed coupon with the appropriate payment to a qualified depository for federal taxes.

✓ **Form 8109-B.** Use Form 8109-B deposit coupons to make tax deposits only in the following two situations:

● You have reordered preprinted deposit coupons (Form 8109) but have not yet received them.

- You are a new entity and have already been assigned an EIN, but have not yet received your initial supply of preprinted deposit coupons (Form 8109).

Form 8109-B may be obtained only from the IRS.

Filing the Quarterly Payroll Tax Forms

Employers must report covered wages paid to their employees by filing Form 941 with the IRS.

Form 941

Church and other nonprofit employers who withhold income tax and both social security and medicare taxes, must file Form 941 quarterly. There is no requirement to file Form 941 if your organization has not been required to withhold payroll taxes even if you have one or more employee-ministers (but without any voluntary withholding).

Most common errors made on Form 941

The IRS has outlined the most common errors discovered during the processing of Form 941, Employer's Quarterly Federal Tax Return, and the best way to avoid making these mistakes. A checklist for avoiding errors follows:

✓ Do not include titles or abbreviations, such as Dr., Mr., or Mrs.

✓ Make sure that taxable social security wages and the social security tax on line 6a, the social security tax on line 6b, and the taxable medicare wages and the medicare tax on line 7 are reported separately. Most employers will need to complete both lines 6a and 7.

✓ The preprinted form sent by the IRS should be used. If the return is prepared by a third-party preparer, make certain that the preparer uses exactly the name that appears on the preprinted form that was sent.

✓ Check the math for lines 5, 10, 13, and 14. Line 14 should always be the sum of lines 5, 10, and 13.

✓ Make sure the social security tax on line 6a is calculated correctly (12.4% x social security wages).

✓ Make sure the medicare tax on line 7 is calculated correctly (2.9% x medicare wages).

✓ Be sure to use the most recent Form 941 that the IRS sends. The IRS enters

Form **941**
(Rev. July 1998)

Department of the Treasury
Internal Revenue Service

Employer's Quarterly Federal Tax Return

▶ See separate instructions for information on completing this return.
Please type or print.

OMB No. 1545-0029

Enter state code for state in which deposits were made ONLY if different from state in address to the right ▶ [:] (see page 3 of instructions).

Name (as distinguished from trade name)	Date quarter ended
Barnett Ridge Church	**3/31/99**
Trade name, if any	Employer identification number
	48-5125445
Address (number and street)	City, state, and ZIP code
P.O. Box 517, Selma, AL 36701	

T	
FF	
FD	
FP	
I	
T	

If address is different from prior return, check here ▶ □

IRS Use

1 1 1 1 1 1 1 1	2	3 3 3 3 3 3 3	4 4 4	5 5 5
6 7 8 8 8 8 8 8 8		9 9 9 9 9	10 10 10	10 10 10 10 10

If you do not have to file returns in the future, check here ▶ □   and enter date final wages paid ▶

If you are a seasonal employer, see **Seasonal employers** on page 1 of the instructions and check here ▶ □

1	Number of employees in the pay period that includes March 12th . ▶	1		4		
2	Total wages and tips, plus other compensation				2	24,811
3	Total income tax withheld from wages, tips, and sick pay				3	4,642
4	Adjustment of withheld income tax for preceding quarters of calendar year				4	
5	Adjusted total of income tax withheld (line 3 as adjusted by line 4—see instructions) .				5	4,642
6	Taxable social security wages	6a	16,340	× 12.4% (.124) =	6b	2,026
	Taxable social security tips	6c		× 12.4% (.124) =	6d	
7	Taxable Medicare wages and tips . . .	7a	16,340	× 2.9% (.029) =	7b	474
8	Total social security and Medicare taxes (add lines 6b, 6d, and 7b). Check here if wages are not subject to social security and/or Medicare tax . . . . ▶ □				8	2,500
9	Adjustment of social security and Medicare taxes (see instructions for required explanation) Sick Pay $ _____ ± Fractions of Cents $ _____ ± Other $ _____				9	
10	Adjusted total of social security and Medicare taxes (line 8 as adjusted by line 9—see instructions)				10	2,500
11	**Total taxes** (add lines 5 and 10)				11	7,142
12	Advance earned income credit (EIC) payments made to employees				12	
13	Net taxes (subtract line 12 from line 11). **This should equal line 17, column (d) below (or line D of Schedule B (Form 941))**				13	7,142
14	Total deposits for quarter, including overpayment applied from a prior quarter				14	7,142
15	**Balance due** (subtract line 14 from line 13). See instructions				15	0
16	Overpayment. If line 14 is more than line 13, enter excess here ▶ $ _____ and check if to be: □ Applied to next return **OR** □ Refunded.					

• **All filers:** If line 13 is less than $1,000, you need not complete line 17 or Schedule B (Form 941).
• **Semiweekly schedule depositors:** Complete Schedule B (Form 941) and check here . . . . ▶ □
• **Monthly schedule depositors:** Complete line 17, columns (a) through (d), and check here . . . . ▶ □

17	**Monthly Summary of Federal Tax Liability.** Do not complete if you were a semiweekly schedule depositor.			
	(a) First month liability	(b) Second month liability	(c) Third month liability	(d) Total liability for quarter
	2,603	2,548	1,991	7,142

Sign Here

Under penalties of perjury, I declare that I have examined this return, including accompanying schedules and statements, and to the best of my knowledge and belief, it is true, correct, and complete.

Signature ▶ *Alan W. Dunn*   Print Your Name and Title ▶ Alan W. Dunn, Treas.   Date ▶ 4/30/99

For Privacy Act and Paperwork Reduction Act Notice, see page 4 of separate instructions.   Cat. No. 17001Z   Form **941** (Rev. 7-98)

Note: File this form to report social security (FICA) and medicare taxes and federal income tax withheld.

Form **941c**	**Supporting Statement To Correct Information**	OMB No. 1545-0256
(Rev. October 1996)	**Do Not File Separately**	Page
Department of the Treasury Internal Revenue Service	▶File with Form 941, 941-M, 941-SS, 943, 945, or 843.	No.

Name	Employer identification number
Little Valley Church	35-6309294

Telephone number		Check one box.

A This form supports adjustments to:

[X] Form 941	Form 941-SS	Form 945
Form 941-M	Form 943	

B This form is filed with the return for the period ending (month, year) ▶ 3/31/99

C Enter the date you discovered the error(s) reported on this form. (If you are making more than one correction and the errors were not discovered at the same time, please explain in Part V.) . . . . ▶3/1/99

Part I Signature and Certification (You **MUST** complete this part for the IRS to process your adjustments for overpayments.) Skip Part I if all your adjustments are underpayments. (See the instructions for Part I.)

I certify that **Forms W-2c**, Corrected Wage and Tax Statement, have been filed (as necessary) with the Social Security Administration, and that (check appropriate boxes):

[ ] All overcollected income taxes for the current calendar year and all social security and Medicare taxes for the current and prior calendar years have been repaid to employees. For claims of overcollected employee social security and Medicare taxes in earlier years, a written statement has been obtained from each employee stating that the employee has not claimed and will not claim refund or credit of the amount of the overcollection.

[ ] All affected employees have given their written consent to the allowance of this credit or refund. For claims of overcollected employee social security and Medicare taxes in earlier years, a written statement has been obtained from each employee stating that the employee has not claimed and will not claim refund or credit of the amount of the overcollection.

[ ] The social security tax and Medicare tax adjustments represent the employer's share only. An attempt was made to locate the employee(s) affected, but the affected employee(s) could not be located or will not comply with the certification requirements.

[ ] None of this refund or credit was withheld from employee wages.

Sign Here Signature ▶ *Curtis R. Lee* Title ▶ Treasurer Date ▶4/30/99

Part II Income Tax Withholding (Including Backup Withholding) Adjustment

(a) Period Corrected (For quarterly returns, enter date quarter ended. For annual returns, enter year.)	(b) Withheld Income Tax Previously Reported for Period	(c) Correct Withheld Income Tax for Period	(d) Withheld Income Tax Adjustment
1 12/31/98	400	600	200
2			
3			
4			

5 Net withheld income tax adjustment. If more than one page, enter total of **ALL** columns (d) on first page only. Enter here and on the **appropriate** line of the return with which you file this form . . . . ▶ | 5 | 200

Part III Social Security Tax Adjustment (Use the tax rate in effect during the period(s) corrected. You must also complete Part IV.)

(a) Period Corrected (For quarterly returns, enter date quarter ended. For annual returns, enter year.)	(b) Wages Previously Reported for Period	(c) Correct Wages for Period	(d) Tips Previously Reported for Period	(e) Correct Tips for Period	(f) Social Security Tax Adjustment
1 12/31/98	2000	4500			155
2					
3					
4					

5 Totals. - If more than one page, enter totals on first page only . . . . ▶

6 Net social security tax adjustment. If more than one page, enter total of **ALL** columns (f) on first page only. Enter here and on the appropriate line of the return with which you file this form . . . . ▶ | 6 | 155

7 Net wage adjustment. If more than one page, enter total of **ALL** lines 7 on first page only. If line 5(c) is smaller than line 5(b), enter difference in parentheses . . . . ▶ | 7 | 2500

8 Net tip adjustment. If more than one page, enter total of **ALL** lines 8 on first page only. If line 5(e) is smaller than line 5(d), enter difference in parentheses . . . . ▶ | 8 |

For Paperwork Reduction Act Notice, see page 3.   Form **941c** (Rev. 10-96)

Note: Use this form to correct income, social security (FICA), and medicare tax information reported on Form 941. It may be necessary to issue Form W-2c to employees relating to prior year data.

the date the quarter ended after the employer identification number. If the form is used for a later quarter, the IRS will have to contact the employer.

✓ Make sure there is never an entry on both lines 18 and 19. There cannot be a balance due and a refund.

Form 941c

Form 941c may be used to correct income, social security, and medicare tax information reported on Forms 941, 941-M, 941SS, or 943. Attach it to the tax return on which you are claiming the adjustment (Form 941, and so on) or to Form 843, Claim for Refund and Request for Abatement. Also issue the employee(s) a Form W-2c for the prior year, if applicable.

Filing the Annual Payroll Tax Forms

Form W-2

By January 31 each employee must be given a Form W-2. To help you in the completion of the 1998 version of the Form W-2, an explanation of certain boxes is provided. For additional help, call 304–263–8700.

Be sure to reconcile the data reflected on Forms W-2, W-3, and 941 before distributing Form W-2s to employees. If these forms do not reconcile, the IRS generally sends a letter to the employer requesting additional information.

Void—Put an X in this box when an error has been made on this W-2.

Box 1—Wages, tips, other compensation. Items to include in Box 1 before any payroll deductions are

✓ total wages paid during the year (including love offerings paid by the church or nonprofit organization to a minister or other employee);

✓ the value of noncash payments, including taxable fringe benefits;

✓ business expense payments under a nonaccountable plan;

✓ payments of per diem or mileage allowance paid for business expense purposes that exceed the IRS specified rates;

✓ payments made by a church or nonprofit organization to an employee's Individual Retirement Plan;

✓ payments for nonexcludable moving expenses;

Checklist for Completing Box 1 of Form W-2

Minister Only	Both	Nonminister Only	
	yes		Salary
no		yes	Housing/furnishings allowance (designated in advance)
no		yes	Parsonage rental value
no		yes	Utilities paid by church or nonprofit
	yes		Social security/medicare "allowance" or reimbursement
	no		Transportation/travel and other business and professional expense reimbursements *only if* paid under a board-adopted accountable reimbursement plan
	yes		"Reimbursements" if not paid under an accountable reimbursement plan
	yes		Love offerings or cash gifts in excess of $25
	no		Contributions to a tax-sheltered annuity plan
	no		Health/dental/long-term care insurance premiums paid directly or reimbursed by the employer
	no		Group term life insurance premiums (for up to $50,000 coverage) paid directly by the employer
	no		Excludable moving expense paid for or reimbursed to an employee
	yes		Nonexcludable moving expenses paid for or reimbursed to an employee
	yes		Value of personal and nonbusiness use of organization's vehicle

Data Included for

✔ all other compensation, including taxable fringe benefits. "Other compensation" represents amounts an organization pays to an employee from which federal income tax is not withheld. If you prefer, you may show other compensation on a separate Form W-2; and

✔ the cash housing allowance or the fair market rental value of housing and utilities must be reported as taxable income for lay employees unless furnished on the employer's premises and the employee is required to accept the lodging as a condition of employment.

Exclude the following:

✔ the fair rental value of a church-provided parsonage or a properly designated housing allowance for ministers;

✔ auto or business expense reimbursements paid through an accountable expense plan; and

✔ contributions to 403(b) tax-sheltered annuities or 401(k) plans.

a Control number				
		OMB No. 1545-0008		
b Employer identification number		1 Wages, tips, other compensation	2 Federal income tax withheld	
35-2946039		14586.00	2039.00	
c Employer's name, address, and ZIP code		3 Social security wages	4 Social security tax withheld	
		15786.00	979.00	
ABC Charity		5 Medicare wages and tips	6 Medicare tax withheld	
2670 N. Hull Road		15786.00	229.00	
Traverse City, MI 49615		7 Social security tips	8 Allocated tips	
d Employee's social security number		9 Advance EIC payment	10 Dependent care benefits	
517-28-6451				
e Employee's name, address, and ZIP code		11 Nonqualified plans	12 Benefits included in box 1	
Michael A. Black		13 See instrs. for box 13	14 Other	
15550 Cleveland Avenue				
Traverse City, MI 49615		E 1200.00		
		P 984.73		

15 Statutory employee	Deceased	Pension plan	Legal rep.	Deferred compensation

16 State Employer's state I.D. no.	17 State wages, tips, etc.	18 State income tax	19 Locality name	20 Local wages, tips, etc.	21 Local income tax
MI 6309294	15786.00	205.00			

Department of the Treasury—Internal Revenue Service

Form **W-2** Wage and Tax Statement **1998**

This information is being furnished to the Internal Revenue Service.

Copy B To Be Filed With Employee's FEDERAL Tax Return

Box 2—Federal income tax withheld. Enter the total federal income tax withheld according to the chart and tables in IRS Publication 15.

A qualified minister may enter into a voluntary withholding arrangement with the employing organization. Based on Form W-4 or other written withholding request, federal income tax withholding may be calculated from the chart and tables in Publication 15 excluding any housing allowance amount.

The minister may request that an additional amount of income tax be withheld to cover self-employment tax. The additional amount withheld is reported as income tax withheld on the quarterly Form 941 and in Box 2 of Form W-2.

An organization that provides additional compensation to the employee-minister to cover part or all of the self-employment tax liability may:

✓ pay the additional compensation directly to the IRS by entering that amount on the organization's Form 941 and in Boxes 1 and 2 of Form W-2, or

✓ pay the additional compensation to the minister with the minister being responsible for remitting the amounts to the IRS with a Form 1040-ES. If this procedure is followed, the organization reports this amount only as additional compensation on Form 941 and only in Box 1 of Form W-2.

Box 3—Social security wages. Show the total wages paid (before payroll deductions) subject to employee social security tax (FICA). This amount must not exceed $68,400 in 1998 (the maximum social security tax wage base). Generally all cash and noncash payments reported in Box 1 must also be shown in Box 3. Include nonaccountable employee business expenses reported in Box 1. Voluntary salary reduction tax-sheltered annuity contributions for nonminister employees are included in Box 3.

Box 3 should be blank for qualified ministers.

Box 4—Social security tax withheld. Show the total FICA social security tax (not including the organization's share) withheld or paid by you for the employee. The amount shown must equal 6.2% of the amount in Box 3 and must not exceed $4,240.80 for 1998. Do not include the matching employer FICA tax.

Some organizations pay the employee's share of FICA tax for some or all nonminister employees instead of deducting it from the employee's wages. These amounts paid by the organization must be included in Boxes 1, 3, and 5 as wages and proportionately in Boxes 4 and 6 as social security and medicare tax withheld. In these instances, the effective cost to the employer is 8.28% instead of 7.45% for wages up to $68,400 and 1.47% rather than 1.45% for wages above $68,400.

Box 4 should be blank for qualified ministers. Any amount of withholding to meet the minister's SECA tax liability must be reported in Box 2, not in Box 4 or Box 6.

Box 5—Medicare wages. The wages subject to medicare tax are the same as those subject to social security tax (Box 3), except there is no wage limit for the medicare tax.

Example: You paid a nonminister employee $69,000 in wages. The amount shown in Box 3 (social security wages) should be $68,400, but the amount shown in Box 5 (Medicare wages) should be $69,000. If the amount of wages paid was less than $68,400, the amounts entered in Boxes 3 and 5 will be the same.

Box 5 should be blank for qualified ministers.

Box 6—Medicare tax withheld. Enter the total employee medicare tax (not your share) withheld or paid by you for your employee. The amount shown must equal 1.45% of the amount in Box 5. Box 6 should be blank for qualified ministers.

Box 9—Advance EIC payment. Show the total paid to the employee as advance earned income credit payments.

Box 10—Dependent care benefits. Show the total amount of dependent care benefits under Section 129 paid or incurred by you for your employee including any amount over the $5,000 exclusion. Also include in Box 1, Box 3, and Box 5 any amount over the $5,000 exclusion.

Box 11—Nonqualified plans. Enter the total amount of distributions to the employee from a nonqualified deferred compensation plan. Include an amount in Box 11 only if it is also includable in Box 1 or Boxes 3 and 5.

Box 12—Benefits included in Box 1. Show the total value of the taxable fringe benefits included in Box 1 as other compensation.

If the organization owns or leases a vehicle for an employee's use, the value of the personal use of the vehicle is taxable income. The value of the use of the vehicle is established by using one of the methods described on pages 52–54. The amount of the personal use must be included in Boxes 1 and 12 (and in Boxes 3 and 5 if a lay employee). The employee is required to maintain a mileage log or similar records to substantiate business and personal use of the vehicle and submit this to the employer. If not substantiated, the employer must report 100 percent of the use of the vehicle as taxable income.

If the employee fully reimburses the employer for the value of the personal use of the vehicle, then no value would be reported in either Box 1 or in Box 12.

Box 13—Additional entries. The following items are most frequently inserted in Box 13 by churches and other nonprofit organizations:

C—Group-term life insurance. If you provided your employee more than $50,000 of group-term life insurance, show the cost of the coverage over $50,000. Also include the amount in Box 1 (also in Boxes 3 and 5 if a lay employee).

D—Section 401(k) cash or deferred arrangement.

E—Section 403(b) voluntary salary reduction agreement to purchase an annuity contract. This amount would not be included in Box 1 for either ministerial or lay employees. This amount would be included in Boxes 3 and 5 for a lay employee.

F—Section 408(k)(6) salary reduction simplified employee pension (SEP).

L—Generally payments made under an accountable plan are excluded from the employee's gross income and are not required to be reported on Form W-2. But if you pay a per diem or mileage allowance, and the amount paid exceeds the amount substantiated under IRS rules, you must report as wages on Form W-2 the amount in excess of the amount substantiated. Report the amount treated as substantiated (the nontaxable portion) in Box 13. In Box 1, show the portion of the reimbursement that is more than the amount treated as substantiated. For lay employees the excess amount is subject to income tax withholding, social security tax, medicare tax, and possibly federal unemployment tax.

P—Qualified moving expenses reimbursed to an employee must be reported on Form W-2, only in Box 13, using Code P to identify them as nontaxable reimbursements. Report nonqualified moving expense reimbursements and payments in Box 1 for either ministerial or lay employees. This amount is included in Boxes 3 and 5 for lay employees.

R—Employer contributions to a medical savings account.

S—Salary reductions to a savings incentive match plan for employees with a SIMPLE retirement account.

T—Employer payments under an adoption assistance plan.

Do not include any per diem or mileage allowance or other reimbursements for employee business expenses in Boxes 1 or 13 if the total reimbursement is less than or equal to the amount substantiated.

Example 1: An employee receives mileage reimbursement at the rate of 32.5 cents per mile in 1998 and substantiates the business miles driven to the organization. The mileage reimbursement is not reported on Form W-2.

Example 2: An employee receives a mileage allowance of $2,000 per year and does not substantiate the business miles driven. The $2,000 allowance is includable in Box 1 as compensation for a minister and Boxes 1, 3, and 5 for a lay employee. The business mileage is deductible as a miscellaneous deduction on the employee's Schedule A, subject to limitations.

Payments made to nonminister employees under a nonaccountable plan are reportable as wages on Form W-2 and are subject to income tax withholding, social security tax, medicare tax, and possibly federal unemployment tax.

Payments made to minister-employees under a nonaccountable plan are reportable as wages on Form W-2 and may be subject to income tax withholding under a voluntary agreement, but are not subject to mandatory withholding or social security (FICA) or medicare tax.

Box 14—Other. You may use this box for any other information you want to give your employee. Label each item and include information such as health insurance premiums deducted or educational assistance payments.

The minister's housing allowance could be included in this box with the words "Housing Allowance." However, some organizations prefer to provide the minister with a separate statement reflecting the housing allowance amount.

Box 15—Check the appropriate boxes. The boxes that apply to employees of churches and nonprofit organizations are:

Pension plan. Check this box if the employee was an active participant (for any part of the calendar year) in a retirement plan (including a 401(k) plan and a simplified employee pension plan) maintained by the organization. An employee is an active participant for purposes of this box if the employee participated in a Section 401(a) qualified plan, Section 403(a) qualified annuity plan (nonvoluntary contributions), Section 403(b) annuity contract or custodial account, Section 408(k) simplified employee pension, or Section 501(c)(18) trust.

Subtotal. Check this box only when submitting 42 or more Forms W-2.

Deferred compensation. Check this box if you made contributions for the employee to a Section 403(b) annuity contract or custodial account (voluntary salary reduction), Section 408(k)(6) salary reduction (SEP), Section 457 deferred compensation plan, or Section 501(c)(18)(D) trust.

DO NOT STAPLE

a Control number	33333	For Official Use Only ▶ OMB No. 1545-0008	

b Kind of Payer ▶	941 ☐ Military ☐ 943 ☐ CT-1 ☐ Hshld. emp. ☐ Medicare govt. emp. ☐	1 Wages, tips, other compensation 243987.00	2 Federal income tax withheld 29142.00
		3 Social security wages 236431.00	4 Social security tax withheld 14659.00
c Total number of Forms W-2 19	d Establishment number	5 Medicare wages and tips 243987.00	6 Medicare tax withheld 3538.00
e Employer identification number 35-2946039		7 Social security tips	8 Allocated tips
f Employer's name ABC Charity		9 Advance EIC payments	10 Dependent care benefits
		11 Nonqualified plans	12 Deferred compensation
2760 N. Hull Road Traverse City, MI 49615		13	
		14	
g Employer's address and ZIP code			
h Other EIN used this year		15 Income tax withheld by third-party payer	
i Employer's state I.D. No.			

Contact person	Telephone number ( )	Fax number ( )	E-mail address

Under penalties of perjury, I declare that I have examined this return and accompanying documents, and, to the best of my knowledge and belief, they are true, correct, and complete.

Signature ▶ *Daniel L. Lewis*   Title ▶ Treasurer   Date ▶ 1/31/99

Form **W-3** Transmittal of Wage and Tax Statements **1998**   Department of the Treasury Internal Revenue Service

---

a Year/Form corrected 19 98 / W-2	Void ☐	OMB No. 1545-0008	For Official Use Only ▶	

b Employee's name, address, and ZIP code ☐ Corrected Name	c Employer's name, address, and ZIP code
Norman R. Tice 418 Trenton Street Springfield, OH 45504	Little Valley Church 4865 Douglas Road Springfield, OH 45504

d Employee's correct SSN 304-64-7792	e Employer's SSA number 69-	f Employer's Federal EIN 35-6309294	g Employer's state I.D. number

h Previously reported ▶	Stat. emp. ☐ De- ceased ☐ Pension plan ☐ Legal rep. ☐ Def'd comp. ☐ Hshld. emp ☐	i Corrected ▶	Stat. emp. ☐ De- ceased ☐ Pension plan ☐ Legal rep. ☐ Def'd comp. ☐ Hshld. emp. ☐	j Employer's use

Complete k and/or l only if incorrect on the last form you filed. Show incorrect item here. ▶	k Employee's incorrect SSN	l Employee's name (as incorrectly shown on previous form)

Form W-2 box	(a) As previously reported	(b) Correct information	(c) Increase (decrease)
1 Wages, tips, other comp.	10000.00	12500.00	2500.00
2 Federal income tax withheld	1800.00	2000.00	200.00
3 Social security wages	10000.00	12500.00	2500.00
4 Social security tax withheld	620.00	775.00	155.00
5 Medicare wages and tips	10000.00	12500.00	2500.00
6 Medicare tax withheld	145.00	181.25	36.25
7 Social security tips			
8 Allocated tips			
17 State wages, tips, etc.			
18 State income tax			
20 Local wages, tips, etc.			
21 Local income tax			

CHANGES

Please do not staple.

See back of Copy D for instructions and the Paperwork Reduction Act Notice.

Form W-2c (Rev. 7-97)   **Corrected Wage and Tax Statement**

Copy A For Social Security Administration Department of the Treasury Internal Revenue Service

Form W-3

A Form W-3 is submitted to the IRS as a transmittal form with Form W-2s. Form W-3 and all attached W-2s must be submitted to the Social Security Administration Center by February 28. No money is sent with Form W-3.

Form W-2c

Use Form W-2c to correct errors on a previously filed Form W-2.

Form W-3c

Use Form W-3c to transmit corrected W-2c forms to the Social Security Administration.

Unemployment taxes

The federal and state unemployment systems provide temporary unemployment compensation to workers who have lost their jobs. Employers provide the revenue for this program by paying federal unemployment taxes, under the Federal Unemployment Tax Act (FUTA), and state unemployment taxes. These are strictly employer taxes and no deductions are taken from employees' wages.

The current federal unemployment tax law exempts from coverage

✔ services performed in the employ of a church, a convention, or association of churches or an organization that is operated primarily for religious purposes and that is operated, supervised, controlled, or principally supported by a church or convention or association of churches;

✔ services performed by a duly ordained, commissioned, or licensed minister of a church in the exercise of ministry or by a member of a religious order in the exercise of duties required by such order.

States may expand their coverage of unemployment taxes beyond the federal minimum. In many states, exemption is also provided for

✔ services performed in the employ of a separately incorporated church school if the school is operated primarily for religious purposes and is operated, supervised, controlled, or principally supported by a church or convention or association of churches;

✔ services performed in the employ of an unincorporated church-controlled elementary or secondary school.

Recent court cases reflect attempts by states to subject religious organizations, including churches, to state unemployment taxes.

FUTA reporting requirements

Nonprofit organizations that are liable for FUTA taxes are required to file Form 940, or 940-EZ Employer's Annual Federal Unemployment Tax Return. This form covers one calendar year and is due on or before January 31. Tax deposits may be required before filing the annual return. You must use Form 8109, Federal Tax Deposit Coupon, when making each federal unemployment tax deposit.

The taxable wage base under the Federal Unemployment Tax Act is $7,000 for 1998. The gross FUTA tax rate is 6.2% for 1998. The credit against FUTA tax for payments to state unemployment funds remains at a maximum 5.4%. The net rate is 0.8%. There are no states with credit reductions for 1997, so employers in all states pay FUTA taxes at the net rate of 0.8% for 1998. The 0.2% FUTA surtax has been extended through 1998.

Refunds and Abatements

In certain instances, Form 843, Claim for Refund and Request for Abatement, is used to file a claim for refund of overpaid taxes, interest, penalties, and additions to tax.

Example 1: On your employment tax return you reported and paid more federal income tax than you withheld from an employee. Use Form 843 to claim a refund.

Example 2: The IRS assessed penalties or interest relating to your employment tax return. You paid the penalties or interest. You later realized that the penalties or interest had been incorrectly calculated or assessed. Use Form 843 to file a claim for refund.

Key Concepts

■ The proper classification of all your workers as employees or self-employed is a crucial matter for both your organization and the workers.

■ Understanding the special tax treatments for ministers is very important.

■ The failure to timely file and pay payroll taxes will leave your organization open to scrutiny by the IRS.

■ Reporting all taxable compensation to the IRS requires considerable understanding of the tax laws and regulations.

CHAPTER FIVE

Information Reporting

In This Chapter
- General filing requirements
- Reporting on the receipt of funds
- Reporting on the payment of funds
- Summary of payment reporting requirements

Information reporting may be required for many noncontribution funds received by your organization. Payments to nonemployees will often require filings with the IRS also.

General Filing Requirements

Information forms (1098 and 1099) must be provided to the payers/recipients on or before January 31 following the calendar year that the funds were paid or received. Copies of the forms (or magnetic media) must be filed with the IRS by February 28, following the year that the funds were paid or received.

An extension of time to file may be requested by filing Form 8809, Request for Extension of Time to File Information Returns, with the IRS by the due date of the returns.

Magnetic media reporting may be required for filing information returns with the IRS. If you are required to file 250 or more information returns, you must file on magnetic media. The 250-or-more requirement applies separately to each type of form. A Form 4419, Application for Filing Information Returns on Magnetic Media, must be filed to apply to use magnetic media.

Payers filing returns on paper forms must use a separate transmittal Form 1096, Annual Summary and Transmittal of U.S. Information Returns, for each different type of information form. For example, if you file Forms 1098, 1099-MISC, and 1099-S, complete one Form 1096 to transmit Forms 1098, another Form 1096 to transmit Forms 1099-MISC, and a third Form 1096 to transmit Forms 1099-S.

Form 1096 — Annual Summary and Transmittal of U.S. Information Returns (1998)

OMB No. 1545-0108

Form 1096 — Department of the Treasury, Internal Revenue Service

FILER'S name: ABC Charity
Street address (including room or suite number): 2670 N. Hull Road
City, state, and ZIP code: Traverse City, MI 49615

If you are not using a preprinted label, enter in box 1 or 2 below the identification number you used as the filer on the information returns being transmitted. Do not fill in both boxes 1 and 2.

Name of person to contact if the IRS needs more information
Telephone number ( )

For Official Use Only

1 Employer identification number	2 Social security number	3 Total number of forms	4 Federal income tax withheld	5 Total amount reported with this Form 1096
35-7431092		10	$	$ 5842.00

Enter an "X" in only one box below to indicate the type of form being filed. If this is your FINAL return, enter an "X" here ▶ ☐

W-2G 32	1098 81	1099-A 80	1099-B 79	1099-C 85	1099-DIV 91	1099-G 86	1099-INT 92	1099-LTC 93	1099-MISC 95	1099-MSA 94	1099-OID 96	1099-PATR 97	1099-R 98
☐	☐	☐	☐	☐	☐	☐	☐	☐	☐	☐	☐	☐	☐

1099-S 75	5498 28	5498-MSA 27
☐	☐	☐

Obtaining correct identification numbers

Organizations required to file information returns with the IRS must obtain the correct taxpayer identification number (TIN) to report income paid, real estate transactions, and mortgage interest paid to or by the organization.

Form W-9 — Request for Taxpayer Identification Number and Certification

(Rev. December 1996) Department of the Treasury, Internal Revenue Service

Give form to the requester. Do NOT send to the IRS.

Name: Richard K. Bennett
Business name, if different from above:

Check appropriate box: ☑ Individual/Sole proprietor ☐ Corporation ☐ Partnership ☐ Other ▶

Address (number, street, and apt. or suite no.): 829 Garner Street
City, state, and ZIP code: Thomasville, NC 27360

Requester's name and address (optional)

Taxpayer Identification Number (TIN)

Enter your TIN in the appropriate box. For individuals, this is your social security number (SSN). However, if you are a resident alien OR a sole proprietor, see the instructions on page 2. For other entities, it is your employer identification number (EIN). If you do not have a number, see How To Get a TIN on page 2.
Note: If the account is in more than one name, see the chart on page 2 for guidelines on whose number to enter.

Social security number: 4 0 3 9 8 1 2 9 7
OR
Employer identification number

For Payees Exempt From Backup Withholding (See the instructions on page 2.)

Certification

Under penalties of perjury, I certify that:

1. The number shown on this form is my correct taxpayer identification number (or I am waiting for a number to be issued to me), **and**
2. I am not subject to backup withholding because: (a) I am exempt from backup withholding, or (b) I have not been notified by the Internal Revenue Service (IRS) that I am subject to backup withholding as a result of a failure to report all interest or dividends, or (c) the IRS has notified me that I am no longer subject to backup withholding.

Certification Instructions.—You must cross out item 2 above if you have been notified by the IRS that you are currently subject to backup withholding because you have failed to report all interest and dividends on your tax return. For real estate transactions, item 2 does not apply. For mortgage interest paid, acquisition or abandonment of secured property, cancellation of debt, contributions to an individual retirement arrangement (IRA), and generally, payments other than interest and dividends, you are not required to sign the Certification, but you must provide your correct TIN. (See the instructions on page 2.)

Sign Here — Signature ▶ Richard K. Bennett   Date ▶ 1/1/99

Form W-9, Request for Taxpayer Identification Number and Certification, is used to furnish the correct TIN to the organization and in certain other situations to:

✓ certify that the TIN furnished is correct;

✓ certify that the recipient of the income is not subject to backup withholding; or

✓ certify exemption from backup withholding.

If the recipient does not furnish a completed Form W-9, the church or nonprofit organization is required to withhold 31% of the payment, deposit the withholding with Form 8109 or 8109-B, and report amounts withheld on Form 1099-INT, 1099-MISC, or 1099-R, as applicable.

Reporting on the Receipt of Funds

Receipt of interest on mortgages

Use Form 1098, Mortgage Interest Statement, to report mortgage interest of $600 or more received by your organization during the year from an individual, including a sole proprietor. You need not file Form 1098 for interest received from a corporation, partnership, trust, estate, or association. A transmittal Form 1096 must accompany one or more Form 1098s.

☐ CORRECTED (if checked)

RECIPIENT'S/LENDER'S name, address, and telephone number	* The amount shown may not be fully deductible by you on your Federal income tax return. Limitations based on the cost and value of the secured property may apply. In addition, you may only deduct an amount of mortgage interest to the extent it was incurred by you, actually paid by you, and not reimbursed by another person.	OMB No. 1545-0901	
Debra Heights Church 1517 Cedar Street Rochester, MN 55902		19**98** Form **1098**	Mortgage Interest Statement

RECIPIENT'S Federal identification no. 35-8814073	PAYER'S social security number 441-09-7843	1 Mortgage interest received from payer(s)/borrower(s)* $ 1819.00	Copy B For Payer
PAYER'S/BORROWER'S name Julie M. Chapman		2 Points paid on purchase of principal residence (See **Box 2** on back.) $	The information in boxes 1, 2, and 3 is important tax information and is being furnished to the Internal Revenue Service. If you are required to file a return, a negligence penalty or other sanction may be imposed on you if the IRS determines that an underpayment of tax results because you overstated a deduction for this mortgage interest or for these points or because you did not report this refund of interest on your return.
Street address (including apt. no.) 125 Orchard Drive		3 Refund of overpaid interest (See **Box 3** on back.) $	
City, state, and ZIP code Cedar Falls, IA 50613		4	
Account number (optional)			

Form **1098**   (Keep for your records.)   Department of the Treasury - Internal Revenue Service

Reporting on the Payment of Funds

Payments of interest

File Form 1099-INT, Statement for Recipients of Interest Income, for each person to whom you paid interest reportable in Box 1 of at least $10 in any calendar year. This form is also required if you withheld any federal income tax under the backup withholding rules (31% rate), regardless of the amount of the payment. In certain instances, the $10 limit increases to $600.

The $10 limit applies if the interest is on "evidences of indebtedness" (bonds and promissory notes) issued by a corporation in "registered form." A note or bond is in "registered form" if its transfer must be effected by the surrender of the old instrument and either the reissuance by the corporation of the old instrument to the new holder or the issuance by the corporation of a new instrument to the new holder.

There is no requirement to file Form 1099-INT for payments made to a corporation or another tax-exempt organization.

□ VOID □ CORRECTED		
PAYER'S name, street address, city, state, ZIP code, and telephone no. **Lancaster Community Church** **1425 Spencer Avenue** **Logansport, IN 46947**	Payer's RTN (optional)	OMB No. 1545-0112 **1998** Form **1099-INT** / **Interest Income**
PAYER'S Federal identification number **35-7921873** / RECIPIENT'S identification number **438-42-9973**	1 Interest income not included in box 3 $ **913.00**	**Copy C** **For Payer**
RECIPIENT'S name **James R. Moore**	2 Early withdrawal penalty $	3 Interest on U.S. Savings Bonds and Treas. obligations $
Street address (including apt. no.) **604 Linden Avenue**	4 Federal income tax withheld $	For Paperwork Reduction Act Notice and instructions for completing this form, see the
City, state, and ZIP code **Wabash, IN 46992**	5 Foreign tax paid	6 Foreign country or U.S. possession	**1998 Instructions for Forms 1099, 1098, 5498, and W-2G.**
Account number (optional)	2nd TIN Not. □ $	
Form **1099-INT**		Department of the Treasury - Internal Revenue Service

Example 1: Sleepy Hollow Church financed a new church by issuing registered bonds. 1099-INT forms must be provided to each bond investor receiving $10 or more in interest during any calendar year.

If Sleepy Hollow engaged a bond broker to handle the issuance of the bonds, the broker would issue 1099-INT forms. If Sleepy Hollow issued the bonds without using a bond broker, the church would issue the 1099-INT forms.

Example 2: Sleepy Hollow Church borrows funds from church members. The notes are transferrable. There is no requirement to return the bonds to the church for reissuance. The $600 limit applies for the issuance of 1099-INT forms for the payment of interest on these notes.

Payments to annuitants

File Form 1099-R for each person to whom you have made a designated distribution that is a total distribution from a retirement plan or a payment to an annuitant of $1 of more. If part of the distribution is taxable and part is nontaxable, Form 1099-R should reflect the entire distribution.

Example: ABC Charity makes payments of $1,000 during the year to one of their annuitants, Mary Hughes. (Several years earlier, Mary entered into the charitable gift annuity agreement by giving a check to ABC.)

A portion of each annuity payment is a tax-free return of principal and the remainder is annuity income for Mary. ABC will generally report the entire $1,000 in Box 1 on Form 1099-R and check Box 2b unless ABC determines the taxable amount for the year.

☐ VOID ☐ CORRECTED		
PAYER'S name, street address, city, state, and ZIP code ABC Charity 8049 Riverside Blvd. Sacramento, CA 95831	**1** Gross distribution $ 1000.00 **2a** Taxable amount $	OMB No. 1545-0119 **1998** Form **1099-R**	Distributions From Pensions, Annuities, Retirement or Profit-Sharing Plans, IRAs, Insurance Contracts, etc.
	2b Taxable amount not determined ☐	Total distribution ☐	
PAYER'S Federal identification number 35-0479214	RECIPIENT'S identification number 703-41-3669	**3** Capital gain (included in box 2a) $	**4** Federal income tax withheld $	Copy D For Payer
RECIPIENT'S name Mary D. Hughes	**5** Employee contributions or insurance premiums $	**6** Net unrealized appreciation in employer's securities $	For Paperwork Reduction Act Notice and instructions for completing this form, see the **1998 Instructions for Forms 1099, 1098, 5498, and W-2G.**
Street address (including apt. no.) P.O. Box 9042	**7** Distribution code	IRA/ SEP/ SIMPLE ☐	**8** Other $ %	
City, state, and ZIP code El Toro, CA 92630	**9a** Your percentage of total distribution %	**9b** Total employee contributions $	
Account number (optional)	**10** State tax withheld $ $	**11** State/Payer's state no.	**12** State distribution $ $
	13 Local tax withheld $ $	**14** Name of locality	**15** Local distribution $ $
Form **1099-R**		Department of the Treasury - Internal Revenue Service

Form W-4P, Withholding Certificate for Pension or Annuity Payments, should be completed by recipients of income from annuity, pension, and certain other deferred compensation plans to inform payers whether income tax is to be withheld and on what basis.

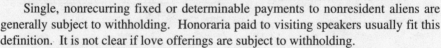

Form **W-4P**
Department of the Treasury
Internal Revenue Service

**Withholding Certificate for
Pension or Annuity Payments**
▶For Paperwork Reduction Act Notice, see page 3.

OMB No. 1545-0415

19**98**

Type or print your full name
Arnold B. Luther

Your social security number
505-19-4129

Home address (number and street or rural route)
P. O. Box 185

Claim or identification number
(if any) of your pension or
annuity contract

City or town, state, and ZIP code
Asheboro, NC 27203

Complete the following applicable lines:

1   Check here if you **do not want** any Federal income tax withheld from your pension or annuity. (Do not complete lines 2 or 3.) . . ▶ [ ]

2   Total number of allowances and marital status you are claiming for withholding from each periodic pension or
ann uity payment. (You may also designate a dollar amount on line 3.) . . . . ▶

Marital status: [ ] Single   [ ] Married   [ ] Married, but withhold at higher Single rate

(Enter number
of allowances.)

3   Additional amount. if any, you want withheld from each pension or annuity payment. Note. *For periodic payments.*
you cannot enter an amount here without entering the number (including zero) of allowances on line 2.. . . . . ▶ $

Your signature ▶ *Arnold B. Luther*

Date ▶ 1/5/99

Payments to nonresident aliens

Payments for personal services made to non-citizens (nonresident aliens) who are temporarily in this country are often subject to federal income tax withholding at a 30% rate. A nonresident alien is a person who is neither a U.S. citizen nor a resident of the United States. Some payments may be exempt from income tax withholding if the person is from a country with which the United States maintains a tax treaty. Salary payments to nonresident aliens employed in the United States are subject to income tax withholding based on the regular withholding tables.

Single, nonrecurring fixed or determinable payments to nonresident aliens are generally subject to withholding. Honoraria paid to visiting speakers usually fit this definition. It is not clear if love offerings are subject to withholding.

All payments to nonresident aliens, other than expense reimbursements and amounts reported on Form W-2, must be reported on Form 1042 and 1042-S. These forms are filed with the IRS Service Center in Philadelphia by March 15 for the previous calendar year, and a copy of Form 1042-S must be sent to the nonresident alien.

Payments of royalties and for other services

File Form 1099-MISC for each recipient (other than corporations) to whom you have paid

✓   at least $10 in royalties, or

✓   at least $600 in rents (for example, office rent or equipment rent), payments for services (nonemployee compensation), or medical health care payments.

Note: For 1998 and later years, you must include payments of attorneys' fees, generally in Box 7, even if the firm providing the legal services is incorporated.

PAYER'S name, street address, city, state, ZIP code, and telephone no.	1 Rents	OMB No. 1545-0115	
ABC Charity 110 Harding Avenue Cincinnati, OH 45963	$ 2 Royalties $ 3 Other income $	**1998** Form **1099-MISC**	**Miscellaneous Income**
PAYER'S Federal identification number 35-1148942	RECIPIENT'S identification number 389-41-8067	4 Federal income tax withheld $	5 Fishing boat proceeds $	**Copy B**

☐ VOID ☐ CORRECTED (if checked)

PAYER'S name, street address, city, state, ZIP code, and telephone no.	1 Rents $	OMB No. 1545-0115	
	2 Royalties $	**1998** Form **1099-MISC**	**Miscellaneous Income**
ABC Charity 110 Harding Avenue Cincinnati, OH 45963	3 Other income $		
PAYER'S Federal identification number 35-1148942 / RECIPIENT'S identification number 389-41-8067	4 Federal income tax withheld $	5 Fishing boat proceeds $	**Copy B** **For Recipient**
RECIPIENT'S name Mark A. Mitchell	6 Medical and health care payments $	7 Nonemployee compensation $ 2400.00	This is important tax information and is being furnished to the Internal Revenue Service. If you are required to file a return, a negligence penalty or
Street address (including apt. no.) 5412 Warren Avenue	8 Substitute payments in lieu of dividends or interest $	9 Payer made direct sales of $5,000 or more of consumer products to a buyer (recipient) for resale ▶ ☐	other sanction may be imposed on you if this income is taxable and the IRS determines that
City, state, and ZIP code Norwood, OH 45212	10 Crop insurance proceeds $	11 State income tax withheld $	it has not been reported.
Account number (optional)	2nd TIN Not. ☐	12 State/Payer's state number	13 $
Form **1099-MISC**	(Keep for your records.)	Department of the Treasury - Internal Revenue Service	

Example: A charity has established a written, nondiscriminatory employee medical expense reimbursement plan under which the charity pays the medical expenses of the employee, spouse, and dependents.

If $600 or more is paid in the calendar year to a doctor or other provider of health care services, a Form 1099-MISC must be filed.

Benevolence payments to nonemployees are not reportable on Form 1099-MISC (or any other information form). Benevolence payments to employees are reportable on Form W-2.

Do not include the payment of a housing allowance to a minister on Form 1099-MISC. Advances, reimbursements, or expenses for traveling and other business expenses of an employee are not reportable on Form 1099-MISC. These payments may be reportable on Form W-2 if they do not comply with the accountable expense plan rules.

Advances, reimbursements, or expenses for traveling and other business expenses of a self-employed person are not reportable on Form 1099-MISC if made under an accountable expense reimbursement plan. Under this type of plan, expenses are reimbursed only if they are substantiated as to amount, date, and business nature, and any excess reimbursements must be returned to the organization.

Advances, reimbursements, or expenses for traveling and other business expenses of a self-employed person that are not substantiated to the paying organization are reportable on Form 1099-MISC.

Example 1: ABC Ministry organizes a seminar and engages a speaker. The speaker is paid a $750 honorarium, and ABC reimbursed the travel expenses of $200 upon presentation of proper substantiation by the speaker. Form 1099-MISC should be issued to the speaker for $750.

Example 2: Same facts as Example 1, except of the $750 payment, $250 is designated for travel expenses and the speaker accounted to ABC for the travel. Since the honorarium of $500, after excluding the substantiated payments, is less than the $600 limit, there is no requirement to issue a Form 1099-MISC to the speaker.

The answer to this example would be different if ABC paid an honorarium to the same speaker during the same calendar year of $100 or more, bringing the total for the year to the $600 level.

Example 3: ABC Ministry contracts for janitorial services with an unincorporated janitorial service and pays $2,000 during the year for this service. ABC should issue a Form 1099-MISC for these payments.

Payments to volunteers

Payments to volunteers that represent a reimbursement under an accountable business expense reimbursement plan for expenses directly connected with the volunteer services are not reportable by the charity.

Payments for auto mileage up to the maximum IRS rate for business miles (32.5 cents for 1998) are generally considered to be tax-free for volunteers. When an organization provides liability insurance for its volunteers, the value of the coverage can be excluded from the volunteer's income as a working condition fringe benefit.

Payments to or on behalf of volunteers that are not business expenses are reported on Form W-2 or Form 1099-MISC, depending on whether or not a common law employee relationship exists. When the relationship between an organization takes the form of an employer-employee relationship, payments other than expense reimbursement are reported on Form W-2. Payments to nonemployee volunteers for medical, education, or personal living expenses must be reported as nonemployee compensation on Form 1099-MISC. Payments to volunteers for lodging, meals, and incidental expenses may be made under the per diem rules if the duration of the travel is under one year.

Moving expenses

Qualified employee moving expense reimbursements are reportable on Form W-2, only in Box 13, using Code P. (See page 11 for reporting changes for 1998.) The payments do not constitute compensation if the expenses would be otherwise deductible by the employee as moving expenses.

A minister must move at least 50 miles to qualify to deduct moving expenses or receive a tax-free reimbursement. Many ministers move less than 50 miles which makes the expenses nondeductible and reimbursements by the church fully taxable for both income and social security tax purposes.

Summary of Payment Reporting Requirements

Below is an alphabetical list of some payments and the forms to file to report them. It is not a complete list of payments, and the absence of a payment from the list does not suggest that the payment is not reportable.

Types of Payment	Report on Form
Advance earned income credit.	W-2
Annuities, periodic payments	1099-R
** Attorneys' fees.	1099-MISC
Auto reimbursements (nonaccountable plan):	
Employee	W-2
Nonemployee	1099-MISC
Awards:	
Employee	W-2
Nonemployee	1099-MISC
Bonuses:	
Employee	W-2
Nonemployee	1099-MISC
Cafeteria/flexible benefit plan	5500, 5500-C, or 5500-R
Car expense (nonaccountable plan):	
Employee	W-2
Nonemployee	1099-MISC
Christmas bonuses:	
Employee	W-2
Nonemployee	1099-MISC
Commissions:	
Employee	W-2
Nonemployee	1099-MISC
Compensation:	
Employee	W-2
Nonemployee	1099-MISC
Dependent care payments	W-2
Director's fees	1099-MISC
Education expense reimbursement (nonaccountable plan):	
Employee	W-2
Nonemployee	1099-MISC
Employee business expense reimbursement (nonaccountable plan)	W-2
Fees:	
Employee	W-2
Nonemployee	1099-MISC
Group-term life insurance (PS 58 costs)	W-2 or 1099-R

Interest, mortgage 1098
Interest, other than mortgage. 1099-INT
Long-term care benefits 1099-LTC
Medical expense reimbursement plan . . . . 5500, 5500-C, or 5500-R
    (employee-funded)
Mileage (nonaccountable plan):
    Employee. W-2
    Nonemployee 1099-MISC
Mortgage interest. 1098
Moving expense:
    * Employee W-2
    Nonemployee 1099-MISC
Prizes:
    Employee. W-2
    Nonemployee 1099-MISC
Real estate proceeds 1099-S
Rents 1099-MISC
Royalties 1099-MISC
Severance pay W-2
Sick pay. W-2
Supplemental unemployment W-2
Vacation allowance:
    Employee. W-2
    Nonemployee 1099-MISC
Wages W-2

*   Qualified reimbursements or payments must be reported on Form W-2, only in Box 13, using Code P.

**   The exemption from reporting payments made to corporations no longer applies to payments for legal services.

Key Concepts

■ The receipt of certain funds, such as mortgage interest, by your organization may trigger information reporting to the IRS.

■ Payments for rent, various services, and other items will often require the preparation of annual information returns.

■ Securing correct taxpayer identification numbers should routinely occur in connection with the filing of information returns.

Your Financial Records

It takes a practical set of accounting records and financial reports to communicate the financial condition of your organization.

Controlling and managing the organization's money is also very important. It is essential that the procedures for the handling of finances be reduced to writing. The governing board should establish and maintain the basic financial procedures for the organization. Too often, a new treasurer is handed a file box of accounting records with no written guidelines to follow. It is little wonder that the accounting system functions effectively one year and is in shambles the next.

Sound procedures should be developed, installed, and maintained year after year. These procedures will be different for every organization depending on the size of the organization, capability, and availability of personnel.

Budgeting

It is possible for a small church or nonprofit organization to operate without a budget. But a budget is an effective tool for allocating financial resources and planning and controlling your spending even for smaller organizations. For larger organizations, a budget is essential.

A budget matches anticipated inflows of resources with outflows of resources.

Preparing a budget requires considerable effort. It includes looking back at revenue and expense trends. Projected plans and programs must be converted into estimated dollar amounts. Too many organizations budget expenses with some degree of precision and then set the income budget at whatever it takes to cover the total expenses. This is often a disastrous approach.

Ideally, separate budgets should be prepared for all funds of an organization. Even capital and debt-retirement funds should be budgeted. The separate budgets are then combined into a unified budget.

Line-item budgets within each fund reflect the projected cost of salaries, fringe benefits, utilities, maintenance, debt retirement, and other expenses. The line-item approach is generally used by a treasurer in reporting to department heads or other responsible individuals.

Program budgets are often presented to the board of a nonprofit organization or a church's membership. In this approach, the cost of a program is reflected rather than the cost of specific line-items such as salaries or fringe benefits.

A good budgeting approach is to divide the budget into quarterly or monthly segments. If a monthly budget is used, the budget for each month is not necessarily one-twelfth of the annual amount. For example, if gifts are typically lower in summer months, the monthly budgets for the summer reflect the projected lower income. When actual activity is compared to monthly or quarterly budgets, it may be possible to make program adjustments as the year progresses.

The Money Comes In

Church offerings are one of the most fundamental elements of church finance. Without them, a church would soon close it doors. The same is true for donations received by nonprofit organizations.

Church offerings come in various forms. Most commonly, the offering plates are passed during the service. In other churches, offerings are placed in containers located outside the sanctuary.

Most offerings received by churches are unrestricted. But nearly every church receives some donor-restricted funds. These donor-restricted funds require special treatment in the process of counting and recording offerings.

Why do money-handling problems so often arise in churches? It's primarily because cash is so easily misappropriated. It is small, lacks owner identification, and has immediate transferability. If offerings are not counted before they go from two-person control to one-person control, some or all of the cash can easily disappear.

Handling offerings with care will generate credibility. Few happenings can cause more consternation in a church than just the possibility that the offerings have been mishandled. And yet many churches leave the door wide open or at least ajar for problems with the handling of offerings. Often overlooked is the fact that sound controls over the offering protect church leaders in the event of false accusations regarding mishandling of funds.

So, how does a church avoid having problems with the handling of offerings? It

Revenue Flow Chart

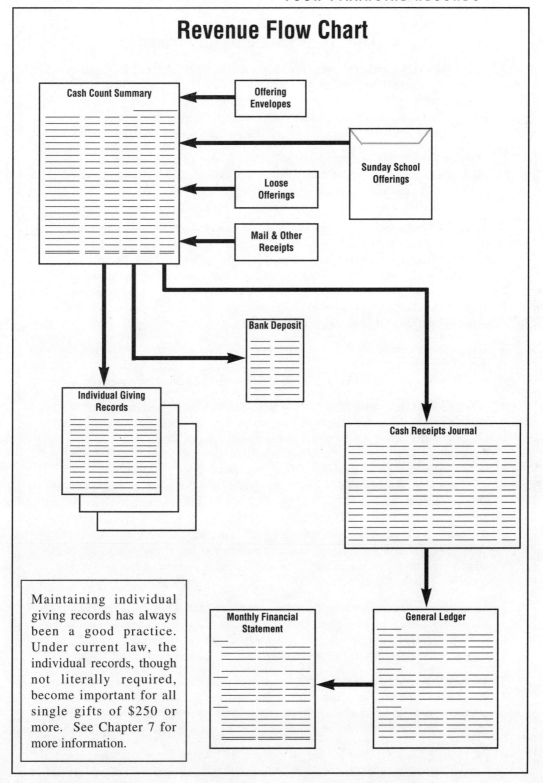

Maintaining individual giving records has always been a good practice. Under current law, the individual records, though not literally required, become important for all single gifts of $250 or more. See Chapter 7 for more information.

Guidelines for Processing Offerings

❏ **Adopt policies to prevent problems.** Written policies are the ounce-of-prevention that could avoid serious problems at your church. Adopt a series of detailed policies that outline the procedures to be followed from the time the money goes into the offering plate—in worship services, Sunday school classes, other services, received in the mail, or delivered to the church—until the money is deposited in the bank.

❏ **Make accountability and confidentiality dual goals.** Too many churches focus so much on confidentiality that accountability takes too low a priority. True, some confidentiality is sacrificed when good accountability exists. But the church that does not balance confidentiality and accountability is treading on dangerous ground.

Example: The Sunday offerings go from the ushers to the head usher and then to the financial secretary, who takes the money, records the donations by donor and then makes the bank deposit. Problem: This violates the principle of having offerings in the control of two individuals until they are deposited in the bank. The head usher and financial secretary both have the opportunity to remove cash. Or, they could be accused of mishandling the funds and have no system of controls to support their innocence.

❏ **Use confidentiality statements.** Counters should sign a written statement of confidentiality before participating in the counting process. If the commitment of confidentiality is broken, the individual(s) should be removed from the team of counters.

❏ **Always follow the principle of two.** When a church leaves the offering in control of a single person—even for a short time period—before the count has been recorded or the uncounted offering has been dropped at the bank, it is a blatant invitation for problems. When sole access to the offering is allowed, most people will not take any money. However, for some, the temptation may be too great.

Even when the principle of joint control is carefully followed, collusion between the two people is still possible—leading to a loss of funds. The risk of collusion can be reduced by rotating ushers and offering-counters so they don't serve on consecutive weeks. Church treasurers, financial secretaries, and other church-elected individuals should serve for limited terms, such as two or three years. A pastor or the church treasurer should not be involved in the counting process. A husband and wife could serve on the same counting team only if a third party is always present.

❏ **Keep the offering plates in plain view.** When the offering is being received, it is important that each offering plate always be kept in plain view of two ushers. When a solo usher takes an offering plate down a hall, upstairs to the balcony, behind a curtain, or out a door, you have created an opportunity of losing cash from the plate.

❏ **Be sure your guidelines cover Sunday school offerings.** Too often churches are very careful with offerings from the worship services but there is little control over offerings received in church school classes. These offerings should be counted in the class and turned over to an usher or counting team comprised of at least two individuals.

❑ **Encourage the use of offering envelopes.** Members should be encouraged to use offering envelopes. The envelopes provide a basis for recording contributions in the church's donor records.

Some churches emphasize this concept by providing each individual or church family with a series of pre-numbered offering envelopes to be used throughout the calendar year. The numbering system identifies the donor. This can ease the process of posting donations and is an excellent approach.

❑ **Count the offerings as soon as possible.** A frequent reason given by churches for not counting offerings immediately is that church members don't want to miss the service. This is very understandable. In many churches, the Sunday offerings are counted on Monday. Adequate control over the money is maintained by providing a secure place to store the funds, usually a safe, and carefully limiting access to the storage location.

However, the greater the length of time between receiving and counting the offering, the greater the potential for mishandling of funds. When offerings are immediately counted, secure storing of the funds is important but not as critical because an audit trail has been established.

❑ **Have counters complete offering tally sheets.** Tally sheets should be completed that separately account for loose checks and cash that was placed in offering envelopes. Checks or cash placed in blank, unidentified offering envelopes should be recorded with the loose funds. This separation of money serves as a control amount for the later posting to donor records.

❑ **Use a secure area for counting.** For safety of the counting team, confidentiality, and to avoid interruptions, provide a secure area in which the offering can be counted. (When offerings are significant, consider providing armed security when offerings are transported to the bank.) The counters should have an adding machine, coin wrappers, offering tally sheets, and other supplies. The adding machine should have a tape (instead of a paperless calculator) so the counting team can run two matching adding machine tapes of the offering.

❑ **Deposit all offerings intact.** Offerings should always be counted and deposited intact. Depositing intact means not allowing cash in the offering to be used for the payment of church expenses or to be exchanged for other cash or a check.

If offerings are not deposited intact, an unidentified variance between the count and the deposit could occur. Additionally, if an individual is permitted to cash a check from offering funds, the church may inadvertently provide the person with a cancelled check that could be used in claiming a charitable tax deduction.

❑ **Verify amounts on offering envelopes with the contents.** As the counting team removes the contents from offering envelopes, any amounts written on the envelope by the donors should be compared with the contents. Any variances should be noted on the envelope.

❑ **Properly identify donor-restricted funds.** All donor-restrictions should be carefully preserved during the counting process. These restrictions are usually noted on an offering envelope, but they can take the form of an instruction attached to a check or simply a notation on the check.

❑ **Use a restrictive endorsement for checks.** During the counting process, it is important to add a restrictive endorsement, with a "For Deposit Only" stamp, to the back of all checks.

❑ **Place offerings in a secure location when they are stored in the church.** If offerings are stored in the church, even for short periods of time, the use of a secure location is important. A safe implies security and an unlocked desk drawer connotes lack of security. But defining security is often not that easy.

Again, the principle is that no one person should have access to the funds at any time. This can be accomplished by

✓ obtaining a safe with two locks,

✓ changing the combination and distributing portions of the new combination to different people, or

✓ placing the safe in a locked room or building and placing the offerings in locked bags before locking them in the safe.

Ideally, offerings are counted during or after the service and a deposit is made immediately. Alternately, the cash portion of the offering is recorded and the uncounted offerings are immediately transported to the bank drop box by two people. When these two preferable options are not used, the offerings are generally stored at the church for a period of time on Sunday or perhaps until Monday morning. This process requires a secure storage location, preferably a safe, and highly structured controls over access to locked bank bags and the safe.

❑ **Use proper controls when dropping uncounted funds at the bank.** If your church drops uncounted offerings at the bank, several key principles should be followed:

✓ The funds should be placed in locked bank bags with careful control of the number of persons who have keys to the bags.

✓ Two individuals should transport the funds to the bank.

✓ Two people should pick up the funds from the bank on Monday morning.

❑ **Control deposit variances.** Provide written instructions to your bank concerning procedures to be followed if the bank discovers a discrepancy in the deposit. The notification should go to someone other than the individual(s) who participated in preparation of the deposit.

❑ **Segregate duties when recording individual contributions.** Someone other than a member of the counting team should record individual gifts in donor records. This segregation of duties reduces the possibility of misappropriation of gifts.

Contributions By Donor

March 6, 199__ (x) A.M. ( ) P.M. ( )

Name of Contributor	Regular Tithes & Offerings	Sunday School	Building Fund	Missions	Other Description	Other Amount
M/M Mark Wilson	50.00		10.00	20.00		
Frank Young	35.00		15.00			
Ellen Jackson	60.00					
Lori Avery	40.00				Benevolence	40.00
M/M Mike Floyd	100.00	10.00				
M/M Harold Long	45.00		5.00	10.00		
Mary Martin	75.00			20.00		
M/M Steve Ross	80.00				School Project	30.00
M/M Joe Harris	65.00		5.00			
Kelly York	50.00					
Peggy Walker	30.00					
M/M Bob Franklin	75.00	5.00		15.00		
Don Gilles	40.00		10.00			
Lou Shields	200.00					
M/M Ron White	80.00		20.00	20.00		
Art Howe	100.00				Choir Robes	50.00
M/M Stan Plunkett	60.00	10.00				
Nancy Robbins	75.00				Youth Trip	40.00
M/M Bill Lyon	50.00			5.00		
M/M David Clark	80.00		20.00			
James Bowers	40.00				Parking Lot	20.00
Cindy Burr	60.00			10.00		
TOTALS	1,490.00	25.00	85.00	100.00		180.00

Cash Count Summary

March 6, 199__

	Sunday School	Sunday A.M.	Sunday P.M.	Received During Week	TOTAL
Coins	83.12	21.82	10.42		115.36
Currency	320.00	431.00	108.00		859.00
Checks	25.00	1,855.00	360.00	185.00	2,425.00
TOTALS	428.12	2,307.82	478.42	185.00	3,399.36

Breakdown By Type Of Gift

	Sunday School	Sunday A.M.	Sunday P.M.	Received During Week	TOTAL
Regular Tithes and Offerings	428.12	1,942.82	368.42	140.00	2,451.24
Sunday School		85.00	50.00	15.00	150.00
Building Fund		100.00	30.00	20.00	150.00
Missions					
Other Designated Funds:					
Benevolence Fund		40.00			40.00
School Project		30.00	10.00		40.00
Choir Robes		50.00			50.00
Youth Trip		40.00	20.00	10.00	70.00
Parking Lot		20.00			20.00
TOTALS	428.12	2,307.82	478.42	185.00	3,399.36

Counted by: Mike Anderson / Helen David / Bob Wells

Deposited on: March 7, 19 99

is impossible to totally eliminate all problems. But following the guidelines on pages 102-4 will certainly reduce your risk.

All funds received should be recorded in detail. The bulk of the income for a church is received in Sunday offerings. Counting sheets are used to record the offerings in detail. Non-offering income for churches and other organizations should be receipted in detail.

Use of offering envelopes

Donors should be encouraged to donate by check and use offering envelopes for designated gifts and cash. Checks, payable to the church, are more difficult to steal than cash. And checks still provide proof of contributions for IRS purposes for single gifts of less than $250. The use of offering envelopes is essential when cash is given. Unless offering envelopes are used, loose cash could more easily be removed without detection during the cash collection and counting process. The money counters should verify that the contents of the offering envelopes are identical to any amounts written on the outside of the envelopes.

Some churches provide 52 numbered envelopes each year plus extra envelopes for special offerings. This system is ideal as a basis of posting contributions to church records. Other churches only provide blank envelopes in the pew racks. Either way, the recording of all gifts by donor with a periodic report of giving to each donor is necessary to provide adequate control over the money given.

Offering envelopes should be retained in the church office. Their retention is important if individual contributions need to be verified.

Bank deposits

Bank deposit slips should be prepared in duplicate with the original going to the bank and the copy kept for the organization's records. It is wise to deposit funds daily as funds are received. If the offering reports and other receipts have been properly prepared, it is generally not necessary to list each check on the deposit slips.

The Money Goes Out

Payment of expenses

One of the most important principles of handling funds is to pay virtually all expenses by check. The use of the petty cash fund should be the only exception to payment by check. Cash from a deposit should never be used to pay expenses.

If checks are prepared manually, a large desk-type checkbook is often helpful. Such a checkbook usually has three checks to a page and large stubs on which to write a full description of each expenditure. Computer-prepared checks should generally have a stub with adequate space to identify the type of expense and account number(s) charged.

Example of Computer-Generated Cash Receipts Journal

Date	Reference	Entry Description	Account No.	Account Name	Amount Debit	Credit
6/06/98	CR1	Weekly receipts	301-000	Regular Offerings		2,511.12
			302-000	Sunday School		304.78
			303-000	Missions		484.11
			304-000	Building Fund		241.50
			305-000	Benevolence Fund		148.70
			101-000	Valley View Bank	3,690.21	
6/13/98	CR2	Weekly receipts	301-000	Regular Offerings		2,604.80
			302-000	Sunday School		411.12
			303-000	Missions		389.00
			304-000	Building Fund		211.00
			306-000	Camp Fund		43.00
			307-000	Choir Fund		30.00
			308-000	School Fund		50.00
			101-000	Valley View Bank	3,738.92	
6/20/98	CR3	Weekly receipts	301-000	Regular Offerings		2,383.70
			302-000	Sunday School		391.42
			303-000	Missions		411.00
			304-000	Building Fund		305.00
			305-000	Benevolence Fund		30.00
			308-000	School Fund		25.00
			101-000	Valley View Bank	3,546.12	
6/27/98	CR4	Weekly receipts	301-000	Regular Offerings		2,780.12
			302-000	Sunday School		393.23
			303-000	Missions		305.00
			304-000	Building Fund		283.00
			305-000	Benevolence Fund		45.00
			307-000	Choir Fund		20.00
			308-000	School Fund		45.00
			101-000	Valley View Bank	3,871.35	
					14,846.60	14,846.60

Example of Computer-Generated General Ledger with Entries Posted from Cash Receipts Journal

Source	Acct. No./ Date	Reference	Description	Beginning Balance	Current Entries	Ending Balance
	301-000		**Regular Offerings**	65,211.12-		
CR	6/06/98	CR1	Weekly receipts		2,511.12-	
CR	6/13/98	CR2	Weekly receipts		2,604.80-	
CR	6/20/98	CR3	Weekly receipts		2,383.70-	
CR	6/27/98	CR4	Weekly receipts		2,780.12-	
					10,279.74-	75,490.86-
	302-000		**Sunday School Offerings**	7,511.82-		
CR	6/06/98	CR1	Weekly receipts		304.78-	
CR	6/13/98	CR2	Weekly receipts		411.12-	
CR	6/20/98	CR3	Weekly receipts		391.42-	
CR	6/27/98	CR4	Weekly receipts		393.23-	
					1,500.55-	9,012.37-
	303-000		**Missions Offerings**	10,211.80-		
CR	6/06/98	CR1	Weekly receipts		484.11-	
CR	6/13/98	CR2	Weekly receipts		389.00-	
CR	6/20/98	CR3	Weekly receipts		411.00-	
CR	6/27/98	CR4	Weekly receipts		305.00-	
					1,589.11-	11,800.91-
	304-000		**Building Fund**	5,612.70-		
CR	6/06/98	CR1	Weekly receipts		241.50-	
CR	6/13/98	CR2	Weekly receipts		211.00-	
CR	6/20/98	CR3	Weekly receipts		305.00-	
CR	6/27/98	CR4	Weekly receipts		283.00-	
					1,040.50-	6,653.20-
	305-000		**Benevolence Fund**	1,411.70-		
CR	6/06/98	CR1	Weekly receipts		148.70-	
CR	6/20/98	CR3	Weekly receipts		30.00-	
CR	6/27/98	CR4	Weekly receipts		45.00-	
					223.70-	1,635.40-

Use preprinted, consecutively numbered checks. All spoiled checks should be marked "void" and kept on file with the cancelled checks.

In some instances, it may be wise to require two signatures on every check or on checks over a certain amount. In other situations, one signature may be appropriate. The level of controls over the funds will help you determine if more than one signature is necessary. Access to a checking account should generally be limited to no more than two or three individuals. A church pastor should not have access to the checking account. Checks should never be signed and delivered to anyone without completing the payee and the amount.

Checks should not be written until near the time there are funds available to cover them. Some organizations write checks when bills are due without regard to available cash. Checks are held for days, weeks, or sometimes months until they are released for payment. This is an extremely confusing practice that makes it very difficult to determine the actual checkbook balance.

Every check should have some type of written document to support it—an invoice, petty cash receipt, payroll summary, and so on. If such support is not available for some good reason, a memo should be written to support the expenditure. For example, an honorarium paid to a visiting speaker would not be supported by an invoice but should be documented by indicating the date of the speaking engagement and the event.

Occasionally it may be necessary to advance funds before supporting documentation is available (for example, a travel advance for future travel). In these instances, the treasurer must devise a system to ensure documentation is provided on a timely basis and any excess funds are returned.

Payments to venders should be based on *original* copies of invoices. Payments should not be based on month-end statements that do not show the detail of the service or products provided. After payment has been made, all supporting material should be filed in a paid-bills file in alphabetical order by payee.

It is important that a treasurer never mix personal funds with organization funds.

Expense approval and recording

If funds are approved in a church or other organization budget, this may be sufficient authority for the treasurer to pay the bills. In other instances, the approval of department heads or supervising personnel may be appropriate. Expenses that exceed the budget may need specific approval.

Although every organization should have a budget, many do not. Even without a budget, routine expenses for utilities, salaries, and mortgage payments normally do not need specific approval before payment by the treasurer.

All checks should be recorded in a cash disbursements journal. The type of expense is reflected in the proper column in a manually prepared journal. Expense account numbers are used to identify the type of expense in a computerized journal. Expenses should be categorized in sufficient detail to provide an adequate breakdown of expenses on the periodic financial statements.

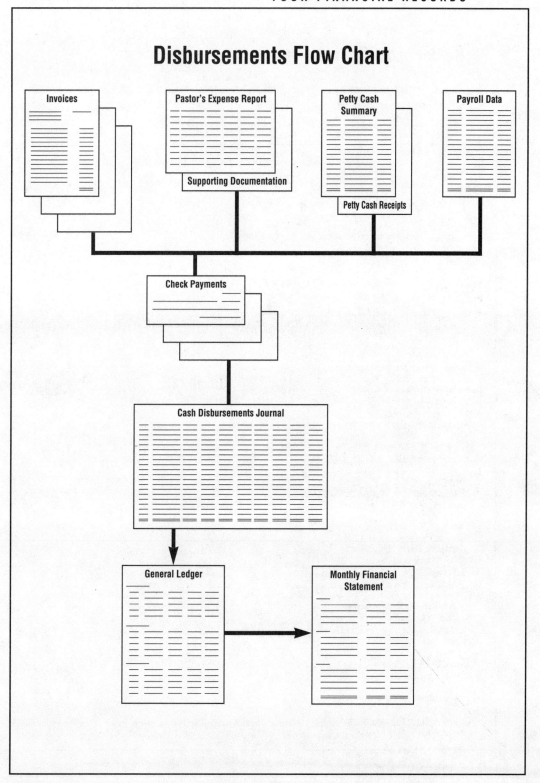

Disbursements Flow Chart

Invoices

Pastor's Expense Report

Supporting Documentation

Petty Cash Summary

Petty Cash Receipts

Payroll Data

Check Payments

Cash Disbursements Journal

General Ledger

Monthly Financial Statement

Bank reconciliation

A written bank reconciliation should be prepared monthly. A sample reconciliation form follows:

BANK STATEMENT RECONCILIATION
As of __March 31__, 199_9_

Balance per bank statement	2,481.40
Add:	
Deposits recorded on books but not credited on bank statement	1,012.80
Subtract:	
Outstanding checks	

Check No.	Amount	
1312	50.00	
1314	17.80	
1318	411.72	
1321	108.14	
1324	791.12	1,378.78

Adjusted balance per bank statement	2,115.42
Balance per check book	2,365.74
Add:	
Interest recorded on bank statement but not reflected in books	10.42

Corrections of checks or deposits:

Check #1250 written for $80.00/ recorded as $90.00	10.00	10.00

Other: 6/18 deposit not recorded in books	175.00	175.00

Subtract:

Bank service charges	29.80
Automatic checks paid by bank	311.12
Nonsufficient fund checks:	
Mike Brown	20.00
Alex Smith	40.00

Corrections of checks or deposits:

6/25 deposit recorded on books as $511.80/should be $501.98	9.82

Other: Check printing	35.00	
		445.74

Adjusted balance per checkbook	2,115.42

These items should be recorded in the checkbook and the cash receipts or disbursements journals after the reconciliation is completed.

Petty cash system

To avoid writing numerous checks for small amounts, it is wise to have a petty-cash fund (with a fixed base amount) from which to make small payments. For example, if the church office needs a roll of stamps, the use of the petty cash fund for the expense is more efficient than writing a check for the minor amount.

A petty cash fund of $50 or $100 is often adequate for small organizations. Large organizations may have multiple petty cash funds in various departments. The amount of the fund may vary based on need.

As funds are disbursed from the petty cash fund, a slip detailing the expense is completed and placed in the petty cash box. If an invoice or receipt is available, it should be attached to the petty cash slip for filing. The petty cash slips are kept with the petty cash. At all times, the total of the unspent petty cash and the petty cash slips should equal the fixed amount of the petty cash fund.

When the cash in the fund is getting low, a check is written payable to "Petty Cash Fund" for an amount equal to the expense slips plus or minus any amounts the fund is out-of-balance. The check is cashed and the cash returns the fund to the fixed balance. Expenses are allocated and recorded based on the purposes reflected on the slips.

Accounting Records

Accounting systems differ in shape, size, complexity, and efficiency. The objectives of the system should be to measure and control financial activities and to provide financial information to the church governing body, the congregation, and donors. In choosing the accounting records for your organization, the most important consideration is the ability of the individual(s) keeping the records.

Single entry vs. double entry

Double-entry bookkeeping is necessary for most organizations. It shows a twofold effect by recording every transaction twice—as a debit entry in one account and as a credit entry in another. Either or both of the entries may be broken down into several items, but the total of the amounts entered as debits must equal the total of the amounts entered as credits.

As the following table shows, when you pay an expense, the amount paid is entered as a debit to expense and as a credit to your cash account (an asset). When you receive a gift, an asset is debited (cash) and an income account is credited.

PETTY CASH RECONCILIATION

DEPARTMENT __Youth__   DATE __June 30, 1999__

Cash On Hand		Payments from Petty Cash — Reconciliation Period From 6/1/99 To 6/30/99										
Currency	Amount	Account	Date	Amount	Date	Amount	Date	Amount	Date	Amount	Date	Total
$20.00 Bills	100 00	626-010	6/2	3 10	6/16	2 00						5 10
10.00 Bills	10 00	633-021	6/10	5 50								5 50
5.00 Bills	20 00	634-120	6/8	1 30	6/20	4 00	6/29	1 00				6 30
2.00 Bills		636-041	6/18	12 89								12 89
1.00 Bills	10 00	637-910	6/4	6 00								6 00
Checks		644-002	6/21	13 80								13 80
$1.00 Coins		645-001	6/10	2 50	6/12	2 00	6/18	1 50				6 00
.50 Coins		647-102	6/26	11 91								11 91
.25 Coins	3 75	649-023	6/19	5 50								5 50
.10 Coins	2 20	651-101	6/3	8 10								8 10
.05 Coins	80	653-001	6/12	12 40								12 40
.01 Coins	36	655-012	6/14	7 12								7 12
SUMMARY		660-001	6/2	1 02	6/8	2 04	6/12	3 11	6/20	4 00		10 17
		663-004	6/8	7 00	6/21	4 00						11 00
1. Total Cash	147 11	665-012	6/29	16 40								16 40
2. Total Petty Cash Slips	150 89	670-080	6/12	4 70	6/20	8 00						12 70
3. Subtotal (1+2)	298 00											
4. Petty Cash Fund	300 00											
5. Overage (3-4)												
6. Shortage (4-3)	2 00											
7. To be reimbursed (2+6 or 2-5)	152 89											
								TOTAL PETTY CASH SLIPS				150 89

__7/2/99__
Date

Dave Mason
Signature of Person Reconciling

When the cash in the petty cash fund is about used up, the custodian summarizes the petty cash receipts on a form like the one illustrated above. A check is then written to replenish the fund.

PETTY CASH RECEIPT

Date __June 7, 1999__

DESCRIPTION OF ITEM / SERVICE PURCHASED	AMOUNT
Office Supplies:	
Pens (1 doz.)	4 90
Envelopes 9x12 (2 doz.)	8 40
Receipt from Complete	
Office Supply is attached	
CHARGE TO ACCOUNT 652-001 TOTAL	13 30

Mary Moore
Money Received By

Dave Mason
Approved By

CASH EXPENSE REPORT

Name: Pastor Frank Morris

Address: 3801 North Florida Avenue

Miami, Florida 33168

Period Covered: From: 6/1/99   To: 6/15/99

| DATE | TRAVEL | | | | | | | | OTHER * | | ACCOUNT TO |
	City	Purpose of Travel	Brkfast	Lunch	Dinner	Snack	Lodging	Trans.	Description	Amount	BE CHARGED
6/2/99									Lunch w/Bob Cox	18.21	641-002
6/6/99	Atlanta, GA	Continuing Ed Seminar		10.80	13.40	2.10	90.50	281.00	Tips	8.00	644-010
6/6/99	✓ ✓	✓ ✓	6.40								644-010
6/8/99									Lunch w/Al Lane	12.80	641-002
6/14/99									Lunch w/Sam Lee	11.10	641-002
	TOTAL CASH EXPENSES		6.40	10.80	13.40	2.10	90.50	281.00		50.11	

*If this is entertainment, please use the entertainment worksheet on the back of this form.

Frank Morris 6/16/99
Signature (person requesting reimbursement)   Date

Bob Davis 6/16/99
Approved by   Date

Total cash expenses	454.31
Personal auto business mileage (Complete worksheet on the back of this form.)	71.82
221 miles X 32.5 per mile	
Less travel advance	⟨300.00⟩
Balance due	226.13
Refund due organization	

PERSONAL AUTO BUSINESS MILEAGE

Date	Purpose/Destination	Miles	Account to be charged
6/1/99	Calls/Valley View Rest Home	23	638-000
6/2/99	Funeral Home / Harold Boone Brown	18	✓
6/3/99	Calls / Various Homes	20	✓
6/4/99	Calls / Memorial Hospital	15	✓
6/5/99	Kiwanis Speaker/Pat's Cafeteria	25	✓
6/7/99	Calls/Various Homes	10	✓
6/8/99	Calls/St. Luke's Hospital	17	✓
6/9/99	Calls/Cannon Nursing Home	12	✓
6/10/99	Calls/Various Homes	8	✓
6/12/99	Calls/Memorial Hospital	15	✓
6/15/99	Ministerial Convention /Webb City	58	✓
	TOTAL MILES TRAVELED	221	

To mileage summary on page one

ENTERTAINMENT WORKSHEET
(Expenses paid in behalf of individual(s) other than the person filing this expense report.)

Date	Persons Entertained	Purpose of Entertainment	Place	Amount
6/2/99	M/m Bob Cox	Prospective Members	Olive Garden	18.21
6/8/99	Frank Lane	Discuss church bldg. plans	Chi Chi's	12.80
6/14/99	Sam Lee	Church goals w/board chair.	Damon's	11.10
	TOTAL AMOUNT SPENT			42.11

To "other" expense column on page one

Example of Computer-Generated Cash Disbursements Journal

Date	Reference	Entry Description	Account No.	Account Name	Amount Debit	Credit
6/01/98	1025	Rev. Glenn Phillips	501-000	Pastor Salary	1,500.00	
			211-000	Income Tax W/H		200.00
6/01/98	1026	Mary Brown	505-000	Secretary Salary	750.00	
			211-000	Income Tax W/H		50.00
			212-000	FICA W/H		57.37
6/03/98	1027	Postmaster	649-000	Postage	29.00	
6/04/98	1028	Bell Telephone	663-000	Telephone	83.92	
6/04/98	1029	City Power & Light	664-000	Utilities	173.12	
6/06/98	1030	Gas Service Co.	664-000	Utilities	20.11	
6/09/98	1031	Harold Reynolds	810-000	Benevolence Expense	50.00	
6/11/98	1032	Blair Insurance	690-000	Insurance Expense	342.00	
6/13/98	1033	Franklin Printing	651-000	Literature & Prtg.	83.29	
6/14/98	1034	Postmaster	649-000	Postage	142.00	
6/15/98	1035	Rev. Glenn Phillips	501-000	Pastor Salary	1,500.00	
			211-000	Income Tax W/H		200.00
6/15/98	1036	Mary Brown	505-000	Secretary Salary	750.00	
			211-000	Income Tax W/H		50.00
			212-000	FICA W/H		57.37
6/20/98	1037	Valley View Bank	505-000	Income Tax W/H	500.00	
			211-000	FICA W/H	114.74	
			212-000	FICA Expense	114.74	
6/20/98	1038	ABC Church Supply	651-000	Literature & Prtg.	200.00	
6/30/98			101-000	Valley View Bank		5,738.18
					6,352.92	6,352.92

Example of Computer-Generated General Ledger with Entries Posted from Cash Disbursements Journal

Source	Acct. No./ Date	Reference	Description	Beginning Balance	Current Entries	Ending Balance
	649-000		**Postage**	316.61		
CD	6/07/98	1027	Postmaster		29.00	
CD	6/14/98	1034	Postmaster		142.00	
					171.00	487.61
	651-000		**Literature & Printing**	702.58		
CD	6/13/98	1033	Franklin Printing		83.29	
CD	6/20/98	1038	ABC Church Supply		200.00	
					283.29	985.87
	653-000		**Kitchen Supplies**	53.72		53.72
	663-000		**Telephone**	648.12		
CD	6/14/98	1028	Bell Telephone		83.92	
					83.92	732.04
	664-000		**Utilities**	1,401.43		
CD	6/04/98	1029	City Power & Light		173.12	
CD	6/06/98	1030	Gas Service Co.		20.11	
					193.23	1,594.66
	810-000		**Benevolence Expense**	200.00		
CD	6/09/98	1031	Harold Reynolds		50.00	
					50.00	250.00
	850-000		**Missions Expense**	2,411.80		2,411.80
	865-000		**Camp Expense**	1,012.80		1,012.80

Type of account	If the transaction will decrease the account, enter it as a —	If the transaction will increase the account, enter it as a —	Typical balance
Asset	credit	debit	debit
Liability	debit	credit	credit
Capital	debit	credit	credit
Income	debit	credit	credit
Expense	credit	debit	debit

Church management software

The accounting records for most organizations are maintained on computers. Even many small churches have a personal computer that is primarily used for word processing. This computer can be used to run software to process church financial data. Many accounting software packages designed for small businesses can be easily adapted for nonprofit use. Most of these packages include the double-entry process. There are also many software packages designed specifically for churches. An excellent summary of church management software prepared by Nick B. Nicholaou, President, Ministry Business Services, Inc., P.O. Box 1567, Huntington Beach, CA 92647 (Tel. 714-840-5900) is reprinted with permission on the following four pages. Feel free to contact the church management software providers.

A compilation of their responses is summarized on the chart on page 116. The symbol ■ is used on those options currently available and that they provide directly. The symbol ☒ is used on those options the provider offers from an outside source. The symbol ☐ is used on those options the provider is working on, but was not ready to offer at press time. If an item on the contact portion of the list was not answered, "n/a" is shown.

Cash and accrual methods

Most small churches and nonprofit organizations use the cash basis of accounting. Other organizations frequently use the accrual method. A common rule of thumb is that organizations with annual revenue of $250,000 and larger probably need to use the accrual method of accounting.

Advantages of cash method

Under this method, revenue is recorded only when cash is received, and expenses are recorded when they are paid. For example, office supplies expense is shown in the month when the bill is paid, even though the supplies were received and used in the previous month.

The primary advantage of the cash method is its simplicity. It is easier for nonaccountants to understand and keep records on this basis. When financial

Church Management Software Comparison Chart

Compiled by
Ministry Business Services, Inc.

Companies (columns):
Valley Software Development, Inc.; Vian Data Systems; Torbert Data Systems; TLC Communications, Inc.; Titus Information Systems; Swan Systems; Summit Systems; Stoner & Wilson; Specialty Software; Software Library; Software For Ministry; Shelby Systems; Servant PC Resources, Inc.; SanSaver; RDS Publishing; PowerChurch Software; Parsons Technology; Parish Data Systems; Micro Information Products; Membership Services (MSI); Logos Research Systems; Logos Management Software; Lieberman Consulting Group; J S Paluch Co.; Icon Systems; Hunter Systems; Greentree Applied Systems; Gronell Computer Service; Focus On Business; Diakonia; Concordia Publishing House; Church Windows/Computer Helper; Church Organizer by The Book; Blackbaud Microsystems; Automated Church System (ACS); AlphaOmega Information Systems

Features (rows):
- Congregation Database
- Attendance Tracker
- Contributions Tracker
- Can Add/Modify Fields
- Photos by Individual/Family
- Mail Merge Interface
- Bulk Mail Bar Codes
- Bulk Mail CASS Certification
- Telephony Services Link
- Facility Scheduler
- Equipment Scheduler
- Retreat Registrations & A/R
- General Ledger
- GAAP Compliant
- Full Audit Trail
- Fixed Budget Tracker
- Variable Budget Tracker
- Graphic Analysis
- Accounts Payable
- Accrual Basis Capable
- Cash Basis Capable
- Annual 1099's
- Laser Checks
- Dot Matrix Checks
- Payroll
- Minister's Salary Capable
- ACH Direct Deposit Capable
- Quarterly 941's
- Annual W2's
- Worker's Comp Audit
- Laser Checks
- Dot Matrix Checks
- Tracks Vacation & Sick
- IBM PC - DOS
- IBM PC - Windows
- Macintosh/Power Mac
- Unix/Xenix
- Midrange System
- Mainframe System
- Novell Networks
- NT Networks
- Other Networks
- Year 2000 Certified

116

Church Management Software Providers
Compiled by Ministry Business Services, Inc.

AlphaOmega Information Systems
12604 Waterfowl Way
Upper Marlboro, MD 20772
Voice: (888) CH-WORKS (249-6757)
Fax: (301) 390-1616
Email: churchwrks@aol.com
Company Founded: 1993
Years Marketing CMS: 5
Active Installed User Base: 1000
Number of Employees: 15
Tech Support Hours: 10a-4p
Last Major Release Date: 1/98
Number of Updates / Year: 1

Automated Church System (ACS)
PO Box 202010
Florence, SC 29502-2010
Voice: (800) 736-7425
Fax: (800) 227-5990
Web: www.acshome.com
Company Founded: 1978
Years Marketing CMS: 20
Active Installed User Base: 9000
Number of Employees: 130
Tech Support Hours: 8a-8p (-6p F)
Last Major Release Date: 1/98
Number of Updates / Year: 2

Blackbaud Microsystems
4401 Belle Oaks Dr.
Charleston, SC 29405
Voice: (800) 443-9441
Fax: (803) 740-5410
Web: www.blackbaud.com
Company Founded: 1981
Years Marketing CMS: 15
Active Installed User Base: 12,000
Number of Employees: 425
Tech Support Hours: 8:30a-11p
Last Major Release Date: 10/97
Number of Updates / Year: 2-3

By The Book
3900 E Grace Blvd.
Highlands Ranch, CO 80126-7801
Voice: (800) 554-9116
Fax: (303) 791-1032
Web: www.btbook.com
Company Founded: 1991
Years Marketing CMS: 7
Active Installed User Base: 450
Number of Employees: 3
Tech Support Hours: 8a-5p
Last Major Release Date: 1/98
Number of Updates / Year: 1-2

Church Organizer
8127 Mesa Dr. #B206-222
Austin, TX 78759
Voice: (512) 342-7917
Fax: (512) 342-7927
Email: organizer@compuserve.com
Company Founded: 1995
Years Marketing CMS: 3
Active Installed User Base: n/a
Number of Employees: none
Tech Support Hours: 8a-10p
Last Major Release Date: 10/97
Number of Updates / Year: 1

Church Windows/Computer Helper
PO Box 30191
Columbus, OH 43230-0191
Voice: (800) 533-5227
Fax: (614) 478-0625
Web: www.churchwindows.com
Company Founded: 1986
Years Marketing CMS: 12
Active Installed User Base: 3000
Number of Employees: 20
Tech Support Hours: 9a-5p
Last Major Release Date: 1/98
Number of Updates / Year: 1-3

Concordia Publishing House
3558 S. Jefferson Ave.
St. Louis, MO 63118-3968
Voice: (800) 325-2399
Fax: (800) 496-2641
Web: www.cphnet.com
Company Founded: 1869
Years Marketing CMS: 17
Active Installed User Base: 6358
Number of Employees: 350
Tech Support Hours: 7:30a-5:30p
Last Major Release Date: 10/97
Number of Updates / Year: 1-3

Diakonia
PO Box 5647
Diamond Bar, CA 91765
Voice: (909) 861-8787
Fax: (909) 861-0335
Web: ourworld.compuserve.com/homepages/diakonia
Company Founded: 1992
Years Marketing CMS: 5
Active Installed User Base: n/a
Number of Employees: n/a
Tech Support Hours: 9a-5p
Last Major Release Date: 3/98
Number of Updates / Year: varies

Focus On Business
116 SW 19th St.
Guthrie, OK 73044
Voice: (800) 255-6223
Fax: (405) 282-1700
No Web Page or Email
Company Founded: 1985
Years Marketing CMS: 11
Active Installed User Base: 800
Number of Employees: 6
Tech Support Hours: 8a-5p
Last Major Release Date: 12/96
Number of Updates / Year: 2

Gosnell Computer Services
1331 Third St.
New Orleans, LA 70130
Voice: (800) 326-2235
Fax: (504) 899-0481
Web: www.bbll.com/ease/ease.html
Company Founded: 1985
Years Marketing CMS: 13
Active Installed User Base: 1600
Number of Employees: 3
Tech Support Hours: 9a-5p
Last Major Release Date: 1997
Number of Updates / Year: 1

Greentree Applied Systems
157 Propserous Pl. #1A
Lexington, KY 40509
Voice: (800) 928-6388
Fax: (606) 263-9824
Web: www.greentreeky.com
Company Founded: 1982
Years Marketing CMS: 2
Active Installed User Base: 500
Number of Employees: 10
Tech Support Hours: 9a-5p
Last Major Release Date: 3/98
Number of Updates / Year: 8

Hunter Systems
100 Century Park South #206
Birmingham, AL 35226
Voice: (800) 326-0527
Fax: (205) 979-3389
Web: www.huntersys.com
Company Founded: 1986
Years Marketing CMS: 12
Active Installed User Base: 400
Number of Employees: 32
Tech Support Hours: 8:30a-5:30p
Last Major Release Date: 1997
Number of Updates / Year: 1-2

Icon Systems
3704 Westmoor Dr.
Moorhead, MN 56560
Voice: (800) 596-4266
Fax: (218) 236-0235

Church Management Software Providers *(continued)*
Compiled by Ministry Business Services, Inc.

Web: www.revelations.com
Company Founded: 1992
Years Marketing CMS: 5
Active Installed User Base: 1200
Number of Employees: classified info
Tech Support Hours: 8:30a-4:30p
Last Major Release Date: 8/97
Number of Updates / Year: 2

J.S. Paluch Co.
3825 N Willow Rd.
Schiller Park, IL 60176
Voice: (847) 678-9300
Fax: (847) 928-5812
Email: pcmsupport@jspaluch.com
Company Founded: 1913
Years Marketing CMS: 14
Active Installed User Base: 600
Number of Employees: 490
Tech Support Hours: 8a-4:30p
Last Major Release Date: 12/97
Number of Updates / Year: 3

Lieberman Consulting Group
2253 South Ave.
Scotch Plains, NJ 07090-4688
Voice: (510) 283-3289
Fax: (510) 283-3289
Web: www.lieberware.com/mem-info
Company Founded: 1982
Years Marketing CMS: 3
Active Installed User Base: 10
Number of Employees: 2
Tech Support Hours: 9a-5p PST
Last Major Release Date: 2/97
Number of Updates / Year: 2

Logos Management Software
15500 W Telegraph Rd.
Santa Paula, CA 93060
Voice: (800) 266-3311
Fax: (805) 525-6161
Web: logoslbe.com

Company Founded: 1980
Years Marketing CMS: 18
Active Installed User Base: 3500
Number of Employees: classified info
Tech Support Hours: 7a-5p
Last Major Release Date: 2/98
Number of Updates / Year: 1

Logos Research Systems
715 SE Fidalgo Ave.
Oak Harbor, WA 98277-4049
Voice: (360) 679-6575
Fax: (360) 675-8169
Web: www.logos.com
Company Founded: 1992
Years Marketing CMS: 2
Active Installed User Base: 3500
Number of Employees: 66
Tech Support Hours: 7a-4p
Last Major Release Date: 3/98
Number of Updates / Year: as needed

Membership Services (MSI)
PO Box 152130
Irving, TX 75038
Voice: (800) 955-0805
Fax: (972) 594-8100
Web: msi@dallas.net
Company Founded: 1966
Years Marketing CMS: 32
Active Installed User Base: 1100
Number of Employees: 14
Tech Support Hours: 7a-5p
Last Major Release Date: 1995
Number of Updates / Year: 6

Micro Information Products
313 E Anderson Ln. #200
Austin, TX 78752
Voice: (800) 647-3863
Fax: (512) 454-2254
Web: www.mip.com
Company Founded: 1982
Years Marketing CMS: 15

Active Installed User Base: 4000
Number of Employees: 80
Tech Support Hours: 8a-6p
Last Major Release Date: 5/97
Number of Updates / Year: 3

Parish Data Systems
14425 N 19th Ave.
Phoenix, AZ 85023
Voice: (602) 789-0595
Fax: (602) 789-0597
Web: www.parishdatainc.com
Company Founded: 1978
Years Marketing CMS: 20
Active Installed User Base: 10,000
Number of Employees: 14
Tech Support Hours: 8a-5p
Last Major Release Date: 1996
Number of Updates / Year: as needed

Parsons Technology
One Martha's Way
Hiawatha, IA 52233
Voice: (800) 644-6344
Fax: (319) 378-0335
Web: www.quickverse.com
Company Founded: 1984
Years Marketing CMS: 8
Active Installed User Base: 25,000
Number of Employees: 500
Tech Support Hours: 7a-7p
Last Major Release Date: 12/96
Number of Updates / Year: as needed

PowerChurch Software
208 Ridgefield Ct.
Asheville, NC 28806-2262
Voice: (800) 486-1800
Fax: (828) 665-1999
Web: www.pchurch.com
Company Founded: 1984
Years Marketing CMS: 14
Active Installed User Base: 10,000

Number of Employees: classified info
Tech Support Hours: 9a-6p
Last Major Release Date: 12/97
Number of Updates / Year: 1

RDS Publishing
6801 N Broadway #120
Oklahoma City, OK 73116
Voice: (405) 840-5177
Fax: (405) 840-0468
Web: www.rdsadvantage.com
Company Founded: 1983
Years Marketing CMS: 15
Active Installed User Base: classified
Number of Employees: classified info
Tech Support Hours: 8a-5p
Last Major Release Date: 10/97
Number of Updates / Year: 1

SaintSaver
9150 Russell Ave. S
Bloomington, MN 55431-2120
Voice: (612) 881-7324
Fax: (612) 346-0842
Web: www.mumac.org/saintsaver.html
Company Founded: 1992
Years Marketing CMS: 6
Active Installed User Base: 100
Number of Employees: n/a
Tech Support Hours: n/a
Last Major Release Date: 1994
Number of Updates / Year: n/a

Servant PC Resources, Inc.
RR5, Box 323
Jersey Shore, PA 17740
Voice: (800) 773-7570
Fax: (717) 398-2501
Web: www.servantpc.com
Company Founded: 1994
Years Marketing CMS: 4
Active Installed User Base: 3700
Number of Employees: 13

Church Management Software Providers *(continued)*
Compiled by Ministry Business Services, Inc.

Tech Support Hours: 9a-6p
Last Major Release Date: 9/97
Number of Updates / Year: 1

Shelby Systems
65 Germantown Ct. #303
Cordova, TN 38018
Voice: (800) 877-0222
Fax: (901) 759-3682
Web: www.shelbyinc.com
Company Founded: 1976
Years Marketing CMS: 22
Active Installed User Base: 4000
Number of Employees: 68
Tech Support Hours: 8a-6p
Last Major Release Date: 9/97
Number of Updates / Year: 4-5

Software For Ministry
PO Box 1165
Yucaipa, CA 92399
Voice: (909) 797-8445
Fax: same
Email: 74617.1146@com-
puserve.com
Company Founded: 1983
Years Marketing CMS: 15
Active Installed User Base: 1250
Number of Employees: 2
Tech Support Hours: 9a-5p
Last Major Release Date: 2/98
Number of Updates / Year: 1

Software Library
3300 Bass Lake Rd. #304
Brooklyn Center, MN 55429
Voice: (800) 247-8044
Fax: (612) 566-2250
Email: 70563.2140@com-
puserve.com
Company Founded: 1985
Years Marketing CMS: 12
Active Installed User Base: 1500
Number of Employees: 10
Tech Support Hours: 8a-5p

Last Major Release Date: 12/97
Number of Updates / Year: 1

Specialty Software
PO Box 5494
Evansville, IN 47716
Voice: (800) 568-6350
Fax: (407) 728-1077
Email: specialsof@aol.com
Company Founded: 1983
Years Marketing CMS: 14
Active Installed User Base: 5000
Number of Employees: 10
Tech Support Hours: 9a-5p
Last Major Release Date: 12/97
Number of Updates / Year: 1

Stoner & Wilson
2022 S National #B
Springfield, MO 65804
Voice: (417) 881-8500
Fax: (417) 881-7707
Email: crsroads@dialnet.net
Company Founded: 1986
Years Marketing CMS: 7
Active Installed User Base: 42
Number of Employees: 3
Tech Support Hours: 8a-5p
Last Major Release Date: 1/98
Number of Updates / Year: 4

Summit Systems
2163 Amicks Ferry Rd.
Chapin, SC 29036
Voice: (800) 228-5857
Fax: (803) 345-3940
Web: www.intraweb.com/sum-
mit.htm
Company Founded: 1984
Years Marketing CMS: 14
Active Installed User Base: 850
Number of Employees: 5
Tech Support Hours: 8a-5:30p
Last Major Release Date: 5/97

Number of Updates / Year: 2

Suran Systems
695 Craigs Creek Rd.
Versailles, KY 40383-8909
Voice: (800) 557-8726
Fax: (606) 873-0308
Web: www.suran.com
Company Founded: 1986
Years Marketing CMS: 12
Active Installed User Base: 2000
Number of Employees: 12
Tech Support Hours: 9a-5p
Last Major Release Date: 3/98
Number of Updates / Year: 1

Titus Information Systems
1528 E Missouri #161
Phoenix, AZ 85014
Voice: (602) 234-8969
Fax: (602) 234-8927
Email: titusinf@dancris.com
Company Founded: 1979
Years Marketing CMS: 17
Active Installed User Base: 6
Number of Employees: 1
Tech Support Hours: 8a-5p
Last Major Release Date: 8/97
Number of Updates / Year: as
needed

TLC Communications, Inc.
1045 Wildwood Blvd. SW
Issaquah, WA 98027-4506
Voice: (425) 392-9592
Fax: (425) 392-9592-4
Email: tlccomm@msn.com
Company Founded: 1984
Years Marketing CMS: 1
Active Installed User Base: 20
Number of Employees: 4
Tech Support Hours: 7a-6p
Last Major Release Date: 11/97
Number of Updates / Year: 1

Torbert Data Systems
PO Box 9218
Chesapeake, VA 23321
Voice: (800) 755-2641
Email: tds@churchsoftware.com
Web: www.churchsoftware.com
Company Founded: 1990
Years Marketing CMS: 8
Active Installed User Base: 1100
Number of Employees: 4
Tech Support Hours: 8a-5p, Sat 9-1
Last Major Release Date: 11/97
Number of Updates / Year: 2

Vian
452 W Hill Rd.
Glen Gardner, NJ 08826-3253
Voice: (908) 537-4642
Fax: none
Web: www.vian.com
Company Founded: 1982
Years Marketing CMS: 13
Active Installed User Base: 1738
Number of Employees: classified info
Tech Support Hours: 4:30p-6:00p
Last Major Release Date: 10/97
Number of Updates / Year: varies

Yaffey Software
Development, Inc.
435 Walhalla Rd.
Columbus, OH 43202-1474
Voice: (614) 268-6353
Fax: none
Email: cyaffey@columbus.rr.com
Company Founded: 1990
Years Marketing CMS: 8
Active Installed User Base: 10
Number of Employees: 1
Tech Support Hours: 9a-5p
Last Major Release Date: 10/97
Number of Updates / Year: varies

statements are required, the treasurer just summarizes the transactions from the checkbook stubs or runs the computer-prepared financial statements with fewer adjusting entries required. For smaller organizations, the difference between financial results on the cash and on the accrual basis are often not significantly different.

Advantages of accrual method

Many organizations use the accrual method of accounting when the cash basis does not accurately portray the financial picture. Under the accrual method, revenue is recorded when earned. For example, a church charges a fee for the use of the fellowship hall for a wedding.

Under accrual accounting, the revenue is recorded in the month earned even though the cash might not be received until a later month. Under accrual accounting, expenses are recorded when incurred. For example, telephone expense is recorded in the month when the service occurs although the bill may not be paid until the next month.

Generally accepted accounting principles for nonprofit organizations require the use of accrual basis accounting. Organizations that have their books audited by Certified Public Accountants, and want the CPAs to report that the financial statement appear according to "generally accepted accounting principles (GAAP)," must either keep their records on the accrual basis or make the appropriate adjustments at the end of the year to convert to this basis. Financial statements prepared on a cash or other comprehensive basis may qualify under GAAP if the financial statements are not materially different from those prepared on an accrual basis.

Modified cash method

The modified cash method of accounting is a combination of certain features of the cash and accrual methods. For example, accounts payable may be recorded when a bill is received although other payables or receivables are not recorded. The modified cash method portrays the financial picture more accurately than the cash method but not as well as the full accrual method.

Some organizations use the modified cash accounting method during the year and then make entries at year-end to convert the accounting data to a full accrual basis for audit purposes. This method simplifies the day-to-day bookkeeping process with interim reports focused on cash management.

Fund accounting

Fund accounting (or accounting by classes of net assets) provides an excellent basis for stewardship reporting. It is a system of accounting in which separate records are kept for resources donated to an organization which are restricted by donors or outside parties to certain specified purposes or use.

GAAP requires that net assets be broken down into the following three classes, based on the presence or absence of donor-imposed restrictions and their nature:

✓ **Permanently restricted.** These assets are not available for program expenses, payments to creditors, or other organizational needs. An example is an endowment gift with a stipulation that the principal is permanently not available for spending but the investment income from the principal may be used in current operations.

✓ **Temporarily restricted.** These assets may be restricted by purpose or time, but the restrictions are not permanent. An example of the purpose-restricted gift is a gift for a certain project or for the purchase of some equipment. An example of a time-restricted gift is a contribution in the form of a trust, annuity, or term endowment (principal of the gift is restricted for a certain term of time).

✓ **Unrestricted.** These net assets may be used for any of the organization's purposes. According to accounting standards, "the only limits on unrestricted net assets are broad limits resulting from the nature of the organization and the purposes specified in its articles of incorporation or bylaws."

Donor-imposed restrictions normally apply to the use of net assets and not to the use of specific assets. Only donors or outside parties may "restrict" funds given to a nonprofit organization. The organization's board may not "restrict" monies— they may only "designate" funds. For example, if a donor gives money for a new church organ, the funds should be placed in a restricted fund. If the church board sets funds aside in a debt retirement fund, this is a designated fund.

Fund accounting does not necessarily require multiple bank accounts. One bank account is all that is usually necessary. However, it may be appropriate to place restricted funds into a separate bank account to ensure that the funds are not inadvertently spent for other purposes.

Depreciation

Some organizations charge-off or record land, buildings, and equipment as expense at the time of purchase. Other organizations capitalize land, buildings, and equipment at cost and do not record depreciation. Other organizations record land, buildings, and equipment at cost and depreciate them over their estimated useful life. GAAP requires this last method. Depreciation is not required for financial statement presentation on any other basis of accounting.

Organizations may set dollar limits for the recording of buildings and equipment as assets. For example, one organization might properly expense all equipment purchases of less than $2,000 per item and record items as assets above that amount.

Chart of accounts

The chart of accounts lists all ledger accounts and their account number to facilitate the bookkeeping process. Assets, liabilities, net assets, support and revenue, and expense accounts are listed. For a sample chart of accounts for a church, see page 119.

Account numbers are used to indicate the source of support and revenue or the object of expense. In computerized accounting systems, the account number is used to post an entry to the general ledger. The same concept can be used in a manually-prepared accounting system to avoid writing out the account name each time.

Financial Reports

In preparing financial reports, there is one basic rule: prepare different reports for different audiences. For example, a church board would normally receive a more detailed financial report than the church membership. Department heads in a nonprofit organization might receive reports that only relate to their department.

Financial statements should

✓ be easily comprehensible so that any person taking the time to study them will understand the financial picture;

✓ be concise so that the person studying them will not get lost in detail;

✓ be all-inclusive in scope and should embrace all activities of the organization;

✓ have a focal point for comparison so that the person reading them will have some basis for making a judgment (usually this will be a comparison with a budget or data from the corresponding period of the previous year); and

✓ be prepared on a timely basis (the longer the delay after the end of the period, the longer the time before corrective action can be taken).

For additional reading on this topic, see the *Accounting and Financial Reporting Guide for Christian Ministries* (published by the Evangelical Joint Accounting Committee and available from the Christian Management Association 800–727–4CMA) and *Financial and Accounting Guide for Not-for-Profit Organizations* by Melvin J. Gross, Jr., and Richard F. Larkin (John Wiley & Sons).

Statement of activity

The statement of activity (also referred to as a statement of revenues and expenses) reflects an organization's support and revenue, expenses, and changes in net assets for a certain period of time. It shows the sources of an organization's income and how the resources were used. The form of the statement will depend on

SAMPLE CHART OF ACCOUNTS FOR A CHURCH

Assets
Cash and cash equivalents
Prepaid expenses
Short-term investments
Land, buildings, and equipment:
   Church buildings
   Parsonage
   Furnishings
Long-term investments

Liabilities
Accounts payable
Notes payable
Long-term debt

Revenues and Support
Contributions
   Regular offerings
   Sunday school offerings
   Missions offerings
   Building fund offerings
   Other offerings
Investment income
   Interest income
   Rental income
Other income
   Tape sales
   Other sales
   Other income

Expenses
Salaries and wages
   Salary including cash housing allowance
   Tax deferred payments (TSA/IRA)
Benefits
   Pension
   Social security (SECA) reimbursement
   Social Security (FICA)
   Medical expense reimbursement
   Insurance premiums

Supplies
   Postage
   Literature and printing
   Office supplies
   Maintenance supplies
   Food
   Kitchen supplies
   Flowers
   Other supplies
Travel and entertainment
   Auto expense reimbursements
   Vehicle rental
   Other travel expense
Continuing education
Insurance
   Workers' Compensation
   Health insurance
   Property insurance
   Other insurance
Benevolences
   Denominational budgets
   Other benevolences
Services and professional fees
   Speaking honoraria
   Custodial services
   Legal and audit fees
   Other fees
Office and occupancy
   Rent
   Telephone
   Utilities
   Property taxes
   Other office and occupancy
Depreciation
Interest expense
Other
   Banquets
   Advertising

Suffix digits may be used to indicate the functional expense category such as

- 10	Program expenses		- 16	Youth	
- 11	Pastoral		- 17	Singles	
- 12	Education		- 18	Seniors	
- 121	Sunday school		- 20	Management and general	
- 122	Vacation Bible school		- 21	Church plant	
- 123	Camps and retreats		- 22	Parsonages	
- 13	Music and worship		- 23	Office	
- 14	Missions		- 30	Fund raising	
- 15	Membership and evangelism				

the type of organization and accounting method used. But the statement must present the change in unrestricted, temporarily restricted, permanently restricted, and total net assets.

Many smaller organizations will have several lines for support and revenue such as contributions, sales of products, investment income, and so on. Expenses are often listed by natural classification such as salaries, fringe benefits, supplies, and so on.

Organizations desiring to meet GAAP accounting standards must reflect functional expenses (for example, by program, management and general, fund raising, and membership development) in the statement of activity or footnotes. Smaller organizations will tend to show expenses by natural classification in the statement of activity and functional expenses in the footnotes. The reverse approach will generally be true of larger organizations. While the reporting of expenses by natural classification is not generally required under GAAP, readers of the financial statements will often find the additional reporting very helpful.

Statement of financial position

A statement of financial position shows assets, liabilities, and net assets as of the end-of-period date. This statement is also called a balance sheet because it shows how the two sides of the accounting equation (assets minus liabilities equal net assets) "balance" in your organization.

Anything an organization owns that has a money value is an asset. Cash, land, buildings, furniture, and fixtures are examples of assets. Anything the organization owes is a liability. Liabilities might include amounts owed to supplies (accounts payable) or to the bank (notes payable, and other amounts due).

Statement of cash flows

The statement of cash flows provides information about the cash receipts and disbursements of your organization and the extent to which resources were obtained from, or used in, operating, investing, or financing activities. The direct method of presenting a cash flow statement starts by listing all sources of cash from operations during the period and deducts all operating outflows of cash to arrive at the net cash flow. The indirect method begins with the change in net assets and adjusts backwards to reconcile the change in net assets to net cash flows. The financial Accounting Standards Board encourages the use of the direct presentation method.

Audit Guidelines

An annual audit of the organization's records is a must. External audits are performed by an independent auditor that has no impairing relationship to the organization and can review the data procedures with maximum objectivity. Internal audits are generally performed by members or those closely associated with the organization.

Fall Creek Church
Statement of Activity
Year Ended June 30, 1998

	Unrestricted	Temporarily Restricted	Permanently Restricted	Total
Support and revenues				
Contributions				
Regular offerings	$260,000			$260,000
Sunday school offerings	45,000			45,000
Missions offerings	50,000			50,000
Other offerings	25,000	$10,000		35,000
Investment income				
Interest income	1,000		$2,000	3,000
Rental income	3,000			3,000
Total revenues	384,000	10,000	2,000	396,000
Expenses				
Program expenses				
Worship	25,000	9,000		34,000
Sunday school	35,000			35,000
Youth	30,000			30,000
Management and general	296,000			296,000
Fund raising	5,000			5,000
Total expenses	391,000	9,000		400,000
Change in net assets	(7,000)	1,000	2,000	(4,000)
Net assets at beginning of year	645,000	4,000	18,000	667,000
Net assets at end of year	$ 638,000	$ 5,000	$ 20,000	$ 663,000

Expenses incurred were for:

	Total	Worship	Sunday School	Youth	Mgt. & Gen.	Fund Raising
Salaries, wages, and benefits	$142,000	$5,000	$6,000		$131,000	
Supplies	73,000	25,000	24,000	$24,000		
Travel	16,000			1,000	10,000	$5,000
Insurance		20,000				20,000
Benevolences						
Denominational budgets	20,000				20,000	
Other benevolences	50,000				50,000	
Services and professional fees	14,000	4,000	5,000	5,000		
Office and occupancy	30,000				30,000	
Depreciation		10,000				10,000
Interest		25,000				25,000
	$400,000	$ 34,000	$ 35,000	$ 30,000	$296,000	$ 5,000

Note: This is a multi-column presentation of a statement of activity. Reporting of expenses by natural classification (at bottom of page), though often useful, is not required.

Castle Creek Church
Statement of Activity
Year Ended June 30, 1998

Changes in unrestricted net assets:
Revenues:

Contributions	$ 141,000
Fees	6,250
Income on long-term investments	5,400
Other	20,100
Total unrestricted revenues	172,500

Expenses (Note A)

Salaries, wages, and benefits	90,500
Supplies	3,000
Travel	5,000
Insurance	7,500
Benevolences	
Denominational budgets	10,000
Other benevolences	20,000
Services and professional fees	8,000
Office and occupancy	7,000
Depreciation	5,000
Interest	20,000
Total expenses	176,000

Net assets released from restrictions:	
Satisfaction of program restrictions	2,000
Expiration of time restrictions	3,000
Total net assets released from restrictions	5,000
Increase in unrestricted net assets	2,500
Changes in temporarily restricted net assets:	
Contributions	23,000
Net assets released from restrictions	(5,000)
Increase in temporarily restricted net assets	19,500
Changes in permanently restricted net assets:	
Contributions	5,000
Increase in permanently restricted net assets	7,000
Increase in net assets	29,000
Net assets at beginning of year	910,000
Net assets at end of year	$941,000

Note A:
Functional expense breakdown:

Program expenses:	
Worship	$16,000
Sunday school	7,000
Youth	5,000
Management and general	145,500
Fund raising	2,500
Total expenses	$176,000

Note: This is an alternate, single-column, presentation of a statement of activity. If the natural classification of expenses is shown in the body of the statement, the functional expenses must be reflected in a footnote to meet accounting standards.

Fall Creek Church
Statement of Financial Position
June 30, 1998 and 1997

	1998	**1997**
Assets:		
Cash and cash equivalents	$20,000	$15,000
Prepaid expenses	5,000	4,000
Short-term investments	10,000	8,000
Land, buildings, and equipment:		
Church buildings	525,000	525,000
Parsonage	110,000	110,000
Furnishings	175,000	160,000
Long-term investments	30,000	25,000
Total assets	875,000	847,000
Liabilities and net assets:		
Accounts payable	$8,000	$7,000
Notes payable	9,000	10,000
Long-term debt	195,000	205,000
Total liabilities	212,000	222,000
Net assets:		
Unrestricted	638,000	601,000
Temporarily restricted (Note 1)	5,000	4,000
Permanently restricted (Note 2)	20,000	20,000
Total net assets	663,000	625,000
Total liabilities and net assets	$875,000	$847,000

Note 1:   Restricted net assets result when a donor has imposed a stipulation to use the funds or assets contributed in a manner which is more limited than the broad purpose for which tax-exempt status is granted for an organization. For example, a church may receive a contribution to establish a scholarship fund with the principal and earnings available for scholarship payments. This gift is a temporarily restricted contribution. If the scholarship funds were all expended in the church's fiscal year when the gift was received, the contribution would be unrestricted.

Note 2:   Permanently restricted contributions are those which contain a stipulation which will always be present. For example, if a scholarship gift is made with the stipulation that only the earnings from the fund may be spent for scholarships, this is a permanently restricted net asset.

The financial statements illustrated on pages 125–27 are presented based on Statement No. 117 issued by the Financial Accounting Standards Board of the American Institute of Certified Public Accountants.

External audits

The ideal is to have an annual audit performed by independent CPAs. However, only medium to large nonprofits generally can afford this extra expense. External audits of smaller organizations are often done on a non-GAAP basis—the statements do not conform to the full accrual method with depreciation recognized. Non-GAAP audits of smaller organizations are often acceptable to banks and other agencies that require audited financial statements.

Internal audits

Members of the organization may form an audit committee to perform an internal audit to determine the validity of the financial statements. (Sample internal audit guidelines for churches are shown on pages 129–32.) If the committee takes its task seriously, the result may be significant improvements in internal control and accounting procedures. Too often, the internal audit committee only conducts a cursory review, commends the treasurer for a job well done, and provides the organization with a false sense of security.

Key Concepts

■ Good accounting records and good stewardship go hand in hand.

■ Your organization is the trustee of the money it receives—handle it carefully.

■ Tailor meaningful financial statements for your organization.

■ Prepare timely financial reports covering all of your funds—not just the operating fund.

■ An annual audit—either external or internal—is a must.

Church Internal Audit Guidelines

Financial statements

✓ Are monthly financial statements prepared on a timely basis and submitted to the organization's board?

✓ Do the financial statements include all funds (unrestricted, temporarily restricted, and permanently restricted)?

✓ Do the financial statements include a statement of financial condition and statement of activity?

✓ Are account balances in the financial records reconciled with amounts presented in financial reports?

Cash receipts

✓ **General**

- Are cash handling procedures in writing?

- Has the bank been notified to never cash checks payable to the church?

- Are Sunday school offerings properly recorded and delivered to the money counters?

- Are procedures established to care for offerings and monies delivered or mailed to the church office between Sundays?

✓ **Offering counting**

- Are at least two members of the counting committee present when offerings are counted? (The persons counting the money should not include a pastor of a church or the church treasurer.)

- Do money counters verify that the contents of the offering envelopes are identical to the amounts written on the outside of the envelopes?

- Are all checks stamped with a restrictive endorsement stamp immediately after the offering envelope contents are verified?

- Are money counters rotated so the same people are not handling the funds each week?

- Are donor-restricted funds properly identified during the process of counting offerings?

✓ **Depositing of funds**

- Are two members of the offering counting team in custody of the offering until it is deposited in the bank, placed in a night depository, or the church's safe?

- Are all funds promptly deposited? Compare offering and other receipt records with bank deposits.

- Are all receipts deposited intact? Receipts should not be used to pay cash expenses.

✓ **Restricted funds**

- Are donations for restricted purposes properly recorded in the accounting records?

- Are restricted funds held for the intended purpose(s) and not spent on operating needs?

Donation records/receipting

✓ Are individual donor records kept as a basis to provide donor acknowledgments for all single contributions of $250 or more?

✓ If no goods or services were provided (other than intangible religious benefits) in exchange for a gift, does the receipt include a statement to this effect?

✓ If goods or services (other than intangible religious benefits) were provided in exchange for a gift, does the receipt

- inform the donor that the amount of the contribution that is deductible for federal income tax purposes is limited to the excess of the amount of any money and the value of any property contributed by the donor over the value of the goods and services provided by the organization, and

- provide the donor with a good faith estimate of the value of such goods and services?

✓ Are the donations traced from the weekly counting sheets to the donor records for a selected time period by the audit committee?

Cash disbursements

✓ Are all disbursements paid by check except for minor expenditures paid through the petty cash fund?

✓ Is written documentation available to support all disbursements?

✓ If a petty cash fund is used, are vouchers prepared for each disbursement from the fund?

✓ Are pre-numbered checks used? Account for all the check numbers including voided checks.

✓ Are blank checks ever signed in advance? This should never be done.

Petty cash funds

✓ Is a petty cash fund used for disbursements of a small amount? If so, is the fund periodically reconciled and replenished based on proper documentation of the cash expenditures?

Bank statement reconciliation

✓ Are written bank reconciliations prepared on a timely basis? Test the reconciliation for the last month in the fiscal year. Trace transactions between the bank and the books for completeness and timeliness.

✓ Are there any checks that have been outstanding over three months?

✓ Are there any unusual transactions in the bank statement immediately following year-end? Obtain the bank statement for the first month after year-end directly from the bank for review by the audit committee. Otherwise, obtain the last bank statement (unopened) from the church treasurer.

Savings and investment accounts

✓ Are all savings and investment accounts recorded in the financial records? Compare monthly statements to the books.

✓ Are earnings or losses from savings and investment accounts recorded in the books?

Land, buildings, and equipment records

✓ Are there detailed records of land, buildings, and equipment including date acquired, description, and cost or fair market value at date of acquisition?

✓ Was an equipment physical inventory taken at year-end?

✓ Have the property records been reconciled to the insurance coverages?

Accounts payable

✓ Is there a schedule of unpaid invoices including vendor name, invoice date, and due date?

✓ Are any of the accounts payable items significantly past-due?

✓ Are there any disputes with vendors over amounts owed?

Insurance policies

✓ Is there a schedule of insurance coverage in force? Reflect effective and expiration dates, kind and classification of coverages, maximum amounts of each coverage, premiums and terms of payment.

✓ Is Workers' Compensation insurance being carried as provided by law in most states? Are all employees (and perhaps some independent contractors) covered under the Workers' Compensation policy?

Amortization of debt

✓ Is there a schedule of debt such as mortgages and notes?

✓ Have the balances owed to all lenders been confirmed directly in writing?

✓ Have the balances owed to all lenders been compared to the obligations recorded on the balance sheet?

Securities and other negotiable documents

✓ Does the church own any marketable securities or bonds? If so, are they kept in a safety deposit box, and are two signatures (excluding a pastor) required for access?

✓ Have the contents of the safety deposit box been examined and recorded?

CHAPTER SEVEN

Charitable Gifts

In This Chapter

- Percentage limitations
- Charitable gift options
- Charitable gift timing
- Charitable contribution acknowledgments
- Gifts that may not qualify as contributions
- Reporting to the IRS
- Quid pro quo disclosure requirements
- Special charitable contribution issues

While most donors care more about the reason for giving than they do about the tax implications, the spirit of giving should never be reduced by unexpected tax results.

A gift is the voluntary transfer of cash or property motivated by something other than "consideration." Consideration is something being received in return for a payment. The mere transfer of funds to a church or charitable nonprofit is not necessarily a gift. Thus, when a parent pays the college tuition for a child, there is no gift or charitable deduction.

If payments are made to a church or other nonprofit organization to receive something in exchange, the transaction is more in the nature of a purchase. The tax law states that a transfer to a nonprofit is not a contribution when made "with a reasonable expectation of financial return commensurate with the amount of the transfer." When one transfer comprises both a gift and a purchase, only the gift portion is deductible.

The two broad categories of charitable gifts are *outright* gifts and *deferred* gifts. Outright gifts require that the donor immediately transfer possession and use of the gift property to the donee. In deferred giving, the donor also makes a current gift, but the gift is of a future interest. Accordingly, actual possession and use of the gift property by the donee is deferred until the future.

Charitable contributions are deductible if given "to and for the use" of a "qualified" tax-exempt organization to be used under its control to accomplish its exempt purposes. ("Qualified" organizations are churches and other domestic 501(c)(3) organizations.) To be deductible, contributions must be unconditional and without personal benefit to the donor.

Three types of gifts commonly given to a church or other nonprofit organization are:

✔ **Gifts without donor stipulations.** Contributions received without donor restriction are generally tax-deductible.

✔ **Donor restricted gifts.** Contributions may be designated (*also referred to as restricted*) by the donor for a specific exempt purpose of the organization rather than being given without donor stipulation. If the gifts are in support of the organization's exempt program activities and not designated or restricted for an individual, they are generally tax-deductible.

   If gifts are designated or earmarked for a specific individual, no tax deduction is generally allowed unless the church or nonprofit organization exercises full administrative control over the funds and they are spent for program activities of the organization.

✔ **Personal gifts.** Gifts made through an organization to an individual, where the donor has specified, by name, the identity of the person who is to receive the gift, are not tax-deductible. Processing of personal gifts through a church or nonprofit organization should be discouraged by the organization unless it is done as a convenience to donors and the ultimate recipients where communication between the two parties might otherwise be difficult (e.g., a misisonary supported by the organization who is serving in a foreign country).

Tax-deduction receipts should not be issued to a donor for personal gifts and the organization should affirmatively advise donors that the gifts are not tax-deductible.

Percentage Limitations

Charitable deductions for a particular tax year are limited by certain percentages of an individual's adjusted gross income (AGI). These are the limitations:

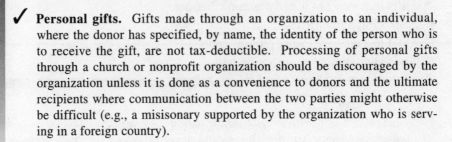

✔ Gifts of cash and ordinary income property to public charities and private operating foundations are limited to 50% of AGI. Any excess may generally be carried forward up to five years.

✔ Gifts of long-term (held 12 months or more) capital gain property to public charities and private operating foundations are limited to 30% of AGI. The same five-year carry-forward is possible.

✓ Donors of capital gain property to public charities and private operating foundations may use the 50% limitation, instead of the 30% limitation, where the amount of the contribution is reduced by all the unrealized appreciation (nontaxed gain) in the value of the property.

✓ Gifts of cash, short-term (held less than 12 months) capital gain property, and ordinary income property to private foundations and certain other charitable donees (other than public charities and private operating foundations) are generally limited to the item's cost basis and 30% of AGI. The carry-forward rules apply to these gifts.

✓ Gifts of long-term (held 12 months or more) capital gain property to private foundations and other charitable donees (other than public charities and private operating foundations) are generally limited to 20% of AGI. There is no carry-forward for these gifts.

✓ Charitable contribution deductions by corporations in any tax year may not exceed 10% of pretax net income. Excess contributions may be carried forward up to five years.

Charitable Gift Options

Irrevocable nontrust gifts

✓ **Cash.** A gift of cash is the simplest method of giving. The value of the gift is easily known. A cash gift is deductible within the 50% or 30% of adjusted gross income limitations, depending on the type of the recipient organization. Generally the 50% limit applies.

✓ **Securities.** The contribution deduction for stocks and bonds held long-term (held 12 months or more), is the mean between the highest and lowest selling prices on the date of the gift where there is a market for listed securities. The contribution deduction is limited to cost for securities held short-term.

Example: An individual taxpayer plans to make a gift of $50,000 to a college. To provide the capital, the taxpayer planned to sell stock that had cost $20,000 some years earlier yielding a long-term capital gain of $30,000. The taxpayer decides to donate the stock itself instead of the proceeds of its sale. The taxpayer receives a contribution deduction of $50,000 and the unrealized gain on the stock is not taxable. By contributing the stock, the taxpayer's taxable income is $30,000 less than if the stock were sold.

✓ **Real estate.** The contribution deduction for a gift of real estate is based on the fair market value on the date of the gift. If there is a mortgage on the property, the value must be reduced by the amount of the debt.

✓ **Life insurance.** The owner of a life insurance policy may choose to give it to a charitable organization. The gift will produce a tax deduction equal to one of several amounts. The deduction may equal the cash surrender value of the policy, its replacement value, its tax basis or its "interpolated terminal reserve" value (a value slightly more than cash surrender value). The deduction cannot exceed the donor's tax basis in the policy.

✓ **Bargain sale.** A bargain sale is part donation and part sale. It is a sale of property in which the amount of the sale proceeds is less than the property's fair market value. The excess of the fair market value of the property over the sale's price represents a charitable contribution to the organization. Generally each part of a bargain sale is a reportable event so the donor reports both a sale and a contribution.

✓ **Remainder interest in a personal residence or life estate.** A charitable contribution of the remainder interest in a personal residence (including a vacation home) or farm creates an income tax deduction equal to the present value of that future interest.

✓ **Charitable gift annuity.** With a charitable gift annuity, the donor purchases an annuity contract from a charitable organization for more than its fair value. This difference in values between what the donor could have obtained and what the donor actually obtained represents a charitable contribution. The contribution is tax-deductible in the year the donor purchases the annuity.

✓ **Deferred charitable gift annuity.** A deferred gift annuity is similar to an immediate payment annuity except that the annuity payments begin at a future date. This date is determined by the donor at the time of the gift.

Irrevocable gifts in trust

✓ **Charitable remainder annuity trust.** With an annuity trust, the donor retains the right to a specified annuity amount for a fixed period or the lifetime of the designated income beneficiary. The donor fixes the amount payable by an annuity trust at the inception of the trust.

✓ **Charitable remainder unitrust.** The unitrust and annuity trust are very similar with an important difference—the determination of the payment amount. The unitrust payout rate is applied to the fair market value of the net trust assets, determined annually, to establish the distributable amount each year.

✓ **Charitable lead trust.** The charitable lead trust is the reverse of the charitable remainder trust. The donor transfers property into a trust, creating an income interest in the property in favor of the charitable organization for a period of years or for the life or lives of an individual or individuals. The remainder interest is either returned to the donor or given to a noncharitable beneficiary (usually a family member).

✓ **Pooled income fund.** A pooled income fund consists of separate contributions of property from numerous donors. A pooled income fund's payout to its income beneficiaries is not a fixed percentage. The rate of return that the fund earns each year determines the annual payout.

Revocable gifts

✓ **Trust savings accounts.** A trust savings account may be established at a bank, credit union, or savings and loan. The account is placed in the name of the depositor "in trust for" a beneficiary, a person, or organization other than the depositor.

   The depositor retains full ownership and control of the account. The beneficiary receives the money in the account either when the depositor dies, or when the depositor turns over the passbook.

✓ **Insurance and retirement plan proceeds.** A nonprofit organization may be named the beneficiary of an insurance policy or retirement plan. The owner of the policy or retirement plan completes a form naming the nonprofit as the beneficiary, and the company accepts the form in writing. The gift may be for part or all the proceeds.

✓ **Bequests.** By a specific bequest, an individual may direct that, at death, a charity shall receive either a specified dollar amount or specific property. Through a residuary bequest, an individual may give to charity the estate portion remaining after the payment of other bequests, debts, taxes, and expenses.

Charitable Gift Timing

   When donors make gifts near the end of the year, the question often arises: "Is my gift deductible this year?" A donor's charitable deduction, assuming deductions are itemized, depends on various factors:

✓ **Checks.** A donation by check is considered made on the date the check is delivered or mailed, as evidenced by its postmark, if the check subsequently clears the donor's bank in due course. That means a check that's mailed with a December 31 postmark and promptly deposited by the charity will be deductible by the donor in the year the check is written, even though the check clears the bank the following year. However, a postdated check is not deductible until the day of its date.

Example 1: Donor mails a check with a postmark of December 31, 1998. The charity does not receive the check until January 7, 1999. The charity deposits the check in its bank on January 7 and it clears the donor's bank on January 10. The gift is deductible by the donor in 1998.

Example 2: Donor delivers a check to the charity on December 31, 1998. The donor asks that the check be held for three months. Complying with the donor's request, the charity deposits the check on March 31, 1999. This gift is deductible by the donor in 1999.

Example 3: Donor delivers a check to the charity on January 5, 1999. The check is dated December 31, 1998. The gift is deductible by the donor in 1999.

✓ **Credit cards.** A contribution charged to a bank credit card is deductible by the donor when the charge is made, even though the donor does not pay the credit card charge until the next year.

✓ **Cyber gifts.** Donors can instruct their banks via phone or computer to pay contributions to your charity. If a donor uses this method to make a donation, it's deductible at the time payment is made by the bank.

✓ **Pledges.** A pledge is not deductible until payment or other satisfaction of the pledge is made.

✓ **Securities.** A contribution of stock is completed upon the unconditional delivery of a properly endorsed stock certificate to your charity or its agent. If the stock is mailed and is received by the charity or its agent in the ordinary course of the mail, the gift is effective on the date of mailing. If the donor delivers a stock certificate to the issuing corporation or to the donor's broker for transfer to the name of the charity, the contribution is not completed until the stock is actually transferred on the corporation's books.

✓ **Real estate.** A gift of real estate is deductible at the time a properly executed deed is delivered to the charity.

Charitable Contribution Acknowledgments

Contributors to your charity seeking a federal income tax charitable contribution deduction must produce, if asked, a written receipt from the charity if a single contribution's value if $250 or more.

Strictly speaking, the burden of compliance with the $250 or more rule falls on the donor. In reality, the burden and administrative costs fall on the charity, not the donor.

The IRS can fine a charity that deliberately issues a false acknowledgement to a contributor. The fine is up to $1,000 if the donor is an individual and $10,000 if the donor is a corporation.

A donor will not be allowed a charitable deduction for donations of $250 or more unless the donor has a receipt from your charity. This applies to any type of donation. For a single donation of $250 or more made by check, the cancelled check is not adequate substantiation

If a donor makes multiple contributions of $250 or more to one charity, one acknowledgment that reflects the total amount of the donor's contributions to the charity for the year is sufficient. In other words, the charity can total all of the contributions for a donor and only show the total amount on the receipt.

 Information to be included in the receipt. The following information must be included in the gift receipt:

- the donor's name,
- if cash, the amount of cash contributed,
- if property, a description, but not the value, of the property,
- a statement explaining whether the church provided any goods or services to the donor in exchange for the contribution,
- if goods or services were provided to the donor, a description and good-faith estimate of their value and a statement that the donor's charitable deduction is limited to the amount of the payment in excess of the value of the goods and services provided, and if services were provided consisting solely of intangible religious benefits, a statement to that effect,
- the date the donation was made (except for out-of-pocket expenses, see below), and,
- the date the receipt was issued.

 When receipts should be issued. Donors must obtain their receipts no later than the earlier of the due date, plus any extension, of their income tax returns or the date the return is filed. If a donor receives the receipt after this date, the gift does not qualify for a contribution deduction even on an amended return.

If your charity is issuing receipts on an annual basis, you should try to get them to your donors by at least January 31 each year and earlier in January if possible. This will assist your donors in gathering the necessary data for tax return preparation.

 Frequency of issuing receipts. The receipts or acknowledgements can be issued gift-by-gift, monthly, quarterly, annually, or any other frequency. For ease of administration, many charities provide a receipt for all gifts, whether over or under $250.

Sample Charitable Gift Receipt

Received from: Jackie J. Burns

Cash received as an absolute gift:
Received on March 6, 1998 $300.00

Property received described as follows:
Received on May 1, 1998, one 1994 Honda Civic, 4-door sedan LX, automatic transmission, 64,231 miles, vehicle ID #1BFHP53L2NH440968.
(*Note:* No value is shown for the property. Valuation of property is the responsibility of the donor.)

Any goods or services you may have received in connection with this gift were solely intangible religious benefits. (*Note:* It is very important for a religious organization to use wording of this nature when no goods or services were given in exchange for the gift.)

This document is necessary for any available federal income tax deduction for your contribution. Please retain it for your records.

Receipt issued on: January 31, 1999
Receipt issued by: Harold Morrison, Treasurer
                       Castleview Church
                       1008 High Drive
                       Dover, DE 19901

Note: 1. This sample receipt is based on the following assumptions:
    A. No goods or services were provided in exchange for the gift(s) other than intangible religious benefits.
    B. The receipt is issued for a single gift (versus one receipt for multiple gifts).
2. Receipts should be numbered consecutively for control and accounting purposes.

Sample Charitable Gift Receipt

Received from: Howard K. Auburn

Cash received as an absolute gift:

Date Cash Received	Amount Received
1/2/98	$250.00
1/16/98	50.00
3/13/98	300.00
3/27/98	100.00
6/12/98	500.00
7/10/98	150.00
8/21/98	200.00
10/16/98	400.00
11/20/98	350.00
	$2,300.00

Property received described as follows:

Received on May 1, 1998, one 1994 Honda Civic, 4-door sedan LX, automatic transmission, 64,231 miles, vehicle ID# IBFHP53L2NH440968. (*Note:* No value is shown for the property. Valuation of property is the responsibility of the donor.)

Any goods or services you may have received in connection with this gift were solely intangible religious benefits. (*Note:* It is very important for a religious organization to use wording of this nature when no goods or services were given in exchange for the gift.)

This document is necessary for any available federal income tax deduction for your contribution. Please retain it for your records.

Receipt issued on: January 10, 1999
Receipt issued by: Harold Morrison, Treasurer
Castleview Church
1008 High Drive
Dover, DE 19901

Note: 1. This sample receipt is based on the following assumptions:
  A. No goods or services were provided in exchange for the gifts other than intangible religious benefits.
  B. The receipt is issued on a periodic or annual basis for all gifts whether over or under $250.
2. Receipts should be numbered consecutively for control and accounting purposes.

✓ **Form of receipts.** No specific design of the receipt is required. The IRS has not issued any sample receipts to follow.

The receipt can be a letter, a postcard, or a computer-generated form. It does not have to include the donor's social security number or other taxpayer identification number.

✓ **Separate gifts of less than $250.** If a donor makes separate gifts during a calendar year of less than $250, there is no receipting requirement since each gift is a separate contribution. The donor's cancelled check will provide sufficient substantiation. However, most charities receipt all gifts with no distinction between the gifts under or over $250.

✓ **Donations payable to another charity.** A church member may place a check in the offering plate of $250 or more payable to a mission organization designed for the support of a particular missionary serving with the mission. In this instance, no reporting is required by your church. Since the check was payable to the mission agency, that entity will need to issue the acknowledgment to entitle the donor to claim the gift as a charitable contribution.

✓ **Donations in support of a missionary.** Donations may be received, payable to your church, for the support of a particular missionary. These gifts generally qualify for a charitable deduction and the church should include the amounts in acknowledgments issued to donors. However, the funds should be remitted to the missionary-sending organization for their disbursement in relation to the individual missionary.

✓ **Donor's out-of-pocket expenses.** You may have volunteers that incur out-of-pocket expenses on behalf of your church. Substantiation from your charity is required if a volunteer claims a deduction for unreimbursed expenses of $250 or more. However, the IRS acknowledges that you may be unaware of the details of the expenses or the dates on which they were incurred. Therefore, the charity must substantiate only types of services performed by the volunteer.

✓ **Individuals.** Gifts made to poor or needy individuals ordinarily do not qualify as charitable contributions. Gifts made personally to employees of a charity are not charitable contributions.

✓ **Foreign organizations.** Donations must be made to domestic organizations to qualify for a charitable deduction.

Example 1: A gift made directly to a missionary group organized and operating in Israel does not qualify for a charitable deduction.

Example 2: A gift to a U.S.-based missionary organization with a

Sample Letter to Noncash Donors

Charitable Gift Receipt
(Receipts should be numbered consecutively for control and accounting purposes.)
RETAIN FOR INCOME TAX PURPOSES

Donor's Name
Address

Thank you for your noncash gift as follows:
    Date of gift:
    Description of gift:
    (*Note:* No value is shown for the gift. Valuation is the responsibility of the donor.)

To substantiate your gift for IRS purposes, the tax law requires that this acknowledgment state whether you have received any goods or services in exchange for the gift. You have received no goods or services. (Note: If goods or services were provided to the donor, replace the previous sentence with: In return for your contribution, you have received the following goods or services __(description)__ which we value at __(good-faith estimate)__. The value of the goods and services you received must be deducted from the value of your contribution to determine your charitable deduction.)

You must follow the IRS's reporting rules to assure your charitable deduction. We have enclosed a copy of IRS Form 8283 (Noncash Charitable Contributions) and its instructions.

If your noncash gifts for the year total more than $500, you must include Form 8283 with your income tax return. Section A is used to report gifts valued at $5,000 or under. You can complete Section A on your own. When the value of the gift is more than $5,000, you will need to have the property appraised. The appraiser's findings are reported in Section B of Form 8283. The rules also apply if you give "similar items of property" with a total value above $5,000—even if you gave the items to different charities. Section B of Form 8283 must be signed by the appraiser. As the donee, we have already signed the form. It is essential to attach the form to your tax return.

You might want an appraisal (even if your gift does not require one) in case you have to convince the IRS of the property's worth. You never need an appraisal or an appraisal summary for gifts of publicly traded securities, even if their total value exceeds $5,000. You must report those gifts (when the value is more than $500) by completing Section A of Form 8283 and attaching it to your return.

For gifts of closely held stock, an appraisal is not required if the value of the stock is under $10,000, but part of the appraisal summary form must be completed if the value is over $5,000. If the gift is valued over $10,000, then both an appraisal and an appraisal summary form are required.

If we receive a gift of property subject to the appraisal summary rules, we must report to both the IRS and you if we dispose of the gift within two years. We do not have to notify the IRS or you if we dispose of a gift that did not require an appraisal summary.

Again, we are grateful for your generous contribution. Please let us know if we can give you and your advisors more information about the IRS's reporting requirements.

      Your Nonprofit Organization

designation that the funds be used for mission work in China may qualify for a charitable deduction.

✓ **Contingencies.** If a contribution will not be effective until the occurrence of a certain event, an income tax charitable deduction generally is not allowable until the occurrence of the event.

Example: A donor makes a gift to a college to fund a new education program that the college does not presently offer and is not contemplating. The donation would not be deductible until the college agrees to the conditions of the gift.

✓ **Charitable remainders in personal residences and farms.** The final charitable gift regulations are silent on the substantiation rules for remainder interests in personal residences and farms. It should be assumed that the $250 substantiation rules apply to those gifts unless the IRS provides other guidance.

✓ **Charitable trusts.** The $250 substantiation rules do not apply to charitable remainder annuity trusts, charitable remainder unitrusts, and charitable lead trusts.

✓ **Gift annuities.** When the gift portion of a gift annuity or a deferred payment gift annuity is $250 or more, a donor must have an acknowledgment from the charity stating whether any goods or services—in addition to the annuity—were provided to the donor. If no goods or services were provided, the acknowledgment must so state. The acknowledgment need not include a good faith estimate of the annuity's value.

✓ **Pooled income funds.** The substantiation rules apply to pooled income funds. To deduct a gift of a remainder interest of $250 or more, a donor must have an acknowledgment from the charity.

Gifts That May Not Qualify as Contributions

Some types of gifts do not result in a tax deduction and no contribution acknowledgment should be provided by the church:

✓ **Beyond due diligence.** Some donors to your charity may want to make sure their gifts are put to good use. As long as your charity clearly owns the gift, and the donor and charity agree that it will further the charity's purposes, the IRS approves. But they draw the line when the donor demands too much control, intending to benefit a private class of people rather than the public at large. For example, a gift made to a church with the requirement that the funds be used to provide scholarships to students from the church with the donor's last name. The IRS would undoubtedly reject an income tax deduction for this type of gift.

✓ **Passing gifts through to pastors or other employees.** A church member may donate a car, a personal computer, or some other asset and specify that the property be given to one of the church pastors. The member expects a charitable contribution receipt and wants the pastor to have the gift without incurring any taxes on the gift. Should the church accept the gift and what are the consequences of the gift?

Before accepting such a gift, the church must determine if it can exercise adequate control over the gift and if the specified use of the gift would result in appropriate compensation for services rendered to the church. If the church does not feel comfortable with these issues, the gift should be declined. If the church feels that it can properly accept the gift, the fair market value of the assets distributed to staff members must be included on Form W-2.

✓ **Strings attached.** A gift must generally be complete and irrevocable to qualify for a charitable deduction. There is usually no gift if the donor leaves "strings attached" that can be pulled later to bring the gift back to the donor or remove it from the control of the church.

Example: A donor makes a "gift" of $10,000 to a church. The "gift" is followed or preceded by the sale from the church to the donor of an asset valued at $25,000 for $15,000. In this instance, the $10,000 gift does not qualify as a charitable contribution. It also raises the issue of private inurement relating to the sale by the church.

✓ **Services.** No deduction is allowed for the contribution of services to a church.

Example: A carpenter donates two months of labor on the construction of a new facility built by your church. The carpenter is not eligible for a charitable deduction for the donation of his time. The carpenter is entitled to a charitable deduction for any out-of-pocket expenses including mileage (14 cents per mile for 1998) for driving to and from the project. If out-of-pocket expenses are $250 or more in a calendar year, the carpenter will need an acknowledgment from the church. See the out-of-pocket discussion later.

✓ **Use of property.** The gift to a church of the right to use property does not yield a tax deduction to the donor.

Example: A donor provides a church with the rent-free use of an automobile for a year. There is no charitable deduction available to the donor for the value of that use. If the donor paid the taxes, insurance, repairs, gas or oil for the vehicle while it is used by the church, these items are deductible as a charitable contribution based on their cost.

Reporting to the IRS

Most gifts do not require any reporting by the charity to the IRS. However, some gifts do require IRS reporting, or execution of a form that the donor files with the IRS and the rules are complicated:

✓ **Gifts of property in excess of $5,000.** Substantiation requirements apply to contributions of property (other than money and publicly traded securities), if the total claimed or reported value of the property is more than $5,000. For these gifts, the donor must obtain a qualified appraisal and attach an appraisal summary to the return on which the deduction is claimed. There is an exception for nonpublicly traded stock. If the claimed value of the stock does not exceed $10,000 but is greater than $5,000, the donor does not have to obtain an appraisal by a qualified appraiser.

The appraisal summary must be on Form 8283, signed and dated by the charity and the appraiser, and attached to the donor's return on which a deduction is claimed. The signature by the charity does not represent concurrence in the appraised value of the contributed property.

If Form 8283 is required, it is the donor's responsibility to file it. The charity is under no responsibility to see that donors file this form nor that it is properly completed. However, advising donors of their obligations and providing them with the form can produce donor goodwill.

✓ **Gifts of property in excess of $500.** Gifts of property valued at $500 or more require the completion of certain information on page one of Form 8283. For gifts between $500 and $5,000 in value, there is not a requirement of an appraisal or signature of the charity.

✓ **Charity reporting for contributed property.** If property received as a charitable contribution requiring an appraisal summary on Form 8283 is sold, exchanged, or otherwise disposed of by the charity within two years after the date of its contribution, the charity must file Form 8282 with the IRS within 125 days of the disposition.

This form provides detailed information on the gift and the disposal of the property. A copy of this information return must be provided to the donor and retained by the charity. A charity that receives a charitable contribution valued at more than $5,000 from a corporation generally does not have to file Form 8283.

A letter or other written communication from a charity acknowledging receipt of the property and showing the name of the donor, the date and location of the contribution, and a detailed description of the property is an

Form **8282**
(Rev. September 1995)
Department of the Treasury
Internal Revenue Service

Donee Information Return

(Sale, Exchange, or Other Disposition of Donated Property)
▶ See instructions on back.

OMB No. 1545-0908

Give Copy to Donor

Please Print or Type

Name of charitable organization (donee)
Oneonta First Church

Employer identification number
35-4829942

Address (number, street, and room or suite no.)
292 River Street

City or town, state, and ZIP code
Oneonta, NY 13820

Part I Information on ORIGINAL DONOR and DONEE Receiving the Property

1a Name(s) of the original donor of the property
Keith E. Chapman

1b Identifying number
512-40-8076

Note: Complete lines 2a-2d only if you gave this property to another charitable organization (successor donee).

2a Name of charitable organization

2b Employer identification number

2c Address (number, street, and room or suite no.)

2d City or town, state, and ZIP code

Note: If you are the original donee, skip Part II and go to Part III now.

Part II Information on PREVIOUS DONEES - Complete this part only if you were not the first donee to receive the property.
If you were the second donee, leave lines 4a-4d blank. If you were a third or later donee, complete lines 3a-4d.
On lines 4a-4d, give information on the preceding donee (the one who gave you the property).

3a Name of original donee

3b Employer identification number

3c Address (number, street, and room or suite no.)

3d City or town, state, and ZIP code

4a Name of preceding donee

4b Employer identification number

4c Address (number, street, and room or suite no.)

4d City or town, state, and ZIP code

Part III Information on DONATED PROPERTY - If you are the original donee, leave column (c) blank.

(a) Description of donated property sold, exchanged, or otherwise disposed of (if you need more space, attach a separate statement)	(b) Date you received the item(s)	(c) Date the first donee received the item(s)	(d) Date item(s) sold, exchanged, or otherwise disposed of	(e) Amount received upon disposition	
Real estate/vacant lot, 82 White Street, Oneonta, NY	9/4/98		11/10/99	3780	

For Paperwork Reduction Act Notice, see instructions on back.

Form **8282** (Rev. 9-95)

Note: The donee must file this form with the IRS if property received as a charitable contribution is sold, exchanged, or otherwise disposed of within two years after the date of its contribution.

Form **8283**
(Rev. October 1995)

Department of the Treasury
Internal Revenue Service

Noncash Charitable Contributions

▶ Attach to your tax return if you claimed a total deduction
of over $500 for all contributed property.

▶ See separate instructions.

OMB No. 1545-0908

Attachment
Sequence No. **55**

Name(s) shown on your income tax return
Mark A. and Joan E. Murphy

Identifying number
392-83-1982

Note: *Figure the amount of your contribution deduction before completing this form. See your tax return instructions.*

Section A—List in this section **only** items (or groups of similar items) for which you claimed a deduction of $5,000 or less. Also, list certain publicly traded securities even if the deduction is over $5,000 (see instructions).

Information on Donated Property—If you need more space, attach a statement.

1	(a) Name and address of the donee organization	(b) Description of donated property
A	Endless Mountain Church, 561 Maple, Rochester, NY 14623	Used bedroom furniture
B		
C		
D		
E		

Note: *If the amount you claimed as a deduction for an item is $500 or less, you do not have to complete columns (d), (e), and (f).*

	(c) Date of the contribution	(d) Date acquired by donor (mo., yr.)	(e) How acquired by donor	(f) Donor's cost or adjusted basis	(g) Fair market value	(h) Method used to determine the fair market value
A	10/1/99	6/91	Purchased	3,400	750	Sale of comparable used furniture
B						
C						
D						
E						

Other Information—Complete line 2 if you gave less than an entire interest in property listed in Part I. Complete line 3 if restrictions were attached to a contribution listed in Part I.

2 If, during the year, you contributed less than the entire interest in the property, complete lines a – e.

a Enter the letter from Part I that identifies the property ▶ _____ . If Part II applies to more than one property, attach a separate statement.

b Total amount claimed as a deduction for the property listed in Part I: **(1)** For this tax year ▶ _____
(2) For any prior tax years ▶ _____ .

c Name and address of each organization to which any such contribution was made in a prior year (complete only if different than the donee organization above):

Name of charitable organization (donee)

Address (number, street, and room or suite no.)

City or town, state, and ZIP code

d For tangible property, enter the place where the property is located or kept ▶ _____

e Name of any person, other than the donee organization, having actual possession of the property ▶ _____

3 If conditions were attached to any contribution listed in Part I, answer questions a – c and attach the required statement (see instructions).

		Yes	No
a	Is there a restriction, either temporary or permanent, on the donee's right to use or dispose of the donated property?		
b	Did you give to anyone (other than the donee organization or another organization participating with the donee organization in cooperative fundraising) the right to the income from the donated property or to the possession of the property, including the right to vote donated securities, to acquire the property by purchase or otherwise, or to designate the person having such income, possession, or right to acquire?		
c	Is there a restriction limiting the donated property for a particular use?		

For Paperwork Reduction Act Notice, see separate instructions.

Cat. No. 62299J

Form **8283** (Rev. 10-95)

Note: This form must be completed and filed with the donor's income tax return for gifts of property valued at $500 or more.

There is no requirement of an appraisal or signature of the donee organization for gifts valued between $500 and $5,000.

Form 8283 (Rev. 10-95)   Page **2**

Name(s) shown on your income tax return

Mark A. and Joan E. Murphy

Identifying number
392-83-1982

Section B—Appraisal Summary—List in this section only items (or groups of similar items) for which you claimed a deduction of more than $5,000 per item or group. **Exception.** Report contributions of certain publicly traded securities only in Section A.

If you donated art, you may have to attach the complete appraisal. See the **Note** in Part I below.

Information on Donated Property—To be completed by the taxpayer and/or appraiser.

4 Check type of property:

☐ Art* (contribution of $20,000 or more)   ☒ Real Estate   ☐ Gems/Jewelry   ☐ Stamp Collections

☐ Art* (contribution of less than $20,000)   ☐ Coin Collections   ☐ Books   ☐ Other

*Art includes paintings, sculptures, watercolors, prints, drawings, ceramics, antique furniture, decorative arts, textiles, carpets, silver, rare manuscripts, historical memorabilia, and other similar objects.

Note: If your total art contribution deduction was $20,000 or more, you must attach a complete copy of the signed appraisal. See instructions.

5	(a) Description of donated property (if you need more space, attach a separate statement)	(b) If tangible property was donated, give a brief summary of the overall physical condition at the time of the gift	(c) Appraised fair market value
A	Residence and two lots:	Good repair	42,500
B	2080 Long Pond Road		
C	Syracuse, New York		
D			

	(d) Date acquired by donor (mo., yr.)	(e) How acquired by donor	(f) Donor's cost or adjusted basis	(g) For bargain sales, enter amount received	(h) Amount claimed as a deduction	(i) Average trading price of securities
A	7/20/91	Purchased	36,900		42,500	
B						
C						
D						

Taxpayer (Donor) Statement—List each item included in Part I above that is separately identified in the appraisal as having a value of $500 or less. See instructions.

I declare that the following item(s) included in Part I above has to the best of my knowledge and belief an appraised value of not more than $500 (per item). Enter identifying letter from Part I and describe the specific item. See instructions. ▶ _____

Signature of taxpayer (donor) ▶   Date ▶

Declaration of Appraiser

I declare that I am not the donor, the donee, a party to the transaction in which the donor acquired the property, employed by, or related to any of the foregoing persons, or married to any person who is related to any of the foregoing persons. And, if regularly used by the donor, donee, or party to the transaction, I performed the majority of my appraisals during my tax year for other persons.

Also, I declare that I hold myself out to the public as an appraiser or perform appraisals on a regular basis; and that because of my qualifications as described in the appraisal, I am qualified to make appraisals of the type of property being valued. I certify that the appraisal fees were not based on a percentage of the appraised property value. Furthermore, I understand that a false or fraudulent overstatement of the property value as described in the qualified appraisal or this appraisal summary may subject me to the penalty under section 6701(a) (aiding and abetting the understatement of tax liability). I affirm that I have not been barred from presenting evidence or testimony by the Director of Practice.

Sign Here   Signature ▶ *Andrew J. Noble*   Title ▶ **President**   Date of appraisal ▶ **9/15/99**

Business address (including room or suite no.)
1100 North Adams Street

Identifying number
541-90-9796

City or town, state, and ZIP code
Elmira, NY 14904

Donee Acknowledgment—To be completed by the charitable organization.

This charitable organization acknowledges that it is a qualified organization under section 170(c) and that it received the donated property as described in Section B, Part I, above on ▶ _____ **9/25/99** _____
                                                                                          (Date)

Furthermore, this organization affirms that in the event it sells, exchanges, or otherwise disposes of the property described in Section B, Part I (or any portion thereof) within 2 years after the date of receipt, it will file **Form 8282**, Donee Information Return, with the IRS and give the donor a copy of that form. This acknowledgment does not represent agreement with the claimed fair market value.

Name of charitable organization (donee)	Employer identification number
Fairlawn Heights Church	**35-4029876**

Address (number, street, and room or suite no.)	City or town, state, and ZIP code
P.O. Box 829	**Oswego, NY 13126**

Authorized signature	Title	Date
James A. Black	**Executive Pastor**	**10/31/99**

✳ *Printed on recycled paper*

149

acceptable contribution receipt for a gift of property.

There is no requirement to include the value of contributed property on the receipt. Most charities are not prepared to value gifts of property. A tension often surrounds a significant gift of property because the donor may request the charity to include an excessively high value on the charitable receipt. It is wise for the charity to remain impartial in the matter and simply acknowledge the property by description with the exclusion of a dollar amount.

Example 1: A charity receives the gift of an automobile. The charitable contribution receipt should reflect the make, model, vehicle number, options, mileage, and condition with no indication of dollar value.

Example 2: A charity receives a gift of real estate. The receipt should include the legal description of the real property and a description of the improvements with no indication of the dollar value.

Quid Pro Quo Disclosure Requirements

A quid pro quo contribution is a payment made partly as a contribution and partly for goods or services provided to the donor by the charity. A donor may deduct only the amount of the contribution above what the goods or services are worth.

The charity is required to provide a receipt for all transactions where the donor makes a payment of more than $75 to the charity and receives goods or services (other than intangible religious benefits or items of token value).

Form of the receipt

The receipt must

✓ inform the donor that the amount of the contribution that is deductible for federal income tax purposes is limited to the excess of the amount of any money and the value of any property other than money contributed by the donor *over* the value of the goods or services provided by the organization, and

✓ provide the donor with a good-faith estimate of the value of goods or services that the charity is providing in exchange for the contribution.

Only single payments of more than $75 are subject to the rules. Payments are not cumulative. It is not a difference of $75 between the amount given by the donor and the value of the object received by the donor that triggers the disclosure requirements, but the amount actually paid by the donor.

Calculating the gift portion

It is not a requirement for the donee organization to actually complete the subtraction of the benefit from a cash payment, showing the net charitable deduction. However, providing the net amount available for a charitable deduction is a good approach for clear communication with your donors.

When to make the required disclosures

The disclosure of the value of goods or services provided to a donor may be made in the donor solicitation as well as in the subsequent receipt. However, sufficient information will generally not be available to make proper disclosure upon solicitation. For example, the value of a dinner may not be known at the time the solicitation is made.

Goods provided to donors

A gift must be reduced by the fair market value of any premium, incentive, or other benefit received by the donor in exchange for the gift to determine the net charitable contribution. Common examples of premiums are books, tapes, and Bibles. Organizations must advise the donor of the fair market value of the premium or incentive and that the value is not deductible for tax purposes.

Donors must reduce their charitable deduction by the fair market value of goods or services they receive even when the goods or services were donated to the charity for use as premiums or gifts or when they were bought by the charity at wholesale. Therefore, charities cannot pass along to donors the savings realized by receiving products at no cost or buying products at a discount.

If donors receive benefits of insubstantial value, they are allowed a full tax deduction for the donation:

✓ **Low-cost items.** If an item has a cost (not retail value) of less than $7.10 and an item that bears the name or logo of your organization is given in return for a donation of more than $35.50 (1998 inflation-adjusted amount), the donor may claim a charitable deduction for the full amount of the donation. Examples of items that often qualify as tokens are coffee mugs, key chains, bookmarks, and calendars.

✓ **De minimis benefits.** A donor can take a full deduction if the fair market value of the benefits received in connection with a gift does not exceed 2% of the donation or $71.00 (1998 inflation-adjusted amount), whichever is less.

Examples of the quid pro quo rules

Here are various examples of how the quid pro quo rules apply:

✓ **Admission to events.** Many organizations sponsor banquets, concerts, or other events to which donors and prospective donors are invited in exchange for a contribution or other payment. Often, the donor receives a benefit equivalent to the payment and there is no charitable deduction available.

151

But if the amount paid is more than the value received, the amount in excess of the fair market value is deductible if there was intent to make a contribution.

✓ **Auctions.** The IRS generally takes the position that the fair market value of an item purchased at a charity auction is set by the bidders. The winning bidder, therefore, cannot pay more than the item is worth. That means there is no charitable contribution in the IRS's eyes, no deduction, and no need for the charity to provide any charitable gift substantiation document to the bidder.

However, many tax professionals take the position that when the payment (the purchase price) exceeds the fair market value of the items, the amount that exceeds the fair market value is deductible as a charitable contribution. This position also creates a reporting requirement under the quid pro quo rules. Most charities set the value of every object sold and provide receipts to buyers.

Example: Your church youth group auctions goods to raise funds for a mission trip. An individual bought a quilt for $200. The church takes the position that the quilt had a fair market value of $50 even though the bidder paid $200. Since the payment of $200 exceeded the $75 limit, the church is required to provide a written statement indicating that only $150 of the $200 payment is eligible for a charitable contribution.

✓ **Bazaars.** Payments for items sold at bazaars and bake sales are not tax deductible to donors since the purchase price generally equals the fair market value of the item.

✓ **Banquets.** Whether your organization incurs reporting requirements in connection with banquets where funds are raised depends on the specifics of each event.

Example 1: Your church sponsors a banquet for missions charging $50 per person. The meal costs the church $15 per person. There is no disclosure requirement since the amount charged was less than $75. However, the amount deductible by each donor is only $35.

Example 2: Your church invites individuals to attend a missions banquet without charge. Attendees are invited to make contributions or pledges at the end of the banquet. These payments probably do not require disclosure even if the amount given is $75 or more because there is only an indirect relationship between the meal and the gift.

✓ **Deduction timing.** Goods or services received in consideration for a donor's payment include goods and services received in a different year. Thus, a donor's deduction for the year of the payment is limited to the amount, if any, by which the payment exceeds the value of the goods and services.

✓ **Good faith estimates.** A donor is not required to use the estimate provided by

Charitable Contribution Substantiation Requirements

	Not more than $75	Over $75 and under $250	At least $250 and under $500	At least $500 and under $5,000	$5,000 and over
Canceled check acceptable for donor's deduction?	Yes	Yes	No	No	No
Contribution receipt required for deduction?	No	No	Yes	Yes	Yes
Charity's statement on donor's receipt of goods or services required?	No	Yes*	Yes*	Yes*	Yes*

*May be avoided if the charity meets the low-cost items or de minimis benefits exceptions described on page 151.

a donee organization in calculating the deductible amount. When a taxpayer knows or has reason to know that an estimate is inaccurate, the taxpayer may not treat the donee organization's estimate as the fair market value.

✓ **Rights of refusal.** A donor can claim a full deduction if he or she refuses a benefit from the charity. However, this must be done affirmatively. Simply not taking advantage of a benefit is not enough. For example, a donor who chooses not to make use of tickets that you made available by your organization must deduct the value of the tickets from his or her contribution before claiming a deduction. However, a donor who rejects the right to a benefit at the time the contribution is made (e.g., by checking off a refusal box on a form supplied by your charity) can take a full deduction.

✓ **Sale of products or a service at fair market value.** When an individual purchases products or receives services at fair market value, no part of the payment is a gift.

Example 1: An individual purchases tapes of a series of Sunday morning worship services for $80. The sales price represents fair market value. Even though the amount paid exceeds the $75 threshold, the church is not required to provide a disclosure statement to the purchaser.

Example 2: The Brown family uses the fellowship hall of the church for a family reunion. The normal rental fee is $300. The Browns give a check to the church for $300 marked "Contribution." No

153

Sample Charitable Gift Receipt

Received from: Nancy L. Wilson

Cash received:
        Received on April 1, 1998 $100.00

Property received on June 30, 1998 and is described as follows:
        (*Note:* If property was given instead of cash or check, describe the
        property here. No value is shown for the property. Valuation of
        property is the responsibility of the donor.)

In return for your gift described above, we provided you with a study Bible with an estimated value of $30.00. *(Note: Insert the description of goods and/or services provided in exchange for the gift.)* You may have also received goods or services consisting solely of intangible benefits, but these benefits do not need to be valued for tax purposes.

The deductible portion of your contribution for federal income tax purposes is limited to the excess of your contribution over the value of goods and services we provided to you. The $30.00 value of benefits you received must be sub-tracted from your cash contribution (or the value of the property you donated) to determine your net charitable contribution. *(Note: For receipting purposes, do not calculate the net contribution for gifts of property to the charity because the charity does not place a value on the property received.)*

This document is necessary for any available federal income tax deduction for your contribution. Please retain it for your records.

Receipt issued on: January 10, 1999
Receipt issued by: Harold Morrison, Treasurer
                          Castleview Church
                          1008 High Drive
                          Dover, DE 19901

Note: 1. The receipt is issued for a single gift (versus one receipt for multiple gifts).
        2. Receipts should be numbered consecutively for control and accounting purposes.

Sample Charitable Gift Receipt

Received from: Charles K. Vandell

Cash received as an absolute gift:

Date Cash Received	Gross Amount Received	Value of Goods or Services	Net Charitable Contribution
1/23/98	$80.00	$25.00 [1]	$ 55.00
3/20/98	300.00		300.00
4/24/98	60.00		60.00
6/19/98	500.00	100.00 [2]	400.00
9/04/98	275.00		275.00
10/30/98	200.00		200.00
12/18/98	1,000.00		1,000.00
			$2,900.00

Property received described as follows:
Received on October 22, 1998, 12 brown Samsonite folding chairs.

In return for certain gifts listed above, we provided you with the following goods or services:

(1) Christian music tapes $25.00
(2) Limited edition art print $100.00

You may have also received goods or services consisting solely of intangible religious benefits, but these benefits do not need to be valued for tax purposes.

The deductible portion of your contribution for federal income tax purposes is limited to the excess of your contribution over the value of goods and services we provided to you.

This document is necessary for any available federal income tax deduction for your contribution. Please retain it for your records.

Receipt issued on: January 15, 1999
Receipt issued by: Harold Morrison, Treasurer
                      Castleview Church
                      1008 High Drive
                      Dover, DE 19901

Note: 1. This sample receipt is based on the following assumptions:
   A. Goods or services were provided in exchange for the gifts.
   B. The receipt is issued on a periodic or annual basis for all gifts whether over or under $250.
2. Receipts should be numbered consecutively for control and accounting purposes.

receipt should be given because no charitable contribution was made.

Example 3: The Brown family uses the church sanctuary and fellow-ship hall for a wedding and the reception. The church does not have a stated use fee but asks for a donation from those who use the facility. The comparable fee to rent similar facilities is $250. The Browns give a check to the church for $250 marked "Contribution." No receipt should be given because no charitable contribution was made.

Example 4: Your church operates a Christian school. The parent of a student at the school writes a check payable to the church for his child's tuition. No receipt should be given because no charitable contribution was made.

Special Charitable Contribution Issues

Gifts of real estate

Gifts of real estate to a charity can bring incredible opportunities and headaches—opportunities because of the potential dollars that may be realized for ministry and headaches because of the administrative effort required to process many of these gifts.

When drafting a real estate gift policy, consider these issues:

✓ **Inspection of the property.** A charity should not accept a gift of real estate without first inspecting the property. A cursory inspection will make sure there are no visible environmental hazards on the property and determine if there are any obvious marketability issues.

✓ **Information about the property.** The prospective donor should provide the following information about the property:
- A survey.
- A legal description.
- The names of any co-owners and their ownership shares.
- A copy of recent tax statements.
- A copy of any recent appraisals.
- Information on any current leases or contracts outstanding on the property.
- A brief description of the current use of the property.

✓ **Debt on the property.** The charity needs to know the details of any debt on the property, and should decide in advance how much debt is acceptable. If the charity assumes a mortgage, it will usually pay unrelated business income tax on the income from either the rental or sale of the property.

✓ **The property's use.** A charity can either use a real estate gift for ministry purposes, hold it for investment, or turn around and sell it. Real property that's not used in connection with your charity's exempt purpose is usually subject to property tax.

✓ **Disposing of the property.** Will it be the charity's policy to sell the property as soon as possible? If so, the charity must have full authority to decide the buyer and the sales price. Too often, donor's have prearranged a sale and expect the property to be immediately sold to the buyer of their choice at a price agreed upon before the donation. This situation places the charity in a very awkward position.

If the sale is prearranged, the IRS may attribute the gain on the sale by the charity to the donor. In this instance, the donor would have to pay tax on the difference between what the donor originally paid for the property and the sales price the charity receives. Also, an immediate resale could fix the value of the donor's gift to an amount lower than the donor would like to claim as a tax deduction.

✓ **Environmental issues.** Avoid property that has signs of environmental problems. Your charity will probably be liable for any clean-up costs—even if the property was contaminated before your charity received it. Your charity should generally not accept gifts of real estate that could result in liability for environmental contamination. It is wise to perform a Level I Environmental Site Assessment before accepting a gift of real estate.

Gifts of inventory

Donors may give some of their business inventory to a charity and ask for a charitable contribution receipt for the retail value of the merchandise. A charity should never provide such a receipt.

Example: Bill owns a lumber yard. The charity is constructing a building and Bill donates some lumber for the project. Bill's company purchased the lumber during his current business year for $10,000. The retail price on the lumber is $17,000 and it would have generated a $7,000 profit if Bill's company sold it. What is the tax impact for Bill's company? Since Bill's company acquired the item in the same business year that the lumber was donated, there is no charitable contribution for his company. The cost of the lumber, $10,000, is deducted as part of the cost of goods sold on the company books.

What is the bottom line of inventory contributions? An inventory item can only be deducted once—there is no contribution deduction and also a deduction as a part of cost of goods sold. The tax benefit to the donor is generally equal to the donor's cost of the items, not their retail value. Acknowledgements issued by a charity for inventory contributions should not state the value of the gift—only the date of the gift and a description of the items donated should be noted.

157

Gifts of church bonds

Individuals who purchase church bonds often keep the bonds for several years and then donate them back to the church. The charitable tax deduction for a gift of bonds is based on the face of the bond plus any accumulated interest on the date of donation. The church should issue a gift acknowledgment that simply identifies the bond(s) donated by bond number and face value.

Gifts of a partial interest

A contribution of less than the donor's entire interest in property is a gift of a partial interest. Generally, there is no charitable deduction for gifts of partial interest in property, including the right to use the property. Gifts of a partial interest which qualify for charitable deductions are

✓ gifts made in qualified trust form (using a so-called "split-interest trust," such as pooled income funds, charitable remainder trusts, and charitable lead trusts),

✓ outright gifts of a future remainder interest (also called a life estate) in a personal residence or farm,

✓ gifts of an undivided portion of one's entire interest in property,

✓ gifts of a lease on, option to purchase, or easement with respect to real property granted in perpetuity to a public charity exclusively for conservation purposes, or

✓ a remainder interest in real property granted to a public charity exclusively for conservation purposes.

Membership fees

Sometimes a membership fee may be partially or fully deductible. If the member receives benefits from the membership, a monetary value must be assigned to the benefits as the nondeductible portion of the payment.

Example 1: An individual pays a $100 membership fee to a nonprofit organization. In exchange, the individual receives publications and admission privileges to certain events. The value of the benefits received approximates the membership amount. Therefore, the membership fee is nondeductible as a charitable contribution.

Example 2: A nonprofit organization solicits funds for a particular program based on membership in a fund-raising "club." The donors do not receive any benefits from the membership. In this instance, membership fees are fully deductible as contributions.

Payments to private schools

Tuition payments to private schools are generally nondeductible since they correspond to value received. The IRS has ruled that payments to private schools are not deductible as charitable contributions

✓ if there is the existence of a contract under which a parent agrees to make a "contribution" and that contains provisions ensuring the admission of the child;

✓ if there is a plan allowing a parent either to pay tuition or to make "contributions" in exchange for schooling;

✓ if there is the earmarking of a contribution for the direct benefit of a particular individual; or

✓ if there is the otherwise unexplained denial of admission or readmission to a school for children of individuals who are financially able, but who do not contribute.

The IRS also will take into consideration other factors to decide deductibility such as

✓ no significant tuition charge;

✓ the parents of children attending a school receive substantial or unusual pressure to contribute;

✓ contribution appeals made as part of the admissions or enrollment process;

✓ no significant potential sources of revenue for operating the school other than contributions by parents or children attending the school; and

✓ other factors suggesting that a contribution policy was created to avoid the characterization of payments as tuition.

Payments to a church that operates a private school

Some churches operate related private schools on a "tuition-free" basis. These churches typically request that families with children in the school increase their contributions by the amount that they would otherwise have paid as tuition.

In reviewing "tuition-free" situations, the IRS often questions the deductibility of gifts to the church if

✔ contributions of several families increased or decreased markedly as the number of their children enrolled in the school changed;

✔ the contributions of parents of students drop off significantly in the summer months when the school is not in session; and

✔ the parents are not required to pay tuition out of their pockets.

Generally, contributions by parents are not deductible as charitable contributions to the extent that the church pays the parent's tuition liabilities.

Contributions to organizations to support specific individual workers

Many charitable organizations raise funds to support the ministry of specific individual workers. The individuals may be missionaries, youth workers, or employees of the organization.

Contributions to support the ministry of specific individual workers of a nonprofit organization may be deductible if

✔ the organization controls and administers the funds following its board-approved policies and procedures, and the work it supports is in the furtherance of its exempt purpose;

✔ the amounts distributed to the recipient missionary/staff members are in salary payments for services rendered for the organization or in payment for business expenses related to the work of the missionary/staff member;

✔ the amounts distributed to the recipient missionary/staff members are properly included for information reporting purposes (such as on Forms W-2 or 1099-MISC); and

✔ the organization clearly distinguishes the funds given to the organization for the support of a missionary/staff member from funds that are nondeductible personal gifts passed on directly to the individual.

Contributions that benefit specific individuals other than staff members and other than the needy

Occasionally individuals give money to a church but request that it be sent to a particular recipient who is not on the staff of the organization, not a missionary related to the organization, and does not qualify as a "needy" individual. When told that this "conduit" role is improper, the donor usually responds, "But I can't get a tax deduction otherwise!" The donor is absolutely correct.

The general rule in a conduit situation is that the donor is making a gift to the ultimate beneficiary. The IRS will look to the ultimate beneficiary to decide whether the gift qualifies for a charitable contribution deduction.

There are certain limited circumstances in which an organization may serve as an intermediary with respect to a gift that will be transferred to another organization or to a specific individual. In such circumstances, it is essential that the organization first receiving the monies have the right to control the ultimate destination of the funds.

Example: Frank Lee makes a gift of $5,000 to Shady Lane Church. Mr. Lee stipulates that the gift must go to a particular music group of which his son is a member. The money will be used to purchase sound equipment. The group will go on tour to present religious music in churches. The group is not an approved ministry of Shady Lane Church. This gift would generally be termed a personal gift to the music group and would not be deductible as a charitable contribution. It is best if the church returns the gift to Mr. Lee. If the church accepts the gift and passes the money on to the music group, the church should advise Mr. Lee that the gift is not deductible and should not provide a charitable receipt.

Donor intent is also a key factor. If the donor intends for a gift to benefit a specific individual instead of supporting the ministry of the charity, the gift is generally not deductible.

Contributions to needy individuals and benevolence funds

Contributions made directly by a donor to needy individuals are not deductible. To qualify for a charitable deduction, contributions must be made to a qualified organization.

Benevolence should be paid from the general fund of an organization. Contributions to benevolence funds may be claimed as charitable deductions if they are not earmarked for particular recipients.

A gift to a charitable organization involved in helping needy people marked "to aid the unemployed" is generally deductible. Yet if the gift is designated or restricted for the "Brown family" and the organization passes the money on to the Browns, the gift is generally not tax-deductible.

If a donor makes a suggestion about the beneficiary of a benevolent contribution, it may be deductible if the recipient organization exercises proper control over the benevolence fund. The suggestion must only be advisory in nature and the charity may accept or reject the gift. However, if every "suggestion" is honored by the organization, the earmarking could be challenged by the IRS.

A church or nonprofit organization may want to help a particular individual or family that has unusually high medical bills or other valid personal financial needs. To announce that funds will be received for the individual or family and receipt the monies through the church or nonprofit organization makes the gifts personal and not deductible as charitable contributions. An option is for the church to set up a trust fund at a local bank. Contributions to the trust fund would not be deductible for tax purposes. Payments from the trust fund would not represent taxable income to a needy individual or family. This method of helping the needy person or family is clearly a legal approach and would represent personal gifts from one individual to another.

Suggested Benevolence Fund Policy

Whereas, New Haven Church has a ministry to needy individuals; and

Whereas, The church desires to establish a Benevolence Fund through which funds for the support of needy individuals may be administered;

Resolved, That New Haven Church establish a Benevolence Fund to help individuals in financial need and will develop written procedures to document the need, establish reasonable limitations of support per person during a specified time period and obtain external verification of the need; and

Resolved, That the church will accept only contributions to the Benevolence Fund that are "to or for the use" of the church and their use must be subject to the control and discretion of the church board. Donors may make suggestions but not designations or restrictions concerning the identity of the needy individuals; and

Resolved, That the church will provide a charitable contribution receipt for gifts that meet the test outlined in the previous resolution. The church reserves the right to return any gifts that do not meet the test.

Payments to retirement homes

The IRS generally treats payments to nonprofit retirement homes and communities (often referred to as "founders' gifts" or "sustainers' gifts") as nondeductible transfers when the payment is made at or near the time of entry.

If the benefit provided by the home is out of proportion to the benefit, the payment is part nondeductible purchase and part deductible contribution. The burden is on the donor to prove that the contribution is not the purchase price of the benefit and that part of the payment does qualify as a contribution.

If an individual pays a tax-exempt retirement home for the right to choose an apartment and live there, the payment is not a deductible charitable gift.

Gifts designated for missionaries

Charitable contributions must be made "to or for the use of" a qualified charitable organization. The IRS has interpreted "for the use of" to mean "in trust for," implying the use of a trust or similar legal arrangement for the benefit of the organization.

Generally, gifts made by an individual directly to a missionary are not deductible as charitable contributions. The funds need to be given to a missionary organization designated for the ministry of a particular missionary to be deductible.

Donated travel and out-of-pocket expenses

Unreimbursed out-of-pocket expenses of a volunteer performing services for a charity are generally deductible. The expenses must be directly connected with and solely attributable to the providing of the volunteer services.

The type of expenses that are deductible include transportation; travel (mileage at 14 cents per mile for 1998), meals, and lodging while away from home if there is no significant element of personal pleasure, recreation, or vacation associated with the travel; postage; phone calls; printing and photocopying; expenses in entertaining prospective donors; and required uniforms without general utility.

It is generally inappropriate to provide a volunteer with a standard charitable receipt because the charity is usually unable to confirm the actual amount of a volunteer's expenses. But a letter of appreciation may be sent to the volunteer thanking the individual for the specific services provided. The burden is on the volunteer to prove the amount of the expense.

Volunteers who incur $250 or more in out-of-pocket expenses in connection with a charitable activity are subject to the acknowledgment rules. The acknowledgment should identify the type of services or expenses provided by the volunteer and state that no goods or services were provided by the charity to the donor in consideration of the volunteer efforts (see page 164 for a sample letter to volunteers).

Gifts to domestic organizations for foreign use

Gifts must be made to recognized U.S. charities to qualify for an income tax deduction. Some taxpayers have attempted to avoid this rule by funnelling gifts for a foreign-organized entity through a U.S. charity.

There are some acceptable situations where a U.S. charity may receive gifts for which a deduction is allowed with the money used abroad:

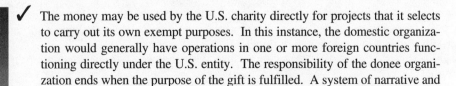

✓ The money may be used by the U.S. charity directly for projects that it selects to carry out its own exempt purposes. In this instance, the domestic organization would generally have operations in one or more foreign countries functioning directly under the U.S. entity. The responsibility of the donee organization ends when the purpose of the gift is fulfilled. A system of narrative and financial reports is necessary to document what was accomplished by the gift.

✓ It may create a subsidiary organization in a foreign country to facilitate its exempt operations there, with certain of its funds transmitted directly to the subsidiary. In this instance, the foreign organization is merely an administra-

Sample Letter to Volunteers

Dear Volunteer:

We appreciate the time, energy, and out-of-pocket costs you devote to our cause as follows:

Description of Services/Expenses Provided

_____

_____

_____

No goods or services were provided to you by our church, except intangible religious benefits, in consideration of your volunteer efforts.

You may deduct unreimbursed expenses that you incur incidental to your volunteer work. So transportation costs (travel from home to our church or other places where you render services), phone calls, postage stamps, stationery, and similar out-of-pocket costs are deductible.

You can deduct 14 cents per mile in computing the costs of operating your car while doing volunteer work as well as unreimbursed parking and toll costs. Instead of using the cents-per-mile method, you can deduct your actual auto expenses, provided you keep proper records. However, insurance and depreciation on your car are not deductible.

If you travel as a volunteer and must be away from home overnight, reasonable payments for meals and lodging as well as your travel costs are deductible. Your out-of-pocket costs at a convention connected with your volunteer work are deductible if you were duly chosen as a representative of our church.

You cannot deduct travel expenses as charitable gifts if there's a significant element of personal pleasure, recreation, or vacation in the travel.

You cannot deduct the value of your services themselves. If you devote 100 hours during the year to typing for us and the prevailing rate for these services is $8.00 per hour, you can't deduct the $800 value of your services. Although deductions are allowed for property gifts, the IRS doesn't consider your services "property." Nor is the use of your home for meetings a "property contribution."

Finally, you may be required to substantiate your deduction to the IRS. Be prepared to prove your costs with cancelled checks, receipted bills, and diary entries. If your expenses total $250 or more for the calendar year, you must have this acknowledgment in hand before you file your income tax return (including any extensions).

Again, thank you for furthering our cause with that most precious commodity: your time.

Castleview Church

tive arm of the U.S. organization, with the U.S. organization considered the real recipient of the contributions. The responsibility of the U.S. organization ends when the purpose of the gift is fulfilled by the foreign subsidiary.

✓ It may make grants to charities in a foreign country in furtherance of its exempt purposes, following review and approval of the uses to which the funds are to be put. The responsibility of the U.S. organization ends when the purpose of the gift is fulfilled by the foreign organization. A narrative and financial report from the foreign organization will usually be necessary to document the fulfillment of the gift.

✓ It may transfer monies to another domestic entity with the second organization fulfilling the purpose of the gift. The responsibility of the first entity usually ends when the funds are transferred to the second organization.

Charity-sponsored tours

Many religious and charitable organizations sponsor cruises and tours. The location is often a resort or tourist area. Can individuals take a charitable deduction for tour expenses? Should the organization give a charitable receipt to tour participants? If tour expenses cannot be deducted as charitable expenses, what about taking a business or education expense deduction? Are work trips to mission fields deductible as charitable contributions?

Tours sponsored by nonprofit organizations rarely provide a tax deduction to the participant. In instances where a tax deduction is available, the deduction is almost always in the business or education expense category. Even these expense deductions are denied if there is a significant element of personal pleasure, recreation, or vacation.

The general rule is that there is no charitable contribution deduction for the cost of a travel or study tour. The only exception is where individuals are actually paying for their expenses and doing work for the organization. Then there is a limited deduction available, subject to a restriction on the amount of pleasure and recreation involved in a particular trip.

Discounts provided charity by a vendor

A business donor may provide a charitable discount for goods or services purchased by a nonprofit organization and denote the discount as a "charitable contribution."

A charitable discount is generally not deductible as a charitable contribution. The donor should not receive a standard receipt, but may receive an appropriately worded acknowledgment.

Interest on restricted gifts

There is often a time period between the receipt of restricted donations and the expenditure of the funds for the specified purpose. If investment income is earned on the monies before their expenditure, do the investment earnings accrue to the gift or may the earnings be used for the general budget of the organization? Unless there are donor or other legal restrictions on the earnings on the funds, state law controls the use of the earnings. Often, the interest earned on restricted funds held for a temporary period prior to expenditure is considered to be unrestricted.

Refunding contributions to donors

Charitable contributions generally should not be returned to donors. However, there are a few instances where donors must be given the option of receiving their contributions back and in some cases the refund should actually occur.

Since contributions must be irrevocable to qualify for a charitable deduction, there is no basis to return an undesignated gift to a donor. Requests from donors to return undesignated gifts should be denied under nearly any circumstances. A practice of refunding such gifts would be an extremely dangerous precedent.

Donors often contribute funds based on the anticipation that a certain event will occur. Their intent is to make an irrevocable gift. For example, a church raises money to buy new pews. However, an insufficient amount is raised and the church board abandons the project. What happens to the money that was designated by donors for the pews? If the donors can be identified, they should be asked whether they would like to remove the designation related to their gift. Otherwise, the money should be returned to the donor. If the donors cannot be identified (as in the case of cash contributions), the congregation could re-direct use of the funds.

If contributions are returned to donors, a written communication should accompany the refund advising donors of their responsibility to file amended tax returns if a charitable deduction was claimed. A written notice should be filed with the IRS to document the initial date of the gift, the date of the refund, the amount, and name and address of the taxpayer.

Key Concepts

■ Since 1917, Congress has provided favored tax treatment to charitable contributions by individuals.

■ Most nonprofit organizations qualify to receive tax-deductible contributions.

■ Not all gifts to your organization are tax-deductible such as gifts of services or the use of property.

■ Certain gifts of property may require you to file reports with the IRS.

■ Gifts that are designated for the benefit of individuals may be inappropriate for your organization to receive or at least receipt as charitable contributions.

CHAPTER EIGHT

Insuring Your Organization

In This Chapter

- Abuse or molestation insurance
- Automobile insurance
- COBRA
- Crime insurance
- Dental insurance
- Director's and officer's liability insurance
- Disability insurance
- General liability insurance
- Group life insurance
- Health insurance
- Key employee insurance
- Long-term care insurance
- Professional liability insurance
- Property insurance
- Travel and accident insurance
- Umbrella liability insurance
- Workers' Compensation

Most nonprofit entities need full insurance coverage similar to for-profit organizations. A frequent review of insurance requirements and a good relationship with an insurance agent or broker is important to provide a complete insurance program at competitive cost.

Setting deductible limits is a very important decision. Generally, the higher the deductible, the lower the premium will be. If the organization is financially strong enough to assume a certain degree of risk, the choice of high deductibles will often save in overall insurance costs.

Abuse or Molestation Insurance

All churches and many other nonprofit organizations should purchase a general liability policy that includes an abuse or molestation endorsement or separate coverage. This coverage should apply to the actual or threatened abuse or molestation by anyone of any person while in the care, custody, or control of your organization. It would also extend to the negligent employment, investigation, supervision, reporting to the proper authorities or failure to so report, or retention of an individual for whom your organization was legally responsible and who was involved in actual or threatened abuse.

Automobile Insurance

Automobile insurance is required if your organization owns one or more automobiles, buses, or other vehicles. If an employee runs an errand for an organization using the employer's car and is in an auto accident, this coverage protects the organization. Even if no vehicles are owned by your organization, hired and non-owned automobile insurance is usually needed.

A commercial auto policy is generally more narrow in coverage than a personal auto policy. For example, personal auto policy coverage usually transfers to other cars that you may drive. This is generally not true with a commercial auto policy.

Medical payments provide a goodwill type of coverage. If someone is injured in your auto, the person may be treated up to the medical payment limit of the policy. Often this helps avoid a lawsuit.

Typical policy coverages are $100,000/$300,000 bodily injury, $100,000 property damage, $50,000 uninsured motorist, and $2,000 or $5,000 for medical payments. Endorsements may be added for towing or road service and for rental car reimbursement. Liability coverage should be at least $100,000. If you only purchase the minimum required by your state, you may be inadequately insured.

In the U.S., auto coverages generally follow the car and any driver who operates the vehicle with permission of the insured is covered. If an employer-provided auto is the only vehicle used by the employee—e.g., there is not a personal auto—it is important to add a "broadform drive other car" endorsement.

COBRA

The Consolidated Omnibus Budget Reconciliation Act of 1985 (COBRA) requires covered employers to offer 18 months of group health coverage beyond the time the coverage would have ended because of certain "qualifying events." Premiums are reimbursable by the former employee to the former employer.

A "qualifying event" includes any termination of the employer-employee relationship, whether voluntary or involuntary, unless the termination is caused by the employee's gross misconduct. COBRA coverage applies even if the employee retires, quits, is fired, or laid off.

Churches are excluded from the COBRA requirements. However, churches may provide continuation benefits similar to COBRA. Other nonprofits are generally subject to COBRA if 20 or more employees are employed during a typical working day.

Crime Insurance

Employee dishonesty coverage is usually essential for nonprofit organizations because of the handling of donations. The coverage usually relates to employees but may be extended to volunteers such as a church treasurer.

Protection against robbery inside and outside is often a desirable part of the crime insurance coverage. A high deductible will lower premium cost.

Dental Insurance

An insured dental care program is among the most popular of benefit options. It is a benefit that employees want to take advantage of and can use regularly.

In the traditional approach, a dental plan is similar to medical insurance in that the employer pays a premium to an insurer who acts as the administrator. Covered employees submit claims and the insurer pays according to a "usual and customary" schedule. Employees are typically free to select their dentists.

Similar to the HMO concept in medical insurance, "managed care" dental programs usually work with a list of contracted care providers who provide service to members in the covered group.

Reimbursed self-insurance represents an alternative approach for dental benefits. This concept allows covered employees to select their dentists, have all work done without exclusion, pay for services themselves, and file for reimbursement from the employer.

For example, a company might choose to pay 100% of the first $200 per employee family and a decreasing percentage up to a ceiling limit of their determination. A plan can be structured flexibly to allow employers to predetermine their maximum costs for budget purposes.

Director's and Officer's Liability Insurance

When it comes to lawsuits, one of the most vulnerable positions in any nonprofit is that of a board member or officer. Employment-related claims and monetary awards are increasing, especially in the areas of wrongful discharge and employment discrimination.

Such claims are especially worrisome for individual board members and smaller nonprofits because of the amount of damages that could be involved. A successful defense against a lawsuit can be very expensive, while losing a suit can totally exhaust an organization's resources, as well as those of the individual board members involved.

The two primary options for nonprofits to provide protection to board members against individual liability are:

✓ **Insurance.** Director's and officer's (D&O) liability insurance is designed to protect board members and officers against certain liabilities they may incur while acting in their official capacities. D&O policies usually cover legal fees and other expenses involved in defending against a claim.

✓ **State law protection.** More than 30 states have legislation limiting the liability of individuals who serve as volunteer directors or officers on nonprofit boards. Generally, these laws provide that a director or officer can be held liable only for willful or wanton behavior, not just for simple negligence. Some states require an affirmative act by the organization in order for the exempting state law to apply. This means that specific language must be included in the articles of incorporation or bylaws describing the essence of the statute and clearly stating that it applies to the organization. Without the required language, directors are not covered by the law.

Even if protection is provided under state laws, it may be wise for the organization to purchase D&O insurance to cover the acts of negligence not covered under the state law.

Disability Insurance

Disability insurance may be provided for nonprofit organization employees. Coverage is usually limited to 60% to 75% of the annual salary of each individual. Social security and pension benefits are often offset against disability insurance benefits. Disability insurance premiums may be paid through a flexible benefit plan to obtain income tax and social security tax (FICA) savings.

If the organization pays the disability insurance premiums, the premiums are excluded from the employee's income. If the organization pays the premiums (and the employee is the beneficiary) as a part of the compensation package, any disability policy proceeds are fully taxable to the employee. This is based on who paid the premiums for the policy covering the year when the disability started. If the premiums are shared between the church and the minister, then the benefits are taxable in the same proportion as the payment of the premiums.

The benefit waiting period is generally in the 90-to-120-day range. Coverage may be extended to age 65 or even life.

General Liability Insurance

General liability insurance provides for the avoidance of unforeseeable payments and also protects against the catastrophic hazards when large groups of individuals gather under the sponsorship of an organization. Endorsements to the liability policy may cover such additional hazards as product liability, premises medical payments, real property fire legal liability, advertising injury, contractual liability, and personal injury.

Coverage is usually written for at least $500,000 for each occurrence, $500,000 aggregate, $500,000 products and completed operations, $500,000 personal and advertising, $50,000 fire damage, and $5,000 medical.

If an umbrella liability policy is not purchased, the $500,000 limits listed above probably should be raised to $1,000,000. If umbrella liability coverage is purchased, the insurance company may require that the general liability limit be $1,000,000.

General liability insurance may be purchased with limits higher than $1,000,000. It is usually more cost-effective to use a $500,000 or $1,000,000 limit for the general liability policy and then purchase an umbrella policy with higher limits.

Many churches and nonprofits need liability insurance for special events such as summer camps, skiing, beach activities, softball, basketball, and other sports. Coverage for these events should be provided with a specific endorsement under a general liability policy.

Group Life Insurance

Group life insurance may be written to provide a minimum amount of insurance for each employee. The first $50,000 of coverage is a tax-free benefit for employees. Premiums may be paid wholly or partially by the employer.

Health Insurance

In recent years there has been a shift to managed care—prepaid health-insurance programs that stress preventive care. But for most churches and other small-to-medium charities, an indemnity plan may be the only avenue available.

Medium-to-larger nonprofits typically offer a group health-insurance plan for the benefit of employees as an important fringe benefit. Very small nonprofits usually help their employees secure individual health policies.

Health insurance purchased through a group policy is usually more expensive than individual policies if the individual can qualify for coverage. Insurers often require that 75% of the full-time employees be enrolled to qualify for a group plan. This enrollment requirement is necessary to avoid adverse selection. Adverse selection occurs when a disproportionate number of employees with very high-cost medical problems are enrolled in a plan.

The basic offerings in employer-provided health-insurance plans include the following:

 Health Maintenance Organization (HMO). Medical treatment is prepaid and delivered by the HMO provider organization.

✓ **Preferred Provider Organization (PPO).** Medical treatment is supplied through a designated network of physicians and hospitals at discounted rates.

✓ **Indemnity plan.** These plans may include cost containment features such as prehospital authorization and a second opinion before surgery, while also offering incentives for outpatient treatment. Indemnity plans typically feature a per-person, per-year deductible and co-insurance factors and a limit on total lifetime claims covered.

Traditional indemnity plans offer little flexibility of employer design. The partially self-funded concept allows the employer to design the exact coverage and build in customized cost-containment features. The two basic indemnity plan concepts are as follows:

● **Fully insured through a carrier.** This is the traditional approach for health insurance with most of the risk borne by the insurance carrier.

● **Partially self-funded by organization.** This method is a shared-risk approach. This concept may make sense if there are 25 or more employees and the maximum annual liability is only slightly higher than the premium under a fully insured plan.

An employee group primarily composed of nonsmokers and nondrinkers and without the incidence of AIDS also may provide an incentive to consider the partially self-funded approach. Traditional fully insured plans must factor the possibility of all types of illness into their rates.

The principles of a partially self-funded plan include payment by the organization of the first-dollar medical costs. The organization buys a high deductible medical plan. For example, the deductible may be $10,000 or $20,000 per person per year. Expenses over the $10,000 or $20,000 are covered by the insurance carrier. This is commonly called a "specific deductible."

An "aggregate stop-loss" policy is also purchased. This policy will provide that annual medical expenses exceeding a total of a certain amount will be paid by the insurance carrier. This is a type of overall stop-loss for the employer.

✓ **Traditional fully insured plan with HMO option.** Under this concept the employer gives the employee the choice of being covered under a traditional indemnity plan or using an HMO.

HMOs are typically more expensive than indemnity plans. Therefore, if the employee chooses the HMO plan, the difference between the cost of the HMO and the fully insured plan usually is paid by the employee.

Current trends in health insurance

✓ **Premium cost-shifting.** Many organizations require some contribution for single coverage and even more require employee contributions toward dependent coverage.

✓ **Deductibles.** While a $100 deductible used to be the norm, today deductibles of $500 to $1,000 per person per year are common.

There is a trend toward setting deductible amounts based on an employee's pay level. For example, a higher paid employee would have a higher deductible than a lower paid employee.

✓ **Co-insurance.** Higher co-insurance limits are common today. An 80%/20% split of the first medical dollar costs after the deductible up to $5,000 or $10,000 per person per year is not unusual.

✓ **Extend the preexisting conditions waiting period.** For plan years beginning after July 1, 1997, health care plans cannot apply preexisting condition limits for periods greater than 12 months (18 months for late enrollees). No limits can be applied in cases involving pregnancy, newborns, or newly adopted children. Furthermore, the 12-month limit for preexisting conditions must be reduced month-for-month by any previous health insurance coverage that a worker had, unless he or she had a break in coverage of more than 63 days.

✓ **Employee health assessment.** Some insurance companies offer health assessment for a per employee fee. Doctors evaluate employees' present conditions and prescribe a personal health program for them. A healthier employee helps to curb premium hikes.

✓ **Second opinions and precertification.** It is more common today to require second opinions before surgery and to precertify hospital stays.

✓ **Prescriptions.** Medical costs can be reduced by providing generic prescriptions by mail.

Medical plan continuation features

Securing medical coverage while an individual is between jobs is often a concern. Churches and small nonprofit employers are exempt from the coverage continuation requirements of COBRA (see page 168) but they may voluntarily comply. Also, some state laws require continued insurance coverage for spouses and children after a divorce.

Some health plans have a conversion feature that allows conversion of group coverage to an individual policy after employment ends. The conversion policy is usually expensive and the benefits are very limited. Still, conversion may be the best alternative for someone with health problems and unable to obtain other insurance.

Flexible benefit plans

Many employers have shifted to a flexible benefit plan (often referred to as a cafeteria plan) to provide health coverage and to allow employees to choose between taxable and nontaxable benefits. In the simplest plans, employees might be offered an opportunity to choose and pay for additional medical benefits or for health benefits to cover family members.

More complex plans offer a full menu of benefits: additional vacation time, disability insurance, child-care allowances or emergency child-care service, life and disability insurance, and legal insurance (long-term care insurance does not qualify). Premiums for a private health insurance plan or for a spouse's plan are not chargeable to a flexible benefit plan. Each benefit has a price. Each employee selects the package of benefits that best meets the employee's needs and ability to pay.

The expense money employees choose to keep in their flexible benefit plan is deducted before taxes. The money is held in reserve, and the employee is reimbursed for expenses as they are incurred.

Depending on the state of employment, employee savings may apply to both federal and state income taxes and social security taxes. This may amount to a discount of around 40% (28% federal tax, 7.65% FICA, 3%-5% state tax) on what was formerly paid personally for health care insurance or child-care expense.

The flexible benefit plan offers some distinct advantages to employers. The organization does not have to pay social security taxes on money that is being withheld from employees under the plan. In some states, lower Workers' Compensation and unemployment insurance payments also result.

Some potential drawbacks for employees are

✓ employees must use the money they have set aside within the plan year or forfeit that money to their employer, and

✓ there might be a slight reduction in some of their social security benefits.

Key Employee Insurance

Key employee insurance reimburses the organization for financial loss resulting from the death of a key employee of the organization. It may be used to build up a fund to be available upon the individual's retirement should death not be a factor.

Long-Term Care Insurance

Long-term care or nursing home insurance provided by the nonprofit is tax-free to the employee effective January 1, 1997. However, long-term care premiums are not excluded from an employee's income if provided through a cafeteria or other flexible spending arrangement.

Professional Liability Insurance

Pastoral counseling is rarely covered in standard policies. Each church should purchase a pastor's professional liability policy to cover any act or omission in the furnishing of pastoral counseling services. The coverage protects both pastor and church. Your pastor will feel more comfortable handling delicate matters because adequate insurance coverage is provided.

Property Insurance

A multi-peril policy provides comprehensive property and general liability insurance tailored to the needs of the insured. Endorsements may be added to provide earthquake, employee dishonesty, and money loss coverages. A general property policy provides fire insurance coverage for structures and fixtures that are a part of the structures. Machinery used in building service, air conditioning systems, boilers, and elevators are covered under a boiler policy.

Endorsements may be added to the general property policy to cover replacement cost, loss caused by windstorm, hail, explosion, riot, aircraft, vehicles and smoke, vandalism and malicious mischief, flood, sprinkler leakage, and earthquake. It may be desirable to eliminate the co-insurance provision by using an agreed amount endorsement. Be sure there is coverage on equipment, such as personal computers and video equipment, that you may take off-premises to conventions or other meetings.

Many church policies do not cover the pastor's personal property located on church premises. Even when some coverage is provided, the limit may be too low, considering the value of books, sermons, and computers.

Try to use your property insurance as catastrophic coverage and not a maintenance policy. Your organization should take care of the small property damage losses.

Travel and Accident Insurance

Travel and accident insurance is often purchased for nonprofit organization executives or perhaps all the employees. It covers injury occurring during travel authorized by the employer. The coverage also may be written on a 24-hour basis.

When purchasing insurance relating to international travel, coverage for emergency medical evacuation and assistance services are additional considerations.

Travel and accident insurance usually does not apply to certain "war zones" unless a special rider is purchased.

Umbrella Liability Insurance

Through an umbrella liability insurance policy, you may purchase liability coverage with higher limits. The particular liabilities covered do not get broader. For example, if your underlying general liability policy has a $500,000 limit and you purchase an umbrella liability policy with a $2,000,000 limit, your total liability coverage will be $2,500,000.

Umbrella policies are usually more liberal in their coverages but tend to be higher priced than excess liability policies (which are only extensions of policy limits).

Workers' Compensation

Workers' Compensation insurance coverage compensates workers for losses caused by work-related injuries. It also limits the potential liability of the organization for injury to the employee related to his job.

Workers' Compensation insurance is required by law in all states to be carried by the employer. A few states exempt churches from Workers' Compensation coverage, and several states exempt all nonprofit employers. Still, churches and nonprofit organizations are covered in most states. Most states also consider ministers to be employees regardless of the income tax filing method used by the minister and therefore they must be covered under Workers' Compensation policy. Contact your state department of labor to find out how your state applies Workers' Compensation rules to churches.

Even if a church or nonprofit organization is exempt from Workers' Compensation, the voluntary purchase of the coverage or the securing of additional general liability coverage may be prudent. This is because other types of insurance typically exclude work-related accidents: health, accident, disability, auto and general liability insurance policies are some examples.

Workers' Compensation premiums are based on the payroll of the organization with a minimum premium charge to issue the policy. An audit is done later to determine the actual charge for the policy.

Most Workers' Compensation insurance is purchased through private insurance carriers. A few states provide the coverage and charge the covered organizations.

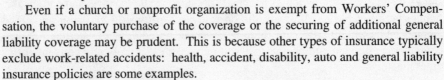

Key Concepts

■ Your nonprofit organization probably needs a broad range of insurance coverages.

■ Obtaining adequate insurance and competitive prices requires working closely with your insurance agent or broker.

■ Providing adequate health insurance for your employees continues to challenge especially smaller organizations.

■ Many organizations overlook the legal requirement to provide Workers' Compensation insurance.

CHAPTER NINE

Laws for Nonprofits

In This Chapter

- Age discrimination
- Americans With Disabilities Act
- Canadian Goods and Services Tax
- Charitable solicitation
- Church-operated child care facilities
- Equal pay
- Environmental issues
- Fair Labor Standards Act
- Family and Medical Leave Act
- Immigration control
- Mailing at third-class rates
- National Child Care Act
- Occupational Safety and Health Act
- Pregnancy discrimination
- Racial discrimination
- Religious discrimination
- Sexual harassment
- State taxes and fees

The non-payroll laws and regulations governing nonprofits, at best, can be confusing, and at worst, very intimidating. Legal assistance may be required to provide interpretation of the laws and regulations for your organization.

This chapter is designed to provide you a very basic explanation of some key laws that may impact your organization. Complying with these laws will often result in good stewardship. There is generally a financial risk if they are ignored.

Age Discrimination

The Age Discrimination in Employment Act of 1967 (ADEA) applies to employers in any industry affecting commerce with 20 or more employees. Churches with 20 or more employees may be exempt from the ADEA because of a lack of involvement in commercial activities.

The ADEA prohibits employment discrimination on the basis of age against applicants for employment and employees who are age 40 and older. The top age limit for mandatory retirement has generally been eliminated. Compulsory retirement is still permissible for certain executives or tenured college faculty members who have reached age 65. Ministers are subject to compulsory retirement.

Americans With Disabilities Act

The employment provisions of the American With Disabilities Act (ADA) became effective July 26, 1994, covering employers with 15 or more workers in 20 or more weeks a year. The public accommodations provisions of the ADA have been effective since January 26, 1992. For ADA questions, you can call a special information line at the Justice Department: 202–514–0301.

The ADA requirements relate to two areas:

✓ **Employment.** Hiring must be without regard to disabilities and also make reasonable accommodation for disabled individuals.

There are limited exceptions to the employment provisions of the ADA for churches and religious employers. Preferential treatment may be given in hiring individuals of a particular religion. Additionally, churches and religious organizations may require employees to conform to their religious tenets.

Example: Two applicants are members of the United Methodist denomination. A Methodist church or Methodist religious organization cannot refuse to hire the disabled applicant simply because of a disability, but it may give preference to a Methodist applicant over a Baptist.

✓ **Public accommodations.** Facilities open to the public must be accessible to the disabled. The primary focus is on facilities like restaurants, museums, hotels, retail stores, and banks.

Religious organizations or entities controlled by religious organizations (including places of worship) are exempt from the public accommodation requirements of the ADA. Caution: Although a church is exempt under the public accommodations provisions, it may still be covered under similar provisions of local building codes.

Canadian Goods and Services Tax

The Canadian Goods and Services Tax (GST) applies to all goods and services introduced into Canada. The GST applies to imports and may have impact on U.S. nonprofit organizations that have even minimal contact in Canada.

The 7% tax may be assessed on all membership dues, publication sales, magazine subscriptions, group insurance sales, advertising revenues, classified ad sales, seminar and training course revenues, and any other product or service offered by a U.S. nonprofit to a Canadian consumer.

There are certain exemptions for membership dues and educational services. Certain products and services offered by U.S. nonprofits to Canadian consumers may be covered under the GST.

For more information on the GST, write the Canadian Society of Association Executives, 45 Charles Street East, Toronto, Ontario, M4Y 1S2 and request the *Goods and Services Tax Booklet.*

Charitable Solicitation

Federal, state, and local governments have enacted laws regulating the solicitation of contributions by nonprofit organizations. These laws are known as "charitable solicitation acts." They have resulted from greater interest in accountability on the part of nonprofit organizations. The laws are designed to assure contributors that funds solicited for a specified charitable purpose will be used for the intended purpose. Many states require the filing of annual registration and reports to comply with the solicitation laws (42 states have some form of solicitation laws). (See Recent Developments.)

Church-Operated Child Care Facilities

Federal funds are available to low-income families for child care through the Child Care and Development Block Grant Act of 1990. States must use 75% of the grants from the federal government to issue child care certificates to qualified low-income parents. The certificates may be redeemed at eligible facilities for child care services. Churches may be eligible to provide child care under this program even if they engage in religious instruction or display religious symbols.

Through another segment of this program, states may provide funds directly to eligible child care facilities, including churches, to assist them in providing child care to children from low-income families. Churches may receive these direct grants only if the funds are not used for religious worship and instruction.

Equal Pay

The Equal Pay Act of 1963 prohibits employers from paying employees of one sex at a lower rate than employees of the opposite sex for equal work for positions that require the same skill, effort, and responsibility and that are performed under similar working conditions.

Environmental Issues

Environmental risks are a major concern for nonprofit organizations purchasing or receiving charitable gifts of real estate. Nonprofits must exercise "due diligence" in conducting an environmental investigation prior to purchasing or accepting donated real estate. These due diligence investigations are usually called "Preliminary Environmental Site Assessments" or "Phase I Environmental Site Assessments." These assessments are performed by qualified environmental consultants.

Environmental laws that may apply to gifts or the purchase of real estate include:

✔ Comprehensive Environmental Response, Compensation, and Liability Act (CERCLA/Superfund, 1980)

✔ Resource Conservation and Recovery Act (RCRA, 1976)

✔ RCRA Underground Storage Tank Regulations (RCRA UST, 1984)

✔ Indoor Radon Abatement Act (IRAA, 1988)

✔ Clean Water Act (CWA, 1977)

✔ Clean Air Act (CAA, 1983)

Fair Labor Standards Act

The Fair Labor Standards Act (FLSA) adopted in 1938 provides protection for employees engaged in interstate commerce concerning minimum wages, equal pay, overtime pay, recordkeeping, and child labor. (Some states even have more restrictive versions of the FSLA.) Commerce is defined by the FLSA as "trade, commerce, transportation, transmission, or communication among the several states or between any state and any place outside thereof."

The employees of nonprofit organizations involved in commerce or in the production of goods for commerce are generally considered covered by the provisions of the FLSA. Conversely, nonprofits that are not engaged in commerce or fall below the $500,000 annual gross sales volume requirement are generally exempt from the Act.

The FLSA clearly applies to schools regardless of whether they are nonprofit entities operated by religious organizations. Church-operated day care centers and

What the FLSA Does Not Regulate

While the Fair Labor Standards Act does set basic minimum wage and overtime pay standards and regulates the employment of minors, there are a number of employment practices which the Act does not regulate. For example, the Act does not require

✓ vacation, holiday, severance, or sick pay;

✓ meal or rest periods, holidays or vacations off;

✓ premium pay for weekend or holiday work;

✓ pay raises or fringe benefits;

✓ a discharge notice, reason for discharge, or immediate payment of final wages to terminated employees; or

✓ any limit on the number of hours of work for persons 16 years of age and over.

elementary and secondary schools are generally considered subject to the FLSA.

Most local churches would not meet the definition of being involved in commerce. However, many churches and nonprofits voluntarily choose to follow the FLSA regulations as an equitable guide and as a precaution against possible litigation.

The overtime compensation requirements of the FLSA do not apply to certain employees in executive, administrative, or professional positions. Ministers are generally exempt under the professional provisions of this exemption. Minors under age 14 generally cannot be hired.

The FLSA minimum wage increased to $5.15 per hour on September 1, 1997 (it was formerly $4.75 per hour). Teenagers may be paid a training wage of $4.25 per hour for the first 90 days of employment.

The minimum wage rates of 13 states and the District of Columbia are tied to the federal minimum wage rate in some way. For example, the minimum wage rates in Alaska and the District of Columbia are generally $0.50 and $1.00 over the federal rate, respectively.

Family and Medical Leave Act

The Family and Medical Leave Act of 1993 (FMLA) requires certain employers to provide up to twelve weeks of unpaid leave to eligible employees. The FMLA does not override more generous state entitlements. The new law became effective on August 5, 1993, and only applies to organizations with fifty or more employees.

There is no exemption for religious employers.

While only large churches and nonprofit organizations may be subject to the Act, some employers will choose to comply with the provisions of the law in an effort to improve employee morale. Even though an organization is not subject to the Act, they may have legal responsibilities to pregnant or ill employees under other federal laws (see other sections of this chapter).

To be eligible under this law, a person must be employed at least twelve months and have worked at least 1,250 hours during the twelve months. Eligible employees are entitled to a total of twelve weeks of unpaid leave for the birth of a child and certain other reasons.

Immigration Control

The Immigration Reform and Control Act of 1986 (IRCA) prohibits all employers from hiring unauthorized aliens, imposes documentation verification requirements on all employers, and provides an "amnesty" program for certain illegal aliens. The law also prohibits employers with three or more employees from discriminating because of national origin. An I-9 Form (see page 183) must be completed and retained on file by all employers for each employee hired after November 6, 1986. The form must be available for inspection at any time. Form I-9 may be obtained by calling 800–755–0777 or at www.usdoj.gov/ins/index.html.

The Form I-551 Alien Registration Receipt Card issued after August 1, 1989, is the exclusive registration card issued to lawful permanent residents as definitive evidence of identity and U.S. residence status.

National Child Care Act

The National Child Care Act (NCCA) of 1993 became effective on December 20, 1993. Under the law, states may designate organizations that will be permitted to obtain a nationwide criminal records check on child care workers. If your state designates churches, this will enable you to quickly check on prospective child care workers by asking a state agency to conduct a criminal records check.

If your state does not designate churches as eligible under the NCCA, you should rely on other methods of screening child care workers in your church.

Occupational Safety and Health Act

The Occupational Safety and Health Act (OSHA) was designed to protect workers from unsafe conditions in the workplace. OSHA generally applies to all employers engaged in commerce who have employees.

States are permitted to adopt standards of their own. Some 23 jurisdictions now have an approved state plan in place.

Churches and other nonprofit employers are not specifically exempt from OSHA. A church must employ at least one person in "secular activities" to be

U.S. Department of Justice
Immigration and Naturalization Service

OMB No. 1115-0136
Employment Eligibility Verification

Please read instructions carefully before completing this form. The instructions must be available during completion of this form. **ANTI-DISCRIMINATION NOTICE.** It is illegal to discriminate against work eligible individuals. Employers CANNOT specify which document(s) they will accept from an employee. The refusal to hire an individual because of a future expiration date may also constitute illegal discrimination.

Section 1. Employee Information and Verification. To be completed and signed by employee at the time employment begins

Print Name: Last	First	Middle Initial	Maiden Name
Hendricks	Fred	W.	

Address (Street Name and Number)	Apt. #	Date of Birth (month/day/year)
406 Forest Avenue		6/12/49

City	State	Zip Code	Social Security #
Cincinnati	OH	45960	514-42-9087

I am aware that federal law provides for imprisonment and/or fines for false statements or use of false documents in connection with the completion of this form.

I attest, under penalty of perjury, that I am (check one of the following):
A citizen or national of the United States
A Lawful Permanent Resident (Alien # A_____
An alien authorized to work until___/___/___
(Alien # or Admission #_____

Employee's Signature	Date (month/day/year)
Fred W. Hendricks	1/20/99

Preparer and/or Translator Certification. (To be completed and signed if Section 1 is prepared by a person other than the employee.) I attest, under penalty of perjury, that I have assisted in the completion of this form and that to the best of my knowledge the information is true and correct.

Preparer's/Translator's Signature	Print Name

Address (Street Name and Number, City, State, Zip Code)	Date (month/day/year)

Section 2. Employer Review and Verification. To be completed and signed by employer. Examine one document from List A OR examine one document from List B and one from List C as listed on the reverse of this form and record the title, number and expiration date, if any, of the document(s)

List A	OR	List B	AND	List C
Document title: _____		Driver's License		Birth Certificate
Issuing authority: _____		Ohio		Ohio
Document #: _____		514-42-9087		_____
Expiration Date (if any): __/__/__		6/30/99		__/__/__
Document #: _____				
Expiration Date (if any): __/__/__				

CERTIFICATION - I attest, under penalty of perjury, that I have examined the document(s) presented by the above-named employee, that the above-listed document(s) appear to be genuine and to relate to the employee named, that the employee began employment on (month/day/year) ___/___/___and that to the best of my knowledge the employee is eligible to work in the United States. (State employment agencies may omit the date the employee began employment).

Signature of Employer or Authorized Representative	Print Name	Title
David L. Brown	David L. Brown	Business Manager

Business or Organization Name	Address (Street Name and Number, City, State, Zip Code)	Date (month/day/year)
Fairfield Church, 110 Harding Ave., Cincinnati, OH 45960		1/31/99

Section 3. Updating and Reverification. To be completed and signed by employer

A. New Name (if applicable)	B. Date of rehire (month/day/year) (if applicable)

C. If employee's previous grant of work authorization has expired, provide the information below for the document that establishes current employment eligibility.

Document Title:_____Document #:_____Expiration Date (if any):__/__/__

I attest, under penalty of perjury, that to the best of my knowledge, this employee is eligible to work in the United States, and if the employee presented document(s), the document(s) I have examined appear to be genuine and to relate to the individual.

Signature of Employer or Authorized Representative	Date (month/day/year)

Note: This form must be completed and retained on file by all employers for employees hired after November 6, 1986. (For more information on completing this form, contact the Immigration and Naturalization Service office in your area for a free copy of the Handbook for Employers/Form M-274.)

covered. A person who performs or participates in religious services is not considered to be involved in secular activities.

Postal Regulations

Churches and other nonprofits may qualify to mail at special standard nonprofit mail rates (formerly called bulk third-class). The application (Form 3624) is available at the post office where you wish to deposit the mail (see page 185 for a sample of Form 3624). The following information must be provided (some apply only if the organization is incorporated):

✔ description of the organization's primary purpose which might be found in the articles of incorporation or bylaws;

✔ evidence that the organization is nonprofit such as a federal (and state) tax exemption determination letter; and

✔ materials showing how the organization actually operated in the previous 6 to 12 months such as program literature, newsletters, bulletins, and any other promotional materials.

The U.S. Postal Service offers rate incentives to nonprofit mailers that provide automation-compatible mail. Automated mail must be readable by an Optical Character Reader (OCR). Contact your local Post Office for more information.

Pregnancy Discrimination

Under the Pregnancy Discrimination Act of 1978, women affected by pregnancy, childbirth, or related medical conditions must be treated the same for all employment-related purposes as other workers who have a similar ability or inability to work.

Racial Discrimination

Form 5578, Annual Certification of Racial Nondiscrimination for a Private School Exempt from Federal Income Tax, must be filed by churches that operate, supervise, or control a private school (see page 48). The form must be filed by the 15th day of the fifth month following the end of the organization's fiscal year. For organizations that must file Form 990, there is no requirement to file Form 5578 since the information is included in Part V of Schedule A.

The "private school" definition includes preschools, primary, secondary, preparatory, or high schools, and colleges and universities, whether operated as a separate legal entity or an activity of a church.

Application to Mail at Special Bulk Third-Class Rates

Section A—Application *(Please read section B on page 2 before completion.)*

Part 1 *(For completion by applicant)*

- All information entered below must be legible so that our records will show the correct information about your organization.

- The complete name of the organization must be shown in item 1. The name shown must agree with the name that appears on all documents submitted to support this application.

- A complete address representing a physical location for the organization must be shown in item 2. If you receive mail through a post office box, show your street address first and then the box number.

- The applicant named in item 5 must be the individual submitting the application for the organization and must be an officer of the organization. Printers and mailing agents may not sign for the organization.

- No additional organization categories may be added in item 6. To be eligible for the special rates, the organization must qualify as one of the types listed.

- The applicant must sign the application in item 12.

- The date shown in item 14 must be the date that the application is submitted to the post office.

No application fee is required. All information must be complete and typewritten or printed legibly.

1. Complete Name of Organization *(If voting registration official, include title)*
   Chapel Hill Charity

2. Street Address of Organization *(Include apartment or suite number)*
   300 South Hillcrest Avenue

3. City, State, ZIP+4 Code
   Athens, OH 45701

4. Telephone *(Include area code)*
   614-832-9061

5. Name of Applicant *(Must represent applying organization)*
   Lewis E. Foster

6. Type of Organization *(Check only one)*

   - [X] (01) Religious
   - [ ] (02) Educational
   - [ ] (03) Scientific
   - [ ] (04) Philanthropic
   - [ ] (05) Agricultural
   - [ ] (06) Labor
   - [ ] (07) Veterans'
   - [ ] (08) Fraternal
   - [ ] (09) Qualified political committee *(Go to item 9)*
   - [ ] (10) Voting registration official *(Go to item 9)*

7. Is this a for-profit organization or does any of the net income inure to the benefit of any private stockholder or individual?
   - [ ] Yes
   - [X] No

8. Is this organization exempt from federal income tax? *(If 'Yes,' you must attach a copy of the exemption issued by the Internal Revenue Service that shows the section of the IRS code under which the organization is exempt. If an application for exempt status is pending with the IRS, you must check 'No.')*
   - [X] Yes
   - [ ] No

9. Has this organization previously mailed at the special bulk rates? If 'Yes,' list the post offices where mailings were most recently deposited at these rates.
   - [ ] Yes
   - [X] No

10. Has your organization had special bulk third-class rate mailing privileges denied or revoked? If 'Yes,' please list the post office (city and state) where the application was denied or authorization was revoked.
    - [ ] Yes
    - [X] No

11. Post office (not a station or branch) where authorization requested and bulk mailings will be made *(City, state, ZIP Code)*

I certify that the statements made by me are true and complete. I understand that anyone who furnishes false or misleading information on this form or who omits material information requested on the form may be subject to criminal sanctions (including fines and imprisonment) and/or civil sanctions (including multiple damages **and** civil penalties).

I further understand that, if this application is approved, a postage refund for the difference between the regular and special bulk rates may be made for only those regular bulk third-class mailings entered at the post office identified above while this application is pending, provided the conditions set forth in Domestic Mail Manual E370.5.0 and E370.9.0 are met.

12. Signature of Applicant
    Lewis E. Foster

13. Title
    Manager

14. Date
    1/20/99

Part 2 *(For completion by postmaster at originating office when application filed)*

1. Signature of Postmaster *(Or designated representative)*

2. Date Application Filed With Post Office *(Round stamp)*

PS Form **3624,** January 1995 *(Page 1 of 3)*

Note: This form may be obtained at the post office where you wish to mail at special third-class bulk rates.

Religious Discrimination

Title VII of the Civil Rights Act of 1964 prohibits discrimination in employment with respect to compensation, terms, conditions, or privileges of employment because of an individual's race, color, religion, sex, or national origin. The law applies to organizations with 15 or more employees.

Title VII does permit religious organizations to discriminate on the basis of religion for all positions. However, religious employers may not discriminate on the basis of race, sex, or national origin.

Sexual Harassment

Under Title VII of the Civil Rights Act of 1964 two types of conduct that can constitute unlawful sexual harassment are: harassment in which concrete employment benefits are conditioned upon acquiescence to sexual advances; and harassment that does not affect economic benefits but creates a hostile working environment.

While the standards in this area are not entirely clear, certain basic precautionary steps still serve to reduce the potential for employer liability:

✓ Establish a comprehensive policy against sexual harassment.

✓ Conduct supervisory training on a regular basis.

✓ Implement a meaningful complaint procedure taking into account both the perspective of the aggrieved employee and the rights of the alleged harasser.

✓ Investigate complaints promptly, thoroughly, and tactfully, and document the investigation.

✓ Take appropriate remedial action in cases of proven harassment.

State Taxes and Fees

Exemption from income, franchise, licensing fees, property, sales, use, or other taxes for qualified nonprofit organizations is allowed by many states. Each organization should contact the appropriate state authorities for information on these exemptions.

In a series of decisions in recent years, the Supreme Court has ruled that taxing churches is perfectly legal. A recent Supreme Court decision that permitted sales tax on a religious organization was so broad that many legal experts believe that other church property—like investment income, donation income, and real estate assets—can now be taxed if a state decides to do so.

Property taxes

Church property is generally exempt from property tax. Whether real estate of a nonprofit organization is exempt from property tax usually depends on its use and ownership. Many states restrict the exemption of church property to property used for worship. It is also important to note that not all religious organizations are churches. Contact the office of the county tax assessor or collector to determine what property tax exemptions are available.

Parsonages are usually exempt from real estate tax. This is true though there may be several ministers on the staff of one church and therefore multiple parsonages. If the pastor owns the parsonage instead of the church, the parsonage is usually subject to property tax.

Church parking lots are usually exempt if properly recorded. It may be possible to obtain an exemption for vacant land. Property tax exemption of church camps and recreation facilities often comes under attack because of income that may be generated through their use. Property partially used for church use and partially leased to a third-party for-profit entity generally results in the proration of the tax exemption.

An initial (and perhaps annual) registration of the property with the proper state authorities is generally necessary to record exempt property. The initial purchase of real estate with notification of state authorities is usually not sufficient to exempt property from tax.

Sales taxes

There are presently four states with no sales tax law. In most states a nonprofit organization is exempt from sales tax as a purchaser of goods used in ministry. It is generally necessary to obtain recognition of sales tax exemption from the state revenue department. Some states will accept a federal tax-exemption as sufficient for a state sales tax exemption.

Even if an organization is exempt from paying sales tax, purchases used for the private benefit of the organization's members or employees are not eligible for exemption.

When a nonprofit organization sells goods to others, a sales tax may or may not be applicable. There are some indications that states may begin a stricter enforcement of laws on the books allowing them to impose sales tax on sales by nonprofit organizations. Occasional dinners and sales of goods at bazaars are typically exempt from sales tax.

Sales by a nonprofit within the state where the nonprofit is located are sometimes taxable. Sales to customers located outside of the state, or interstate sales, may not be subject to sales tax. A 1992 Supreme Court case cleared the way for Congress to decide whether states can require organizations to collect state sales taxes on out-of-state mail order purchases. Until Congress acts, nonprofits may continue to ship publications and other taxable materials into states where they have no employees or other significant contacts without having to collect taxes.

When a nonprofit organization operates a conference or convention outside of its home state, it is often possible to obtain sales tax exemption for purchases made within the state where the meeting is held. Sales of products at the convention would generally be covered under sales tax laws without an approved exemption.

Use taxes

Besides sales taxes, many states also have use taxes. A use tax is imposed on the purchaser of a product or service. The use tax is designed to prevent avoidance of a local sales tax by buying property through the mail or in person in another state.

Churches and nonprofit organizations should determine whether they are subject to a use tax on various types of transactions.

Municipal service fees

Several states have recently proposed legislation to permit municipalities to impose "service fees" on property owned by tax-exempt organizations. Cities and counties would be authorized to collect a fee from tax-exempt property to pay for certain municipal services, typically fire and police protection, road construction and maintenance, and snow removal.

While the proposed legislation refers to the amounts to be collected as municipal service charges or fees, the assessments have the characteristics of property taxes. The fees are based on the value of property, not the services consumed. Property owners other than tax-exempt organizations would not be subject to the fees, yet would receive the same services.

Key Concepts

■ A nonprofit organization is subject to many workplace and other laws.

■ Some churches that operate day-care centers, elementary, or secondary schools are unaware that they are generally subject to the Fair Labor Standards Act.

■ The immigration control forms are required to be completed by all nonprofit organizations.

■ Many nonprofits are subject to the payment of sales or use taxes on purchases and the collection of sales taxes on sales.

Citations

Internal Revenue Code (Code): The Code is the "tax law" as enacted and amended by Congress and is the highest authority in all tax matters.

Federal Tax Regulations (Reg.): These are regulations published by the Department of the Treasury (it oversees the IRS) that seek to explain the sometimes vague language of the Internal Revenue Code. The Regulations give definitions, examples, and more plain-language explanations.

Treasury Decisions (T.D.): These are instructions and interpretations issued by the IRS Commissioner with the approval of the Treasury Secretary.

Private Letter Rulings (Ltr. Rul.): A private letter ruling is issued by the IRS at the request of a taxpayer. It is requested for the purpose of getting the IRS's opinion on a specific transaction or issue facing a taxpayer. Although it cannot be used as precedent by anyone else, it usually reflects the IRS's current attitude toward a particular tax matter.

Field Service Advice (F.S.A.): IRS national office personnel prepare FSAs in response to tax law questions from agents in the field. While they can only be relied upon by the recipient of the ruling, they may provide insights into the IRS view of matters that have not been decided by the courts.

Revenue Rulings (Rev. Rul.): A revenue ruling is issued by the IRS and is similar to a letter ruling, but it is not directed to a specific taxpayer. It is designed to give the public the IRS's opinion concerning how the tax law applies to some type of transaction, giving examples and explanations. It also gives the tax consequences of specific transactions.

Revenue Procedures (Rev. Proc.): A revenue procedure is similar to a revenue ruling, but it gives more general guidelines and procedural information. It usually does not give tax consequences of specific transactions.

Technical Advice Memoranda (T.A.M.): These consist of written counsel or guidance furnished by the IRS National Office on the interpretation and proper application of the tax law to a specific set of facts.

Court cases: Taxpayer disputes with the IRS may end up in court if a taxpayer is issued an unfavorable ruling by the IRS and is hit with back taxes. There are two routes to take if the taxpayer wants to take the IRS to court. The taxpayer can elect not to pay the back taxes and petition the Tax Court to find that the proposed back tax assessment is incorrect. Or, the taxpayer can pay the disputed amount and sue the IRS for a refund in a district court. A taxpayer can appeal an adverse court decision in an appellate court, and if unsuccessful, can take it to the U.S. Supreme Court.

    The IRS is bound by decisions of the Supreme Court for all taxpayers. It is bound by the decisions of the other courts only for the particular taxpayer involved and only for the years involved in the litigation.

Chapter 2, Tax-Exemption

- Criteria for qualifying as a church
  Spiritual Outreach Society v. Commissioner,
  T.C.M. 41 (1990)

  Joseph Edward Hardy v. Commissioner,
  T.C.M. 557 (1990)

- Exemption from filing Form 990 for certain missions organizations
  Treas. Reg. 1.6033-2(g)(1)(iv)

- General
  501(c)(3) organization established for religious purposes

  Treas. Reg. 1.511-2(a)(3)(ii)

- Private benefit/private inurement
  Treas. Reg. 1.501(a)-1(c)

  G.C.M. 37789

- Public Disclosure of Information Returns
  P.L. 100-203

- Tax-exempt status revoked for excessive UBI
  United Missionary Aviation, Inc. v.
  Commissioner, T.C.M. 566 (1990)

  Frazee v. Illinois Department of
  Employment, 57 U.S.L.W. 4397, 108 S. Ct.
  1514 (1989)

  Hernandez v. Commissioner, 819 F.2d 1212,
  109 S. Ct. 2136 (1989)

- Unrelated business income: general
  Code Sec. 511-13

- Unrelated business income: affinity credit card programs
  T.C.M. 34 (1996)

  T.C.M. 63 (1996)

- Unrelated business income: jeopardy to exempt status
  Ltr. Rul. 7849003

- Unrelated business income: organization's tour programs
  Ltr. Rul. 9027003

- Unrelated business income: affinity card programs
  Ltr. Rul. 9029047

  G.C.M. 39827, July 27, 1990

- Unrelated business income: mailing list profits
  Disabled American Veterans v. U.S., 94 TC
  No. 6 (1990)

  American Bar Endowment v. U.S., 477 U.S.
  105 (1986)

- Unrelated business income: other
  Hope School v. U.S., 612 F.2d 298 (7th Cir.
  1980)

  Rev. Rul. 64-182

Chapter 3, Compensation Planning

- Accountable expense reimbursement plans
  Treas. Reg. 1.62-2

  Treas. Reg. 1.274-5(e)

  Ltr. Rul. 9317003

- Medical expense reimbursement plans
  Code Sec. 125

- Moving expense exclusion
  Code Sec. 132(g)

- Tax-sheltered annuities
  Code Sec. 403(b)

  Code Sec. 1402(a)

  Code Sec. 3121(a)(5)(D)

  Rev. Rul. 78-6

  Rev. Rul. 68-395

Azad v. Commissioner, 388 F.2d 74
(8th Cir. 1968)

Rev. Rul. 66-274

Chapter 4, Employer Reporting

- Classification of workers
  Rev. Proc. 85-18

  Sec. 530 of the Revenue Act of 1978

- Employee v. self-employed for income tax purposes
  Rev. Rul. 87-41

- Moving expenses
  Code Sec. 82

  Code Sec. 3401(a)(15)

- Noncash remuneration
  Code Sec. 3401(a)

- Payment of payroll taxes
  Triplett 115 B.R. 955 (N.D. Ill. 1990)

  Carter v. U.S., 717 F. Supp. 188 (S.D. N.Y. 1989)

- Per diem allowances
  Rev. Proc. 97-59

- Personal use of employer-provided auto
  Temp. Reg. Sec. 1.61-2T

  IRS Notice 91-41

- Rabbi trusts
  Rev. Proc. 92-64

- Reasonable compensation
  Truth Tabernacle, Inc. v. Commissioner of Internal Revenue, T.C.M. 451 (1989)

  Heritage Village Church and Missionary Fellowship, Inc., 92 B.R. 1000 (D.S.C. 1988)

- Taxability of benefits paid under cafeteria plans
  Ltr. Rul. 8839072

Ltr. Rul. 8839085

- Temporary travel
  Rev. Rul. 93-86

  Comprehensive National Energy Policy Act of 1992

- Unemployment taxes
  Code Sec. 3309(b)

  St. Martin Evangelical Lutheran Church v. South Dakota, 451 U.S. 772 (1981)

  Employment Division v. Rogue Valley Youth for Christ, 770 F.2d 588 (Ore. 1989)

- Voluntary withholding for ministers
  Rev. Rul. 68-507

Chapter 5, Information Reporting Requirements

- Backup withholding
  Code Sec. 3406

- Cash reporting rules for charities
  T.D. 8373

  G.C.M. 39840

- Issuing Form 1099-MISCs
  Rev. Rul. 84-151

  Rev. Rul. 81-232

- Medical expense reimbursements to employees
  Ltr. Rul. 9112022

- Moving expense reporting
  IRS Announcement 94-2

- Nonresident alien payments
  Code Sec. 1441

  Code Sec. 7701(b)

- Volunteer fringe benefits
  Prop. Reg. 1.132-5(r)

- Withholding of tax on nonresident aliens
  Pub. 515

Chapter 7, Charitable Gifts

- Church school gifts
  Rev. Rul. 83-104

- Contributions denied/indirectly related school
  Ltr. Rul. 9004030

- Contributions earmarked for a specific individual
  Ltr. Rul. 9405003

  IRS Announcement 92-128

  Ltr. Rul. 8752031

  Rev. Rul. 79-81

- Contributions sent to children who are missionaries
  Davis v. U.S., 110 S. Ct. 2014 (1990)

- Contribution of church bonds
  Rev. Rul. 58-262

- Contribution of promissory note
  Allen v. Commissioner, U.S. of Appeals,
  89-70252 (9th Cir. 1991)

- Contributions designated for specific missionaries
  Hubert v. Commissioner, T.C.M. 482 (1993)

- Contribution of unreimbursed travel expenses
  Vahan Tafralian v. Commissioner, T.C.M.
  33 (1991)

  Rev. Rul. 84-61

  Rev. Rul. 76-89

- Contributions of services
  Rev. Rul 67-236

  Grant v. Commissioner, 84 T.C.M. 809 (1986)

- Contributions to needy individuals
  Stjernholm v. Commissioner,
  T.C.M. 563 (1989)

  Ltr. Rul. 8752031

  Rev. Rul. 62-113

- Contributions that refer to donor's name
  IR-92-4

- Criteria used to determine deductibility of payments to private schools
  Rev. Rul. 83-104

  Rev. Rul. 79-99

- Deduction of out-of-pocket transportation expenses
  Treas. Reg. 1.170A-1(g)

  Rev. Rul. 76-89

- Deductibility of membership fees as contributions
  Rev. Rul. 70-47

  Rev. Rul. 68-432

- Deductibility of payments relating to fund-raising events
  Pub. 1391

  Rev. Rul. 74-348

- Deductibility of gifts to domestic organizations for foreign use
  Ltr. Rul. 9211002

  Ltr. Rul. 9131052

  Ltr. Rul. 9129040

  Rev. Rul. 75-65

  Rev. Rul. 63-252

- Determining the value of donated property
  IRS Pub. 561

  Rochin v. Commissioner, T.C.M. 262 (1992)

- Gifts of inventory
  Code Sec. 170(e)

  Reg. 1.161-1

  Reg. 1.170A-1(c)(2), (3), (4)

Reg. 1.170A-4A(c)(3)

Rev. Rul. 85-8, superseding

- Gifts of life insurance
  Ltr. Rul. 9147040

  Ltr. Rul. 9110016

- Incentives and premiums
  IRS. Pub. 1391

  Rev. Proc. 96-59

  Rev. Proc. 92-102

  Rev. Proc. 92-49

  Rev. Proc. 90-12

- Payments in connection with use of ministry services
  Rev. Rul. 76-232

- Payments to a retirement home
  T.A.M. 9423001

  U.S. v. American Bar Endowment, 477 U.S.105 (S. Ct. 1986)

  Rev. Rul. 72-506

  Rev. Rul. 67-246

- Scholarship gifts
  Ltr. Rul. 9338014

  Rev. Rul. 83-104

  Rev. Rul. 62-113

- Substantiation rules
  Omnibus Budget Reconciliation Act of 1993

  T.D. 8690

- Travel tours
  Ltr. Rul. 9027003

- Unitrusts
  IRS Notice 94-78

Chapter 9, Laws for Nonprofits

- Americans With Disabilities Act
  Public Law 101-336, 42 U.S.C. 12101 et sec.

- Child care and Development Block Grant Act of 1990, 42 U.S.C. 9801

- Equal Pay Act
  EEOC v. First Baptist Church of Mishawaka, N.D. Ind., S91-179M (1991)

  EEOC v. First Baptist Church N.D. Ind., S89-338 (1990)

- Fair Labor Standards Act
  DeArment v. Harvey, No. 90-2346 (8th Cir. 1991)

  U.S. Department of Labor v. Shenandoah Baptist Church, 899 F.2d 1389 (4th Cir.) cert. denied, 111 S. Ct. 131 (1990)

- Local sales taxes
  Thayer v. South Carolina Tax Commission, 413 S.E. 2d 810 (S.C. 1992)

  Quill Corp. v. North Dakota, S. Ct. No. 91-194

  Jimmy Swaggart Ministries v. Board of Equalization of California, 110 S. Ct. 688 (1990)

- Political activity
  Treas. Reg. 1.501(c)(3)-1(c)(1)(iii)

  IR-92-57

- Property taxes
  Trinity Episcopal Church v. County of Sherburne, 1991 WL 95745 (Minn. Tax 1991)

Index

401(k) plans, *55-56*
Fringe benefits,
    Dependent care, *57*
    Medical expense reimbursement, *58-59*
    Social security tax reimbursement, *60-61*
Fund accounting, *120-21*
Fundraisers,
    Compensation, *25*
Fundraising fees, *4*

G

General ledger, *107, 114, 122, 123*
General liability insurance, *170-71*
Gift annuity, *7, 93-94, 136*
Gift planners, *23*
Gifts to employees, *62*
Gifts-in-kind, *25, 163, 164*
Group exemption, *31, 34*
Group term life insurance, *171*

H

Health insurance, *171-74*
Highly compensated employees, *2, 63*
Housing,
    Allowance, *50-51*
    Resolutions, *50*

I

Immigration control, *182, 183*
Incentives, *2, 24, 150-156*
Incorporation, *30*
Independent contractors, *9, 67-70*
Insurance,
    Abuse, *168*
    Automobile, *168*
    COBRA, *168*
    Crime, *169-69*
    Dental, *169*
    Director's and officer's liability, *169-70*
    Disability, *170*
    Flexible benefit, *174*
    Health, *171-74*
    Key employee, *174*
    Liability, *170-71*
    Life, *136, 171*
    Long-term care, *174*
    Medical, *171-74*
    Molestation, *168*
    Professional liability, *175*
    Property, *175*
    Travel and accident, *175*
    Umbrella, *175-76*
    Workers' Compensation, *176*
Interest,
    Paid, *92-93*
    Received, *91*

Inurement *(see private inurement)*
Inventory, *157*

K

Key employee insurance, *174*

L

Lead trust, *137*
Lease value, autos, *52-54*
Life insurance, *136, 171*
Loans to employees, *60*
Lodging *(see housing)*
Long-term care insurance, *174*

M

Magnetic media reporting, *89*
Mailing rates, *184, 185*
Medical insurance plans,
    Flexible benefits, *174*
    Self-funded, *172*
Medical expense reimbursement plan, *58-59*
Membership fees, *158*
Minimum wage, *12, 180-81*
Ministers,
    Assignment, *71*
    Classification, *70-71*
    Housing allowance, *50-51*
    Special tax provisions, *70*
Missionaries, gifts designated for, *162-63*
Molestation insurance, *168*
Mortgage, interest received, *91*
Moving expenses, *61-62, 96*
Municipal service fees, *188*

N

National Child Care Act, *182*
NCIB, *14*
Nonaccountable expense-reimbursement plans, *62, 65*
Nondiscrimination rules, *62-63*
Nonresident aliens, *94*

O

Occupational Safety and Health Act, *182, 184*
Offering envelopes, *106*
Organizational change, *44*
Out-of-pocket expenses, *163*
Overfunding of projects, *23, 166*
Overtime,
    Payment of, *180-81*

P

Payroll taxes,
    Depositing withheld taxes, *8, 76-77*
    Filing annual returns, *80-88*
    Filing quarterly returns, *77-80*
    Personal liability, *75*

10 Biggest Tax Mistakes Made By Churches And Nonprofit Organizations

1. Not setting up an accountable expense reimbursement plan for employees. Chapter 3.

2. Improperly classifying employees as self-employed. Chapter 4.

3. Not reporting taxable fringe benefits and social security reimbursements as additional compensation to employees. Chapter 4.

4. Deducting FICA tax from the salary of qualified ministers. Chapter 4.

5. Failing to file Form 1099-MISC for independent contractors. Chapter 5.

6. Failing to have offerings controlled by two individuals until the funds are counted. Chapter 6.

7. Failure to issue a receipt for all transactions where the donor makes a payment of more than $75 and receives goods or services. Chapter 7.

8. Providing receipts for the donation of services and the rent-free use of property. Receipting contributions designated for individuals without proper control by the donee organization. Placing a value on noncash gifts. Chapter 7.

9. Not providing Workers' Compensation coverage where required by law and not coordinating Workers' Compensation with health insurance coverages. Chapter 8.

10. Failure to comply with the Fair Labor Standards Act for church-operated schools, including day-cares, preschool, elementary, and secondary. Chapter 9.